Enter THE DRAGON

China is a nation like no other. Once a constellation of fractured states, today it reigns supreme as the greatest power in the Eastern Hemisphere. The story of how a country that comprises over six per cent of the planet's land mass and is home to more than 1 billion people broke free of the shackles of foreign overlords is a fascinating tale of war, empire, invention and, above all, ambition. From its ancient origins to the birth of the People's Republic, the rise of Xi Jinping and the race to dominate the world of tomorrow, the land of the dragon is an endlessly intriguing place, one whose past continues to shape its future. ★

 6

 46

 22

Contents

006
IMPERIAL CHINA
The 13 dynasties that ruled for over 2,000 years

012
LEADING LIGHTS OF ANCIENT CHINA
Meet the fighters, philosophers and politicians who shaped a nation

014
TERRACOTTA ARMY
Unearthing the First Emperor's soldiers of the afterlife

022
THE GREAT WALL OF CHINA
How was this monumental structure built?

030
THE SILK ROAD
Trade and travel in the ancient world

034
THE THREE KINGDOMS
War in the wake of the Han's collapse

036
FAITH IN THE FAR EAST
How Confucianism, Buddhism and Taoism spread throughout Asia

038
10 GREATEST CHINESE INVENTIONS
From paper to gunpowder, Chinese ingenuity changed the world

042
THE TANG DYNASTY
Discover China's golden age

62 · 12 · 108 · 84 · 66

 42

 72

 30

 94
 120

046
CONQUERING CHINA
How the Mongols brought a nation to its knees

056
THE RED TURBAN REBELLION
Overthrowing the Yuan dynasty

062
THE MING DYNASTY
Founding the greatest imperial family in China's history

065
THE PORCELAIN TOWER OF NANJING
Marvel at a medieval wonder of engineering

066
ZHENG HE
Take to the seas with China's intrepid explorer

072
THE FIRST OPIUM WAR
Driven by pure greed, the West humiliated a proud people in its bid to retain control of the drugs trade

078
THE TAIPING REBELLION
When visions of the divine visited hell upon China and fatally wounded a dynasty

082
THE SECOND OPIUM WAR
Death and devastation in the name of narcotics

084
THE BOXER REBELLION
How anti-foreign sentiments sparked a bloody uprising in 1899

092
1911 REVOLUTION
Why did a rebel faction establish a republic?

094
THE CHINESE CIVIL WAR
Understanding the rise of communist China

100
JAPAN 1937
Determined to realise its dreams of territorial expansion, imperial Japan showed its neighbour no mercy

108
MAO'S DISASTER PLAN
A deadly mix of Marxism and madness condemned millions to starvation under Mao

114
TIANANMEN SQUARE MASSACRE
What really happened in 1989?

116
HONG KONG RETURNS
Britain hands the city back in 1997

118
EPIC ENGINEERING
Taming the wilds of China and taking to the skies

120
CHINA'S FIRST OLYMPICS
Relive the 2008 Beijing Olympics

124
THE DRAGON ROARS
Hailed as an economic colossus and potential military rival to the U.S., Xi Jinping's China is a formidable force. But what does the future hold for a nation ruled by a leader who harbours dreams of conquest and building a surveillance state in which dissent is not an option?

 100
 124

中國歷史

Imperial

THE CHINESE EMPIRE STOOD FOR MILLENNIA AT THE CENTRE OF THE EAST ASIAN WORLD AND AT THE FOREFRONT OF HUMAN CIVILISATION

WRITTEN BY **MARC DeSANTIS**

For centuries, China was riven by wars between its rival states. These were bitter enemies, and though there were royal dynasties during these long years, such as the semi-legendary Xia of c.2070-1600 BCE, the warrior aristocrats of the Shang who ruled from c.1600 to 1122 BCE, and the feudal Zhou of c.1046-256 BCE, actual power tended to rest in the hands of the local rulers of its many sub-kingdoms and duchies.

The land was also repeatedly beset by invaders from outside – nomadic, horse-riding peoples from the steppes of Central Asia seeking to claim a piece of China's fertile lands. Many Chinese states on the northern frontier would build long walls to keep them out.

Geographically, China, with its origin along the Yellow River, was separated from the other great world civilisations by distance and difficult terrain, such as mountains and deserts. Though there certainly was contact, the nation primarily developed along its own course without extensive influence from outside.

The country was always the largest polity in eastern Asia. Because of its central location, it came

CHINA

to see itself as the Middle Kingdom between the lesser states that clustered around it – both literally and figuratively – because of its greater size and importance. Culturally, the latter period of this seemingly endless era of internal conflict, the Warring States period, was one of great achievement. It was during this time that the greatest of all Far Eastern philosophers, Confucius, lived. The teacher and politician taught extensively on morality and the correct ordering of the family, society and the state.

But when it came to unifying China, this would be accomplished by the highly militaristic state of Qin, which lay on the western periphery. Qin was extremely militaristic and its soldiers were renowned for their ferocity.

King Zheng came to power in the state in 238 BCE and rapidly gobbled up his neighbours' lands with his massive and powerful army, including Chu, Zhao and lastly Qi in 221 BCE. China was finally brought together under one sole ruler. Zheng took for himself the title Qin Shi Huangdi, or First Emperor Qin, and in this position he was elevated above the old kings of the Shang and Zhou. He also adopted the ancient idea that he, as the Son of Heaven, enjoyed the Mandate of Heaven to rule.

Qin got to work building the first version of the Great Wall of China, though at an enormous cost in lives. He codified Chinese law, standardised weights and measures and developed a common written language. He also built thousands of miles of roads to connect the once-separate states. But he was extremely paranoid – perhaps with good reason as he had been the target of assassins before. He ruled as a tyrant, harsh and cruel. Huge numbers of intellectuals were killed and books burned to destroy the unapproved knowledge in them. The tyranny of Qin soon fostered revolts and his dynasty would be short-lived.

Qin's usurper would rise from humble beginnings. The peasant-born Liu Bang, the founder of what would become the Han dynasty, which reigned from 202 BCE to 220 CE, was originally a police official in

ABOVE People have inhabited the land that comprises what we call China for 1.7 million years

Jiangsu until he became a major leader of rebel forces against the hated Qin. Upon becoming emperor, he took the throne name Han Gaozu.

The greatest of his descendants was Emperor Wudi, who conquered huge territories and incorporated them into the empire, as well as beginning the Silk Road to acquire high-quality horses for his cavalry from Central Asia. Confucianism became the guiding philosophy of government and society, and entry into prestigious civil service was permitted by competitive examinations. It was also a period of technological innovation, seeing the appearance of silk production and paper-making and the invention of the wheelbarrow and the ploughshare.

However, the Han weakened over the centuries. The economy worsened and military problems multiplied, especially on the northern frontier where nomadic peoples stood ready to raid China whenever possible. The Han collapse began in 189 CE when the army mutinied. The capital of Loyang was sacked, including the imperial palace. The last of the Han emperors gave up his throne in 220 CE, but over three and a half centuries of chaos and division ensued. The influence of the Han was undeniably enormous. Today, most Chinese call themselves Han after this remarkable dynasty.

After the collapse of the Han, the Three Kingdoms Period followed. Control of China was divided between three states: Wei, Wu and Shu. The north of the country was overrun by invaders from the steppe, and petty warlords of non-Chinese origin ruled over numerous regions.

Yang Jian became the ruler of a reunited China in 589 CE and took the throne name of Sui Wendi. He had been the Duke of Sui and initially served in the government of a small state, the Northern Zhou. In 581 he convinced its child emperor to abdicate and then announced himself to be the new Son of Heaven. He defeated the last of his opponents in the Chen dynasty in 589, thus beginning the Sui dynasty.

The approximately 1,800-kilometre-long (1,118-mile) Grand Canal from Beijing to Hangzhou, connecting the Yellow River with the Yangtze River, was constructed by the Sui. The dynasty quickly faltered when a terrible flood ravaged the country, convincing many that Heaven had withdrawn its mandate from the Sui and sparking a number of uprisings. Like the birth of the Han, one rebel leader would soon sit on the throne.

The Sui would be succeeded by the Tang dynasty from 618 to 907 when Li Yuan, a Sui general, seized the capital city of Chang'an on the Yellow River in 618. Ruling as Tang Gaozu, he would remain on the throne for eight years. The Tang dynasty he founded presided over a golden age of cultural brilliance during which the arts, literature and scholarship flourished. The vast wealth of the empire owed much to imperial stability, and foreigners from all directions came bearing goods to trade. In accordance with age-old tradition, admission to the imperial civil service was governed by competitive examination.

Like all golden ages, this one too came to an end. A Turkic general, An Lushan, raised his standard in rebellion in 755. The revolt was suppressed but only after eight bloody years, leaving the Tang severely weakened. Power fell into the hands of local officials and aristocrats, and the Tang emperors' control over the huge empire was never as secure as it had once been. The dynasty failed in 907, ushering in a half-century of disorder.

For about five decades, from 907 to 960, a period known as the Five Dynasties Era, China was ruled by a constellation of small states, but this period of division came to an end in 960 with the rise of the Song. One Taizu, the former commander of the palace guard, founded the dynasty and the empire was gradually reassembled. The period would be one of enormous economic growth and great technological progress.

ABOVE Emperor Gaozu was the founder of the Tang dynasty, which presided over a golden age of Chinese culture

ABOVE The world's earliest paper money appeared during the time of the Song dynasty

ABOVE Kublai Khan, the grandson of Genghis Khan, completed the conquest of China by defeating the Southern Song in 1279

ABOVE The ruins of a Han dynasty watchtower at Dunhuang in western China

> "The revolt was suppressed but only after eight bloody years, leaving the Tang severely weakened"

It was not without its problems, however. In the north, the Song were troubled by the nomads of the steppe who had settled on large tracts of Chinese territory. Foremost among these were the non-Chinese Khitans of the Liao dynasty from Manchuria. In the far west, there were troubles with the Tibetans. Later, the Jurchen of the Jin dynasty vexed China's rulers and dominated extensive areas of northern China. By the 12th century, northern China had largely been lost to the Khitans, and the Southern Song, as the dynasty later became known, ruled only the lands south of the Yangtze River.

The most dangerous of all of the northern steppe nomads to lay claim to territory in China were the Mongols. United in 1206 under their greatest leader, Genghis Khan, Mongol cavalry armies swept into northern China and overwhelmed the various non-Chinese dynasties that ruled there. After completing the conquest of north China, the Mongols turned west and stormed into the Middle East, their hard-riding armies reaching as far west as Hungary, Poland and Russia, where they smashed their European opponents. The Mongols created an empire of which China was a major part.

The conquest of the Southern Song would take longer and would not be completed until later in the century during the reign of Kublai Khan, Genghis' grandson, who would found China's Yuan dynasty, which reigned from 1271 to 1368.

The Silk Road flourished with the stability and security that the Mongols provided. It was during this period, in the late 13th century, that the famed Italian traveller Marco Polo journeyed from Venice to China.

In time, the Mongols succumbed to the lure of superior Chinese culture and became sinicised, but not all of their military ventures were successful – two attempted invasions of Japan in the latter 13th century ended in abject failure. Sitting in comfortable Chinese garrisons, the Mongol soldiers themselves became soft, a far cry from their hardy ancestors who had conquered China on horseback. Revolts among the native Chinese, who resisted Mongol rule, broke out. In 1368, Beijing fell. The Yuan dynasty was finished.

The Ming dynasty came next. Its first emperor, Hongwu, had been born a peasant named Zhu Yuanzhang but rose to become the leader of a rebel band that captured Nanjing in 1356, which became the imperial capital. By 1368, he had captured Beijing, with the last of the Mongol leaders fleeing before his approach.

Between 1403 and 1424, the Ming built a large portion of the structure that is today most commonly thought of as the Great Wall. Great seafaring expeditions under Admiral Zheng He were sent out, visiting foreign nations in giant 'treasure ships' as far away as India, the Persian Gulf and Africa between 1405 and 1433.

Yet the Ming were uninterested in continuing these expensive voyages and Chinese sea power atrophied. Later it would become vulnerable to Japanese pirates and overtaken at sea by Western Europeans, such as the Portuguese and Spanish, who began to appear in China in the 16th century.

By the early 16th century the Ming empire was tottering. Peace had brought about a big increase in population, but this meant that there were more people than the land could easily support and rebellions occurred. The northern tribes were constantly making trouble on the frontier, and Japanese pirates raided China's coasts at will. The Ming were incapable of coping with them all. Revolts broke out and the Manchus of Manchuria took advantage of the chaos and captured Beijing in 1644. China was once more ruled by foreigners.

The Manchus founded the country's last dynasty, the Qing, which would govern China until the collapse of imperialism in 1912. During its rule the outside world begin to impinge more forcefully despite the Qing's resistance to change. Western nations, undergoing their own industrialisation, began to insist on favourable trading relations, weakening China.

China suffered defeat in both the First and Second Opium Wars in the mid-1800s, which were fought largely over the opium trade between Britain and China, and it subsequently lost much of its sovereignty in the treaties that followed. But the humiliation didn't stop there; China was incapable of protecting itself from foreign aggression and was overpowered by Japan's modern military in the First Sino-Japanese War of 1894-1895. Then the anti-foreign Boxer Rebellion of 1899-1901 was crushed by the armies of several foreign powers.

Revolts against the foreign and decrepit Qing dynasty multiplied and the last emperor, Pu Yi, formally abdicated in 1912. One revolt was led by Sun Yat-sen, who had lived in the United States as a young man. He became the leader of the newly proclaimed Republic of China in 1912. And thus the imperial system that had prevailed in China for over 2,000 years was extinguished. ★

KEY EVENTS & RULERS

221 BCE – Unification of China
The ruthless King Zheng of Qin becomes the first ruler of a unified China. He declares himself emperor.

589 – China reunited
After over three centuries of division, the Chinese Empire is reunited by Emperor Sui Wendi.

1209 – Mongol invasions of China
The mounted Mongol army invades northern China.

1839-1842 – First Opium War
China and Britain go to war over diplomatic relations and trade. The British ultimately defeat a weakened Qing China in 1842.

139 BCE – Heavenly horses
Emperor Wudi of the Han dynasty sends a mission to find quality horses for his army in Central Asia.

960 – Founding of the Song dynasty
Song emperor Taizu unites China after over 40 years of disunity.

1661 – Ascension of the Kangxi Emperor
Kangxi, the longest-reigning Chinese emperor of the Qing dynasty, assumes the imperial throne. He reigns until 1722.

1912 – Republic of China
Sun Yat-sen becomes the leader of the Republic of China, bringing the country's imperial era to an end.

RIGHT First Emperor Qin codified Chinese law and developed a common written language for the new empire

The Forbidden City

A fortress of palaces and gardens

When Yongle of Ming decided to restore Beijing as the imperial capital, his aim was strategic: to oversee the northern frontier marked by the Great Wall. He ordered a palace more stupendous than anything that had come before. It took most of his reign to build but was far enough advanced by 1420 for the emperor to live in it for four years before his death.

Construction continued for generations, until it covered 72 hectares and contained almost 9,000 rooms – four times the number in the Palace of Versailles, Buckingham Palace, the White House and the Kremlin combined.

The centre of Beijing was built as a set of boxes nested inside each other. In the middle was the moated Forbidden City, which was surrounded by the Imperial City's parks, temples and warehouses. The Forbidden City, containing the residences for the emperor and his family and retainers, was the nerve centre for 14 Ming emperors and ten Qing emperors until 1912. Its axis is the Imperial Way, linking the Outer Court, once used for ceremonies, and the Inner Court, used for imperial residences and administration.

Today, the surrounding Imperial City is very different from the original and most of the walls and gate towers have gone. In the 1950s, buildings were razed to create the space that is today's Tiananmen Square. But the Forbidden City retains its original appearance, with great front courts and halls, which still have their white marble terraces and carved railings, while the Hall of Supreme Harmony is still one of the biggest wooden buildings in China. Many of the rooms now form the National Palace Museum.

The Hall of Supreme Harmony
The smallest of the three Outer Court halls, this was used as an antechamber and imperial rest room. A throne is flanked by gargoyles of unicorns, which symbolise wisdom. After being burned down three times the hall was restored for the last time in 1627 to its original form.

The Meridian Gate
This is the entrance to the Forbidden City. The central arch was once reserved for the emperor alone, but the empress was allowed to enter it on the day of her wedding, and the top three scholars in the Imperial Service examinations could leave their exams through it. All other officials had to use the side entrances.

The Gate of Supreme Harmony
Here, across five bridges spanning a meandering stream, the Ming emperor met his ministers daily in a formal display of his 'diligence'. The original was rebuilt in 1894 after a fire. It leads along the city's north-south central axis to the three halls of the Outer Court.

IMPERIAL CHINA

The Gate of Heavenly Purity
This divides the Outer from the Inner Court and is guarded by two lions with limp ears. An official website claims that "these two lions with flipperty-flopperty ears alarm the Inner Court concubines and court ladies," warning them to avoid the Outer Court and its concerns with government.

Palace of Earthly Tranquillity
This was the empress' residence during the Ming dynasty, and in Qing times it was the wedding chamber for the emperor and empress. Since the Qing were Manchu, not Chinese, they also used the hall to worship shamanistic deities.

Gate of Divine Might
At the northern end of the garden, this gate leads out of the Forbidden City. A bell and drum were used to mark the time of day.

Imperial Garden
160 cypress and locust trees are centred on the Hall of Imperial Peace, with its 400-year-old tree, the Consort Pine, symbolising the harmony between emperor and empress. They and the women of the court liked to read while strolling along the paved pathways. Four pavilions at the garden's corners symbolise the four seasons.

Hall of Union
Sometimes called the Hall of Celestial and Terrestrial Union, it was used for ceremonies to promote harmony. It contains two 18th-century clocks, a water-clock (a clepsydra) and a huge chiming mechanical clock more than five metres (16 feet) tall. Here the empress met with other women of the court – the princesses and concubines.

Palace of Heavenly Purity
The emperor's residence is a smaller version of the Hall of Supreme Harmony. The raised throne is surrounded by incense burners, red candles and mirrors to ward off evil spirits. When Qing emperors died their coffins were placed here for ritual mourning.

The Hall of Preserving Harmony
Mainly used for banquets for governors, princes and officials, this was also where the emperor donned ritual clothing for the installation of the empress and crowned prince. In the 18th century, under Emperor Qianlong, it was used for the top level of nationwide examinations.

Leading lights of ancient China

TEN PEOPLE WHO SHAPED THE POLITICAL, CULTURAL, SOCIAL AND GEOGRAPHICAL FOUNDATIONS OF THE ANCIENT KINGDOM

Confucius
551-479 BCE

The most famous of Chinese philosophers, Confucius was also an influential politician and poet of the Spring and Autumn Period. With an emphasis on morality, justice and kindness in relationships, his teachings have been widely read through the ages. He was a strong proponent of loyalty and reverence for ancestors and is noted as the author of numerous classical Chinese literary works, including the *Five Classics*. Politically, he sought to restore the Mandate of Heaven and asked rulers and the people to remember earlier times of peace and prosperity. His teachings remain prevalent in modern Chinese and East Asian culture today.

> After exiling himself from his home state of Lu in 497 BCE, Confucius spent 14 years travelling around China's war-torn states.

Fu Hao
UNKNOWN-C.1250 BCE

One of King Wu Ding's numerous wives, Fu Hao entered the ruling house through an arranged marriage intended to strengthen the allegiance of neighbouring clans. She rose to prominence as a military leader, commanding troops during long campaigns. Fu Hao was mother of the heir to the Shang dynasty throne and a high priestess, participating in religious rituals. Her tomb, containing a trove of artefacts, was discovered during the mid-1970s. Inscriptions on oracle bones attest to her prominent role.

Sun Tzu
544-496 BCE

The author of the seminal work on military strategy and tactics, *The Art of War*, Sun Tzu, or Master Sun, lived during the Eastern Zhou period of ancient China. Sun Tzu is a prominent military and literary figure in Chinese history and is thought to have led soldiers in battle. While his theories on conflict, cooperation and society have been prominent in Asian thought for centuries, Western scholars popularised his writings in the 20th century, finding applications in everyday living.

Emperor Yu the Great
UNKNOWN-C.2025 BCE

Emperor Yu the Great is the semi-mythical king of the ancient Xia dynasty, the earliest in Chinese history and whose existence is the substance of scholarly debate. Yu is credited with establishing Xia and the tradition of dynastic rule in China and is believed to have exerted great effort to implement flood control along the Yellow River. Revered as an upright and moral ruler, he earned the nickname 'Tamer of Waters' and promoted the establishment of villages and agricultural practices through his outstanding leadership, project management and problem-solving capabilities.

Ban Zhao
49-120 CE

Ban Zhao is considered one of the first female historians and was also a prominent politician and philosopher. The daughter of the influential historian Ban Biao, she completed the history of Western Han, the *Book of Han*, begun by her brother, Ban Gu. Ban Zhao was also the author of *Lessons for Women*, a guide to the conduct of women in ancient Chinese society. She also developed a keen interest in mathematics and astronomy. Ban Zhao became the most influential female scholar of her day, wrote poetry and commentaries, and even advised the Han court on numerous matters, including the intricacies of Taoist sexual practices.

> Ban Zhao gained great political influence by teaching in the royal library.

LEADING LIGHTS OF ANCIENT CHINA

Zhang Heng
78-139 CE

Zhang Heng lived during the Han dynasty, rising to prominence as an astronomer, writer, engineer and mathematician. He came to the imperial court and fashioned calendars for emperors, although he was not born of a royal family. He practised Confucianism and declined promotion to posts of greater responsibility, claiming he had little ambition. During his lifetime Zhang Heng invented a water-powered armillary sphere – a device used in astronomy – and mathematical equations to calculate the volume of three-dimensional objects.

> "He declined promotion to greater posts"

Zhuang Zhou
369-286 BCE

Zhuang Zhou was a Chinese philosopher of the Hundred Schools of Thought, influential during the concurrent Warring States Period. He is remembered as the author of one of the basic texts of Taoism, the *Zhuangzi*. His works have been acknowledged as influencing Western thinkers as well, and though his actual existence has been questioned by modern scholars he is believed to have served as a government official in the state of Song.

Lao Tzu
C.500- LATE 4TH CENTURY BCE

The founder of the philosophical school of Taoism, Lao Tzu is the historically acknowledged author of the *Tao Te Ching*. The figure of Lao Tzu is surrounded by legend, and some scholars of ancient China theorise that the actual individual behind the persona was in fact Li Er, a high-ranking figure in the court of King Wu of Zhou who served as head of the royal library. Another legend describes an encounter between Lao Tzu and Confucius in which the latter stood in awe of Tzu's immense knowledge and wisdom.

Emperor Qin Shi Huangdi
259-210 BCE

Considered by many scholars to be the first emperor of China, Qin Shi Huangdi was also the first emperor of the Qin dynasty, coming to the throne at the tender age of 13 and asserting control at the age of 38. From 230 to 221 BCE, Qin Shi Huangdi succeeded in unifying the seven warring states of ancient China. He began the construction of the Great Wall as a defensive measure against invasion from the north, established a universally accepted currency and standardised units of measure. The emperor is famous for being buried with the Terracotta Army of thousands of soldiers, horses and chariots, which was discovered by chance in the 1970s in Shaanxi.

King Wen of Zhou
1152-1050 BCE

The first emperor to claim rule via the Mandate of Heaven, Wen of Zhou espoused the divine right to govern through natural order and the will of the universe. Many writings in classical Chinese poetry praise Wen, and he is considered by some historians as the first epic hero of ancient China. Through sound economic policy he engendered prosperity among the people, while military campaigns extended the Zhou dynasty's territory.

> Qin Shi Huangdi was obsessed with immortality, seeking the mythical elixir of life while taking poisonous mercury pills intended to help him live forever.

中國歷史

Secrets
FROM ANCIENT CHINA

IN THE 1970s, FIVE MEN DIGGING A WELL MADE A STARTLING DISCOVERY THAT TRANSFORMED OUR UNDERSTANDING OF CHINA'S HISTORY AND THE BRUTAL EVENTS OF 2,000 YEARS AGO

WRITTEN BY JOHN MAN

March, 1974. A conical hill looms over an orchard near Xian, north-central China. We're surrounded by fields, but the trees are bare and the grass is dusty. A drought is ravaging the countryside. Five peasants, the Yang brothers, are digging a well. They are two metres down, taking turns to dig while the others haul out soil in baskets. Suddenly the one in the pit, Yang Zhefa, shouts, "An earth god!"

Sticking out of the soil is a head made of clay - it has two eyes, long hair tied in a bun and a moustache. This is bad luck, because it's underground, where the dead live. The men toss the head aside and keep digging, but some local kids see it and throw stones at it. A few adults arrive. An old woman picks up the head, takes it home and puts it on her table. Meanwhile, the Yang brothers make other finds: bricks, bits of bronze and some arrowheads.

A month later, a 24-year-old archaeologist named Zhao Kangmin, who's working in a local museum, hears about the finds. He gets on his bike, rides to the orchard and finds the Yangs, still busy on their well. By now there are more clay bits on their heap of rubbish: legs, arms, two more heads. He takes charge of matters and has the finds brought to his museum in nearby Lintong. He guesses they are important as he knows the historical background.

Over 2,000 years ago, this was the heartland of the state known as Qin (pronounced Chin). That hill in the background, a massive pyramid of earth, was the tomb of the emperor who united China's warring states into a single nation. Kangmin, like most educated people, knew all about the First Emperor, because the story of his rise to power was told in dramatic terms by Sima Qian, one of China's greatest historians, who was writing a century after the events that he describes.

Qin had been one of seven warring states, all with their own armies and systems of government. But Qin had made itself the most powerful by becoming a military dictatorship in which the ruler had total control. For example, as one chronicler recorded, "Anyone who failed to report criminal activity would be chopped in two at the waist." The system worked. By 238 BCE, Qin was a rich, self-confident kingdom under the control of a new 22-year-old ruler, King Zheng.

Zheng was fanatical about security. He thought he could make Qin even safer by using his tough, mobile army to extend his control

THE TERRACOTTA ARMY

The warring states in 250 BCE

Zhao fought off the northern nomads, the Xiongnu, by replacing chariots with mounted archers. This enabled Zhao to withstand Qin until weakened by a bloody defeat in 260 BCE. Qin defeated and occupied it in 222 BCE.

Wei was the birthplace of Lord Shang, a military theorist who advised rulers to be ruthless. He moved to Qin and helped it become an efficient police state. He surrendered to Qin in 225 BCE after the Qin diverted the Yellow River and flooded the Wei capital Daliang.

Qin From 350–250 BCE it absorbed several weaker neighbours. Between 230–221 BCE its ruthless leader, Zheng, conquered Qin's six remaining rivals, formed the heart of modern China, and named himself Qin Shi Huangdi – the First Sovereign Emperor.

Han controlled the eastern approaches to Qin. Smaller and weaker than all the other states, it could not expand. Since it blocked Qin's access to the rich lowlands of eastern China, it was the first of the states to fall to Qin, in 230 BCE.

Yan Fearful of Qin, Yan's heir apparent, Prince Dan, planned to assassinate the First Emperor. The plot failed, but it reinforced the emperor's sense of insecurity and his imperial ambitions. Yan was the penultimate state to fall to Qin, in 222 BCE.

Qi After defeat in 284 BCE, Qi won back lost land when its great general Tian Dan had the tails of oxen coated with grease, set alight and released to trample the enemy. It was the last state to surrender to Qin, which it did peacefully in the end.

Chu dominated China's rich lowlands and the Yangtze River. It joined other states to attack Qi in 284 BCE but went into swift decline when Qin seized its capital four years later. It was the birthplace of Li Si, who became the First Emperor's top adviser.

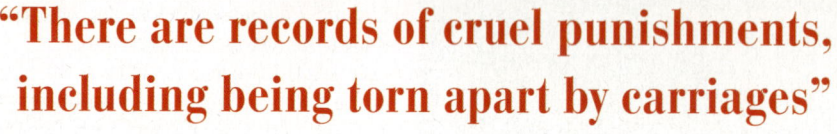

"There are records of cruel punishments, including being torn apart by carriages"

over the other six states. To ensure victory he turned his nation into a war machine fuelled by good food supplies, ruthless tax gatherers, military service for almost all men, and highly trained soldiers.

We have no details of his conquests, which started in 230 BCE, but in nine years he defeated all the other six kingdoms. In 221 BCE, he was master of a unified China, which gets its name from his kingdom. This was not China as it is today, just the central and northern bits, but ever since then the idea of unity has been at the heart of Chinese history. Zheng gave himself a suitably grand title: Qin Shi Huangdi, meaning Qin (or China) First Sovereign Emperor. Non-Chinese usually call him the First Emperor.

Now he needed to weld his conquests together with a revolution in government and vast building projects that would control his people and keep enemies out. First, he ordered wide-reaching administrative reforms, setting up a government of 36 regions, each one divided into counties run by both civil and military governors who oversaw tax collectors and judges. All the different systems of law, money, weights, measures and even styles of clothing were standardised.

Dissent of any kind was crushed. According to Sima Qian, when a scholar dared criticise the emperor for breaking with tradition, Prime Minister Li Si pointed out that the roots of rebellion lay with scholars and books: "Those who use the past to criticise the present should be put to death!" So the royal archives "were all destroyed. How regrettable!" According to Sima Qian the texts om question were burned. This episode, known as the Burning of the Books, is generally accepted as true, as is another claim that "over 460" scholars were buried alive. But Sima Qian, writing during the next dynasty,

ABOVE The level of detail in the terracotta statues' design is astounding

RIGHT Every terracotta warrior discovered so far has a unique feature

ABOVE Many of the damaged terracotta warriors have been meticulously pieced back together

BELOW Qin Shi Huangdi proclaimed that his dynasty would last "10,000 generations"

was keen to discredit his predecessors, and experts question the true meaning of the words widely translated as "burned" and "buried". Anyway, countless Qin books survived. These record cruel punishments, including being torn apart by carriages and being boiled to death. But there are no records of the execution of scholars. It seems the emperor's new legal system actually prevented gross abuses of power.

Peace had one startling result: the king's vast army - millions of soldiers from all seven nations - was no longer needed. Something had to be done with them or risk rebellion. So the soldiers were set to work on huge projects: over 6,000 kilometres (3,728 miles) of paved roads, half a dozen royal palaces, military bases, and - most famously - the first Great Wall.

One the First Emperor's grandest projects was his tomb, built near the ancient capital, Xian, at the foot of a sacred mountain, Mount Li. Records claim that 700,000 worked on it, although 40,000 is a more accurate figure, and they spent a year digging out a pit for the tomb itself. Later, after his death, the tomb would be covered with the hill that is still there today - 50 metres

THE EMPEROR'S GREATEST ACHIEVEMENTS

Unification
The First Emperor is referred to as China's First Unifier. There have been many others since, including Mao Zedong, who created communist China from the ruins of war and revolution in 1949. There have been many periods of division and China has changed shape often. Today's China is around 3.4-times the size of Qin, but for 2,000 years China has looked back to the First Emperor as a symbol of the ultimate ideal: unity.

Standardisation of coins, axles, colours and weights
The Qin Empire was held together by a series of measures that made Qin standards universal. Black was the colour of flags and uniforms. Every state abandoned its own coins for round copper ones with a square hole in the middle. Cartwheels were given a single gauge, so that they all ran in the same ruts. Weights and measures became uniform. Law and order was harsh but equal.

Standardisation of writing
China had used a script for 1,500 years, but it changed with the centuries and each state had its own variant. Under the First Emperor, all regional variations gave way to a single 'seal script'. This was perhaps his most significant reform, because all officials could understand his orders and each other, whatever their dialects. Today, China's script still binds the nation together. Mandarin speakers may not understand spoken Cantonese, but both understand the same written characters.

Roads
Fast travel was vital for messengers, troops and royal retinues, so the emperor put his labourers to work building roads - almost 7,000 kilometres (4,350 miles) in all. All the nation's 270 palaces were connected. In part, this was for security. He travelled between them in secret and executed anyone who revealed where he was. One of the roads ran 800 kilometres (497 miles) northward across the Ordos semi-desert so that troops and workers could get to the border - and the Great Wall - as quickly as possible.

Great Wall of China
This was nothing like today's Great Wall, which dates from 1,500 years later. At the time, there were many walls. After unification, there was only one enemy: the nomadic 'barbarians' of the north. Fearsome mounted archers, they often galloped south on raids. The emperor's huge workforce joined up many small walls along the northern borders of Zhao and Yan, creating a single barrier that stretched for 2,500 kilometres (1,553 miles).

The Painted Warriors

The warriors today are clay-coloured, as are the reproductions bought by tourists. That's what seems 'authentic', but it's wrong. They were originally painted in vivid colours, which were stripped away by their earthy blanket. In the First Emperor's day, the rich loved colours because they were expensive to make and thus symbols of luxury. Surviving flecks of paint reveal what the statues were like, with pink (for faces), red, green, brown and purple – especially so-called 'Chinese purple', made from a complex mixture of barium, copper, quartz and lead.

(164 feet) high, 350 metres (1,148 feet) per side; equivalent in size to the Great Pyramid.

What was it all for? The answer is fitting given the First Emperor's lofty ambitions: to live forever in the spirit world. The emperor, like his whole society, was obsessed with life after death. He believed the next world mirrored this one and that a dead person needed familiar objects in the grave to recreate life. The rich and powerful needed big tombs, filled with grave goods like chariots, weapons, animals and servants, both real ones, killed and buried with their lord, and models, for a life-like image could in some magical way become 'real' in the spirit world. Everything was designed to remake the emperor's life on Earth – government, banquets, entertainments, hunting, fighting.

The tomb itself was perhaps devoted to government. Sima Qian says it contains a model of the empire, with the rivers picked out in flowing mercury, the night sky portrayed in the ceiling, and all defended by crossbows ready to fire on intruders. It sounds unlikely, but in 1982 archaeologists probed the tomb with 560 drillings that revealed the outlines of a building and slight traces of mercury vapour. The truth will only be known if and when the tomb is opened.

But the emperor would also need an army, and so he commissioned something that was totally original and unique. He had his artisans, hundreds of them, make thousands of full-size warriors out of clay, all painted in vivid colours and carrying real bronze weapons (which was why they had to be full-size).

Much of this work must have been done before his death at the age of 50 in 210 BCE. However, for his burial, tens of thousands of workers rushed to finish the tomb and its many outlying graves. The terracotta warriors were placed in three pits 1.5 kilometres (0.9 miles) to the east of the tomb. Well armed with spears, lances, swords and crossbows, they were lined up on a tiled floor as if on a parade ground, ready to help their lord fight off any spirit armies coming to take over his empire. The pits, nine metres deep, were roofed with wooden beams, twice as thick as telegraph poles, weighing 500 kilograms (1,102 pounds) each, over 6,000 (13,227) in all. The beams were covered with matting, on top of which workers piled three metres (9.8 feet) of earth.

Then they vanished. There were no records. Sima Qian makes no mention of them. After a generation or two, they were forgotten, the memory of them erased by the chaos and civil war that destroyed the Qin Empire.

So when the warriors were found in 1974 they were a total surprise. And when archaeologists got to work there was another surprise: not a single soldier was found intact. All had been shattered. Today's display is the result of painstaking reconstruction. So far, 1,000 have been restored, though all their bright colours vanished into the earth that buried them. The rest are still buried, awaiting techniques that can ensure better preservation. No one knows exactly how many there are: 7,000–8,000 is an estimate, as is the number of 670 horses. But this is not enough for an army. The emperor's

> "The emperor, like his whole society, was obsessed with life after death"

real army numbered in the tens of thousands. Perhaps there are more to be discovered. After all, there have been many other finds over the years, including horse skeletons, tombs of officials, other types of terracotta statues, bronze birds, and two astonishing half-sized chariots, complete with horses and drivers.

Without question, the star turn is the army, now partly restored from jigsaw puzzles of bits and pieces. Not a single one in the main pit has been found complete. All were broken – but how? Fire was somehow responsible, for the earth above them was baked solid. But how did the fire start, and how could it possibly have broken every single statue?

To answer this we must become detectives. It must have had something to do with the rebels who rose against the Qin dynasty after the First

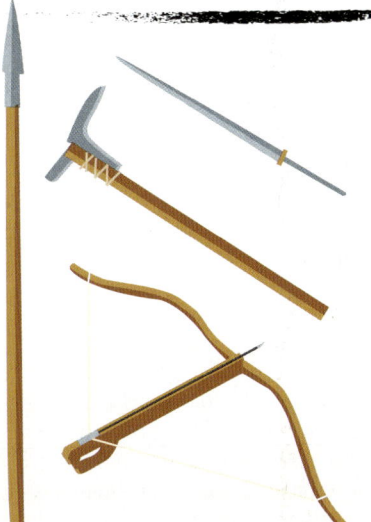

WEAPONS

The mock soldiers carried real weapons made of bronze and wood. Swords were for high-ranking officers, while specialists used bows and crossbows. Rank-and-file soldiers were equipped with halberds and spears.

UNIQUE DESIGNS

Of the 7,000–8,000 buried and broken figures, about 1,000 have been restored, and each one is different. They are not portraits, but ideals – handsome, well built, serene. The artists just varied the details, like eyebrows, beards and moustaches.

THE ELIXIR OF LIFE

Some people thought that the body could be made incorruptible by death, and so become a xian – an immortal. For centuries, Daoists experimented with elixirs – mixtures including gold, mercury, arsenic and lead – undeterred by the often fatal results. The First Emperor believed in the elixir and took seriously a charlatan named Xu Fu, who told him it could be found in islands off the east coast. Xu promised to find it but did nothing. In 210 BCE, the emperor, when touring the east, found and questioned Xu, who claimed he had been prevented from sea travel by a large fish. The emperor, deranged by paranoia, believed him and fired arrows into the sea to kill the non-existent monster. Soon afterward he died.

LEFT Many terracotta horses were also made for the emperor's tomb

LEFT Restoration of the terracotta warriors is currently in progress

RIGHT A depiction of what is believed to be buried under the mound – the transparent pyramid in the picture representing the earth on top of it

Emperor's death in 210 BCE, beginning eight years of civil war before the Han dynasty took over in 202 BCE. In a film shown to tourists in the Terracotta Army museum, rebel soldiers break through doors and torch the place. But there were no doors, nor a mass break-in. There is no evidence of the roof being dug up. So there was no oxygen to sustain a fire. That's the mystery: a fire, but no means to keep it burning.

Another theory posits that as the empire fell apart, a rebel army approached the tomb, with no one around to stop them. Historian Ban Gu, writing 200 years later, says the Qin generals advised: "There are forced labourers at the Mount Li grave complex. Grant them amnesty and supply them with arms." This was done, which temporarily blocked the rebel army, and also stopped work on the First Emperor's tomb. This explains why there are three pits full of soldiers – but a fourth pit is completely empty, awaiting more warriors, which never arrived.

In Lintong, rebels knew about the Terracotta Army from the hastily recruited labourers. So in early 206 BCE, with the Qin palaces ablaze, rebels arrived at the tomb site, eager for more booty. The vast tomb itself was too much of a challenge, but they knew of the buried army and that it contained real weapons.

There was no time to dig up the earth and beams. The best way in was to dig straight down. The evidence is there. In Pit No 2, a hole like a small mineshaft bypasses the roof and enters the pit. It's a metre or so wide – big enough for one person at a time to enter; big enough to hand weapons to the surface.

Imagine the first rebel soldier breaking through, seeing nothing, calling for a blazing torch. Its flickering light reveals the front lines of clay soldiers in their original painted finery, with pink faces and brightly coloured coats. In

The burial site

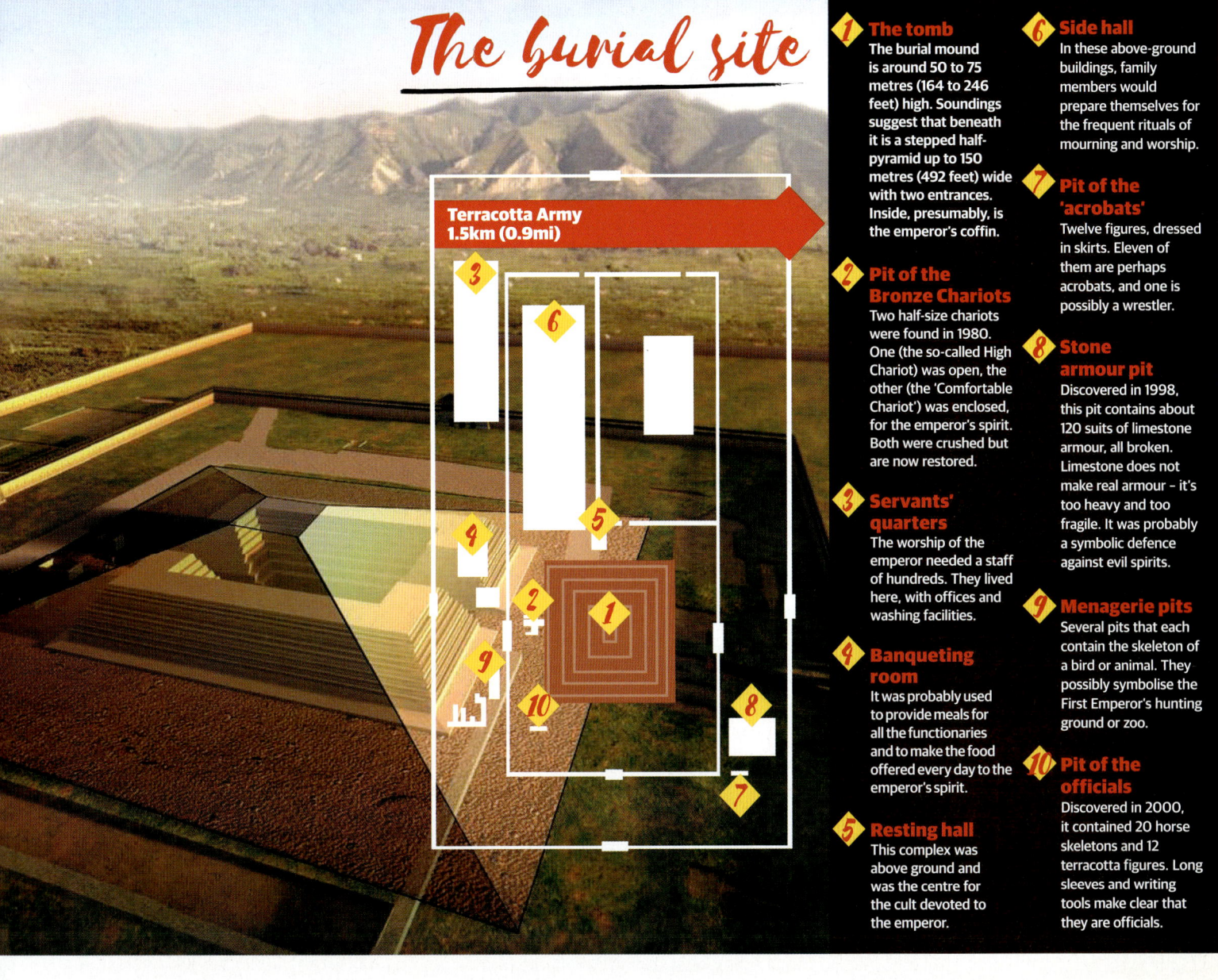

Terracotta Army 1.5km (0.9mi)

1. The tomb
The burial mound is around 50 to 75 metres (164 to 246 feet) high. Soundings suggest that beneath it is a stepped half-pyramid up to 150 metres (492 feet) wide with two entrances. Inside, presumably, is the emperor's coffin.

2. Pit of the Bronze Chariots
Two half-size chariots were found in 1980. One (the so-called High Chariot) was open, the other (the 'Comfortable Chariot') was enclosed, for the emperor's spirit. Both were crushed but are now restored.

3. Servants' quarters
The worship of the emperor needed a staff of hundreds. They lived here, with offices and washing facilities.

4. Banqueting room
It was probably used to provide meals for all the functionaries and to make the food offered every day to the emperor's spirit.

5. Resting hall
This complex was above ground and was the centre for the cult devoted to the emperor.

6. Side hall
In these above-ground buildings, family members would prepare themselves for the frequent rituals of mourning and worship.

7. Pit of the 'acrobats'
Twelve figures, dressed in skirts. Eleven of them are perhaps acrobats, and one is possibly a wrestler.

8. Stone armour pit
Discovered in 1998, this pit contains about 120 suits of limestone armour, all broken. Limestone does not make real armour – it's too heavy and too fragile. It was probably a symbolic defence against evil spirits.

9. Menagerie pits
Several pits that each contain the skeleton of a bird or animal. They possibly symbolise the First Emperor's hunting ground or zoo.

10. Pit of the officials
Discovered in 2000, it contained 20 horse skeletons and 12 terracotta figures. Long sleeves and writing tools make clear that they are officials.

"Something cut the tomb break-in short"

cavernous corridors the soldiers range backward into darkness and – most importantly – they're all armed. For fighting men, it's a treasure-trove.

Others slither down the hole, holding more torches. The intruders begin to weave and shove their way through, grabbing weapons, passing them back to the tunnel. "There is no evidence of organised destruction," says the army's senior archaeologist, Yuan Zhongyi. "We found remains of warriors which seem to have fallen in a zig-zag pattern, which suggests they were pushed over as people forced their way through."

Then, in the chaos, something cut the break-in short. Fire. A torch smouldering beside a wooden pillar or one of the wooden chariots.

For what happened next, we must rely on modern fire-protection engineers, like Joe Lally, an archaeologist with the U.S. Department of the Interior's Bureau of Land Management in Albuquerque, New Mexico. In his computerised scenario, there is no exit for the smoke. The corridors fill with smoke in about four minutes, forcing the thieves to crawl to the exit, toppling more warriors and horses. They have only a few precious minutes to escape, and there is only room for one at a time up the exit shaft. They all made it because no charred skeletons were found with the smashed soldiers.

There is something odd about this fire. It takes a powerful hold, but it needs a flow of oxygen to keep it going. There's not enough coming in through the small entrance, so the flames go out. Yet we know that fire completely destroyed the pit. How? This was a special sort of fire, like those that spread underground along seams of coal. Coal-seam fires are started by bush fires or lightning, and there are thousands of them around the world, burning very slowly for a very long time. There's one under the town of Centralia, Pennsylvania, that has been smouldering for half a century, and it may go on doing so for another 250 years.

Imagine the scene: in the main pit, the flames are dead, the pit dark again, smoke drifting along the corridors. But the fire has found a home in the ceiling, where the earth keeps a lid on it. Traces of oxygen seep in, just enough to keep the ceiling smouldering. Slowly, the fire eats away at the beams. At some point, charred timbers fall, breaking a piece off a warrior or two. A section of earth follows.

And so it goes, for years, the warriors, chariots and crossbow-men crushed by the falling beams, the surface subsiding bit by bit, filled again by water-borne mud, until not a trace remains of what lies beneath – until five brothers start digging a well.

中國歷史

THE Great Wall

SPANNING THOUSANDS OF KILOMETRES AND CENTURIES OF CONSTRUCTION, THIS ENDURING FORTIFICATION REMAINS ENVELOPED IN MYTH AND WONDER

WRITTEN BY JOHN MAN

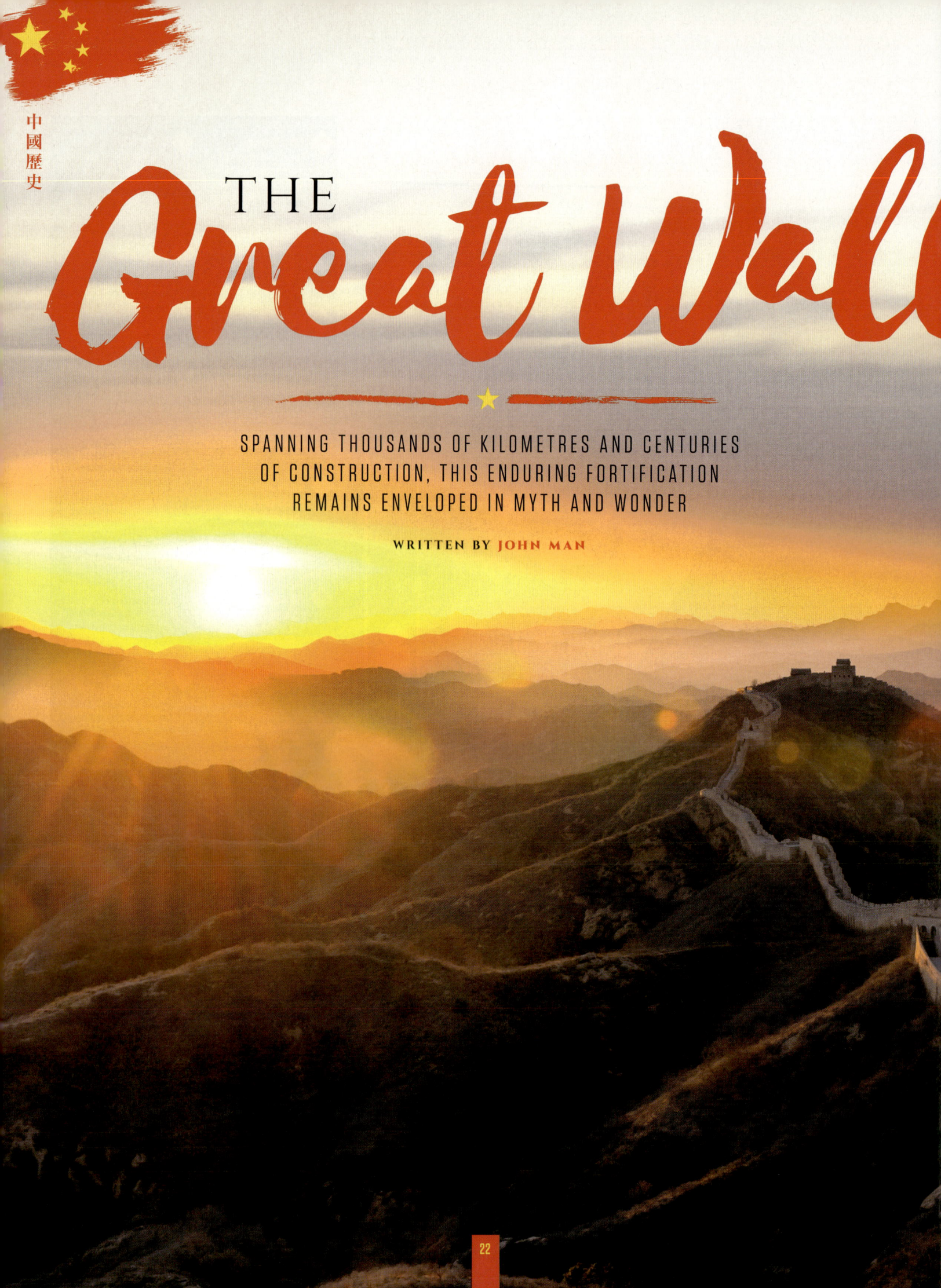

OF CHINA

THE GREAT WALL OF CHINA

The Great Wall is one of the world's most popular tourist sites and one of the best known of all the world's national icons. It sounds simple enough, and it looks it when seen on a tourist T-shirt proclaiming "I climbed the Great Wall", yet it is a thing of mystery. That very phrase - 'a thing of mystery' - is a paradox. The Wall is not a single thing: it is plural. It loops, soars, duplicates itself and often vanishes completely. Bits of it have been rebuilt many times. Tourists see the stone sections north of Beijing and assume that it runs across all of northern China, but to the west stone gives way to earth, sometimes wind-blasted ridges, sometimes nothing at all. There is also much more to the Wall than wall: fortresses, guard towers and beacon towers range out along, ahead and behind it. It is an immeasurable mass of parts.

The Chinese term for the Wall adds to the mystery. They call it the Changcheng, which means both Long City and Long Wall. To English speakers it makes no sense, but some 2,500 years ago when China was a collection of warring states, walls and cities were synonymous, because all cities had walls. The Wall, of course, is rather more than a city wall, which is why Chinese adds the adjective. Imagine a city wall cut open and stretched out,

23

中國歷史

Building the Great Wall

Inheriting a tradition of wall building that stretched back almost 2,000 years, the Ming dynasty (1368-1644) committed itself to sealing the northern frontier against the 'barbarian' nomads – the Mongols – with a wall of unprecedented strength. To the west of the Yellow River it was mainly made of rammed earth. To the east, its many sections were of stone. It took almost two centuries to build.

Road
The brick and stone wall, about seven to nine metres (23 to 29.5 feet) high, also served as a road up to six metres wide. Horses could gallop five abreast or pass each other in safety.

Defences
Crenellations allowed bowmen to shoot without being shot.

Bricks
Brick kilns produced the standardised oblong Great Wall brick, which was 36x19x9 centimetres (14x7x3 inches).

Stones
Quarries supplied stone. Some slabs weighed 500 kilograms (1,102 pounds), while a few were more than a ton.

Foundation
A core was made of anything available locally: earth, stones and wood.

24

"To the north, beyond the Gobi Desert, was another very different empire, one ruled by predatory horsemen: the Xiongnu"

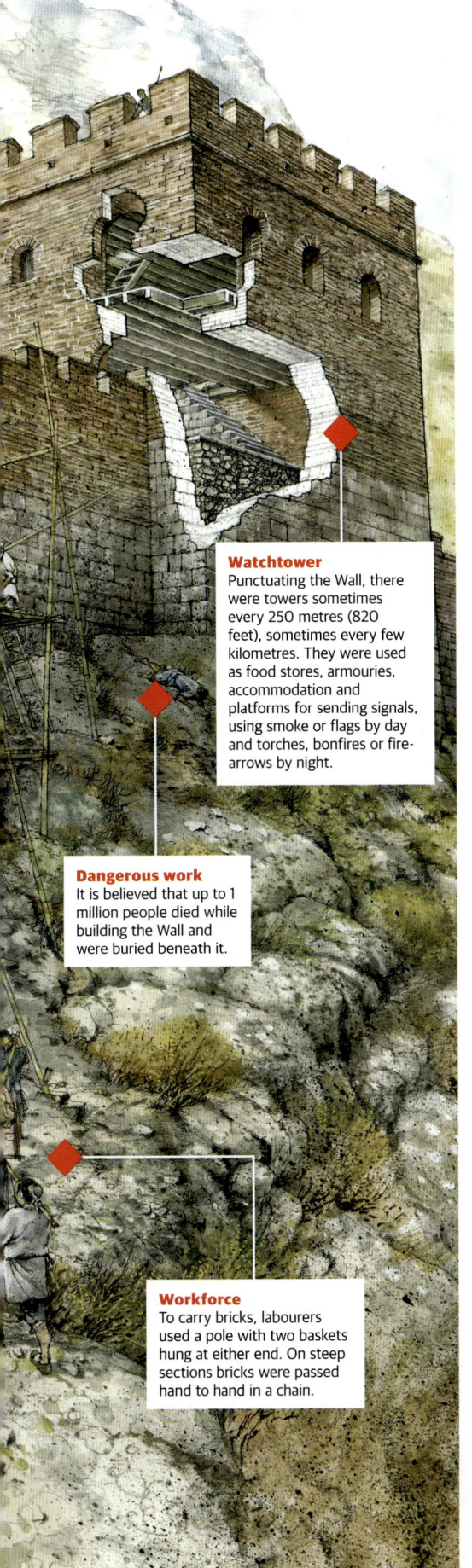

Watchtower
Punctuating the Wall, there were towers sometimes every 250 metres (820 feet), sometimes every few kilometres. They were used as food stores, armouries, accommodation and platforms for sending signals, using smoke or flags by day and torches, bonfires or fire-arrows by night.

Dangerous work
It is believed that up to 1 million people died while building the Wall and were buried beneath it.

Workforce
To carry bricks, labourers used a pole with two baskets hung at either end. On steep sections bricks were passed hand to hand in a chain.

with farms and garrisons along it – that's how to make a Long City into a Great Wall.

The first Great Wall – though it was not called that until the 20th century – guarded the first Chinese Empire, ruled by the strongest of the warring states, the Qin dynasty. Qin (pronounced 'chin', giving its name to China) was originally a backwater on the southern edge of the Ordos semi-desert. Hardened by 400 years of constant war, Qin grew even harder under its most ruthless leader, Qin Shi Huangdi, the First Sovereign Emperor, usually known simply as the First Emperor. It was he who unified the nation in 221 BCE and later created the vast mausoleum near Xian that contains the famous Terracotta Army.

After unification, the First Emperor found he had several problems. To the north, beyond the Gobi Desert, was another very different empire, one ruled by predatory nomadic horsemen: the Xiongnu (pronounced 'shung-nu', and often equated with the Huns, though the evidence for this is hotly debated by scholars). In addition, the emperor had a vast army that needed employment and millions of peasants to be controlled and taxed.

In 214 BCE, he ordered many pre-existing walls to be joined to make a prototype of the Great Wall that was some 2,500 kilometres (1,553 miles) in length. It took approximately four years to build. With millions of peasants dragooned into forced labour, an army to guard them and the Xiongnu locked out, the Wall came to define China, dividing the civilised from the barbarous hordes beyond the border.

So it remained for the next dynasty, the Han, except more so. Han Wudi – Emperor Wu (140–87 BCE) of Han – expanded his empire into Central Asia, despatching explorers and armies to build alliances with local tribes and building the Wall further westwards into the deserts of the Western Regions. To do this demanded control both of Ordos and the Gansu Corridor, which is hemmed in by the Qilian Mountains on one side and deserts on the other, with rivers forming pastures down the middle. Through this bottleneck, only 25 kilometres (15.5 miles) across at its narrowest point, nomads galloped to raid north China. Whoever wished to rule China had to rule the Gansu Corridor.

The consequences were far-reaching and enduring. To seal this frontier involved a range of interlinked strategies, all leading step by step to a Great Wall. Wu had the manpower (1 million conscripts and some 10-13 million available for forced labour). He needed horses by the tens of thousands, mostly acquired through trade. He needed to make allies of a score of oasis kingdoms to the west, bribing them with lavish gifts, especially silk rolls by the thousand. He needed to subdue the Xiongnu. The newly conquered borderlands had to be secured with garrisons, who would have to be fed, which meant sending in colonists to grow grain, and there would have to be the Wall – made of rammed earth, plastered and whitewashed – and fortresses, farms and beacon towers, all creating the Long City we now know as the Great Wall.

Of war there was no end. Almost every year there were invasions and counter-invasions

SAVED BY A BRICK

On a shelf above the gateway into Jiayuguan, at the Wall's far western end, lies a single brick. Legend has it that the architect of the Jiayuguan (Jiayu Pass) was a certain Yi Kaizhan. Yi's boss was a corrupt official, Lu Fu, who had his eyes on the fee. He told Yi to calculate exactly how many bricks would be needed; one brick wrong would mean Yi's death. Yi agreed. But when the fort was finished, there was one brick over. Happily, Lu Fu planned to have Yi killed and to seize his money. But Yi engraved the brick with his name, placed it on a shelf above the gate and made it known that this was a magic brick. "If anyone takes it," he said, "the fort will fall." Lu admitted defeat, and a brick is kept there to this day as a symbol of the architect's expertise and a guarantee of the fort's survival.

THE GREAT WALL OF CHINA

ABOVE During the Ming era Mongol raids were common on the Wall

with tens of thousands of cavalry and infantry. In 103 BCE, a Han force of 20,000, which had advanced 1,000 kilometres (621 miles) across the Gobi Desert, was surrounded and massacred. In 99 BCE, a Han army killed '10,000' Xiongnu yet lost 60-70 per cent of its men. An expeditionary force of 5,000 was trapped by Xiongnu horsemen in southern Mongolia. "The enemy was lodged in the hills, shooting arrows like drops of rain," according to the official Han history. Just 400 made it back home.

To cap it all, the Xiongnu remained a constant presence. Their ruling class had built a rich and varied life for themselves in the mountains of northern Mongolia and southern Siberia. One town was well fortified and served by carpenters, masons, farmers, iron workers and jewellers. Some houses even had under-floor heating, Roman style. To the west, beyond the Great Wall, the Xiongnu controlled some 30 city-states in the Western Regions, mainly in what is today's Gansu province.

With both sides unified neither could win. And what use was the Wall? Very little. The main historian of the period, Sima Qian, records many invasions, but never does he say that the Wall stopped one. Playing many roles – proclaiming the frontier, employing thousands, preventing defections and displaying imperial power – the one thing the Wall could not do was keep out the barbarians.

But there was no alternative strategy. The Wall headed ever further westwards, to Yumenguan, the Jade Gate Pass, on the edge of the vast and impenetrable Taklamakan Desert. Once, the fort was the centre of a thriving city. Now it is a sun-baked stub with few visitors. Beyond, for a few more kilometres, the Han Wall is still there, a low ridge of sand-blasted earth layered with dried grass. The 2,000-year-old grass, preserved by the bone-dry air, looks as if it had been cut last week.

The Xiongnu collapsed in about the 3rd century to be replaced by other nomadic empires. Dynasty followed dynasty. Some wished to save cash and backed away from maintaining the Wall, but always there were generals and bureaucrats who argued for the old policy. The Wall had become part of Chinese identity and could not be abandoned.

The Mongols, the latest of the ever-shifting tribes to dominate today's Mongolia, forced a

BELOW Smoke signals can be sent from one tower to another along vast sections of the Wall to relay messages

HOW TO SEND A SMOKE SIGNAL

In the case of an enemy sighting, beacons were lit during the night and smoke signals sent during the day in order to alert soldiers further down the Wall.

change. In the early 13th century, Genghis Khan united Mongolia's feuding clans with a vision of world rule, and he led them into conquest. North China had lost all semblance of unity, having been divided between a succession of non-Chinese tribes. At the time of Genghis' rise, the dominant powers were the Jurchen (from Manchuria in the northeast) and the Tanguts (of Tibetan origin) ruling most of the far west. The Great Wall was a shadow of its former self.

Under Genghis, the Mongols invaded and conquered until, on his death in 1227, they ruled the greatest land empire the world had ever seen, and it was still only half made. Genghis' vision of world rule was inherited by his grandson Kublai Khan, who conquered all of China, establishing a dynasty that lasted until the Mongols were thrown out of China in 1368. Since the Mongols were ruling on both sides of the Wall, it was completely redundant.

But then came a final, astonishing revival under the successor regime, the Ming. They had seen what happened when China was divided and undefended. It could happen again, for back in the northern grasslands, Mongol princes still claimed they were China's rightful rulers. So the Ming rebuilt – but not well enough. In 1449, a Mongol force advanced on Beijing, destroyed a Ming army and captured the 21-year-old emperor Yingzong. For a moment China lay at their feet. But their leader, Esen, did not have Genghis' vision. He dithered, giving the Chinese time to retrench. When he tried using the emperor as a bargaining chip, it was too late. A successor had been chosen, and Yingzong was worthless. Esen meekly sent him back and retreated into insignificance.

The Ming learned their lesson. Though divided by bitter rivalries, the one thing they agreed on was that the Mongols must never, ever return. There were several options – diplomacy, trade, marriage – but all would imply that the barbarians were equals. Conventional thinking won. The Ming would make the Wall so strong that no nomad would ever appear south of it without permission.

A first step was taken in 1455, when rebuilding around Beijing got under way at the Juyong Pass. It would go on, in fits and starts, for another 170

"Of war there was no end. Almost every year there were invasions and counter-invasions with tens of thousands of infantry"

BELOW Between 1567 and 1570, about 1,200 watchtowers were built along the Wall

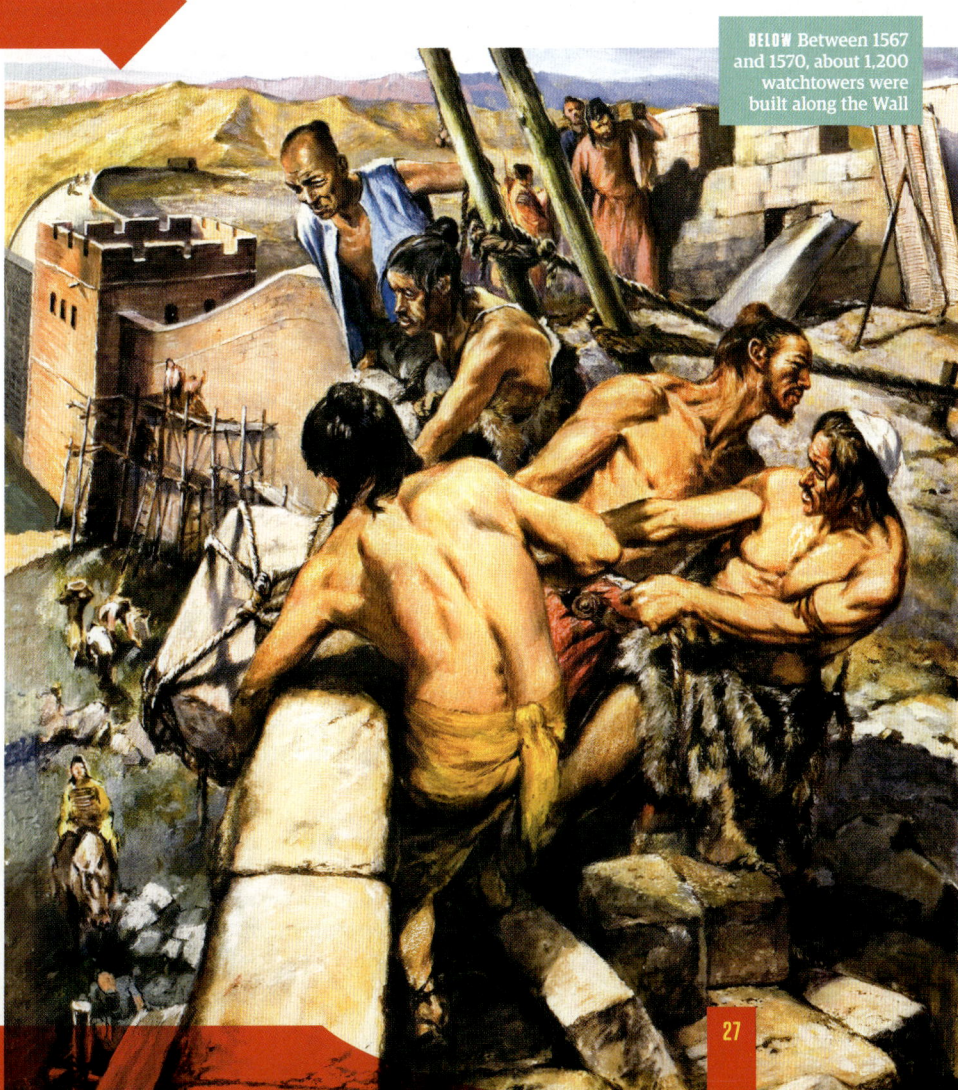

GUARDING THE WESTERN DESERTS

In the bone-dry sands of the Western Regions, wooden strips used as stationery have been perfectly preserved. They contain records of life on the Wall at a time when the Han dynasty was imposing tough laws. This is a composite picture of Xu, a young soldier, from around 100 CE.

Maintain the records
One of his tasks is to catch criminals and deserters, recording names, ages, height, clothing, equipment and baggage. He has to check that travellers are not subject to a court case and are qualified to receive a passport (wood split into two parts, one held locally, so that the traveller will be allowed back into China only when the two are matched).

Oversee the workers
Xu's job includes looking after contingents of three types: convicts, conscripts (men between 20 and 56 on their compulsory two years of service) and volunteers like himself. Arriving in squads, exhausted by their march, they must be listed, clothed, equipped, fed, allocated to a group and set to work. They will dig earth for the body of the wall, mine clay for baked bricks, make horse-dung plaster, apply whitewash, gather reeds, tend orchards and till vegetable gardens.

Check weaponry
The 26 watchtowers in Xu's section do not have staircases but handholds and ropes, which he has to climb to inspect heavy crossbows on their mountings, making sure they are well greased. He also has to count the helmets, armour and pots of grease.

Signal practice
His duties also involve organising signal practice, with flags and smoke-baskets by day and torches and fires by night. Different combinations are used depending on the number of attackers. Mostly, there's nothing to report, but any signal that Xu sends is passed 300 kilometres (186 miles) from tower to tower to Wuwei, where its arrival will be logged. Sometimes, someone will arrive from HQ to check how long the whole operation took.

LEFT Many sections of the Wall were built using forced labour

HOW LONG IS THE WALL?

The Chinese term for the Wall says it's 10,000-li (5,000 kilometres/3,107 miles) long. But '10,000' is simply a traditional phrase for a very big number. In fact, the Wall's nature makes it impossible to measure accurately. It is not a single object. Even the Wall of tourist brochures, the stone section that runs north of Beijing to the Pacific, consists of bits that double, triple and even quadruple each other. Much has vanished under roads and reservoirs. These sections, which straggle for 400 kilometres (248 miles – as the crow flies) to the Pacific, are only the most recent ones, built some 500 years ago. Meandering westwards for almost 1,609 crow-flying kilometres (1,000 miles) over hills, plains and deserts are more ancient walls, mostly of rammed earth, a few restored, many eroded into saw teeth by wind and rain or worn away entirely. Should the gaps be included? What of the low embankments marking the borders of long-gone kingdoms often labelled as parts of the Great Wall on maps yet scores of miles from the 'real' Great Wall?

Why should 5,000 kilometres be favoured? It shouldn't be, and it isn't. Estimates vary from 2,694 kilometres (1,684 miles) according to *Time* magazine at the time of Nixon's visit to China in 1972 to 50,000 kilometres (31,068 miles). In 2012, the first-ever formal measurement of the Wall concluded that its length, including all of its branches, is 21,196 kilometres (13,173 miles) – more than twice the circumference of the Moon.

years. A peace treaty with the Mongols in 1571 ended Mongol raids, but not wall building. When the last bits of this vast edifice clunked into place around 1600, the Nine Border Garrisons (as the Ming called it) ran from the Pacific westwards. It switch-backed over the mountains that are Beijing's natural bastions; it headed over the hills that border Inner Mongolia; jumped the Yellow River into Ordos; and struck westward through the Gansu Corridor to end at the great fort of Jiayuguan, gateway to Central Asia (not so far west as the older Han fort of Yumenguan but better placed).

It is fantastically over-engineered. Of its many architects, the most effective was an austere polymath named Qi Jiguang (1528–88). Brilliant in martial arts, tactics, poetry and writing, he saw the Wall as an all-or-nothing enterprise. "If there is one weak point, and then 100 strong points," he wrote, "then the whole is weak." From this concept grew the Wall as most people know it today: a roller coaster of masonry riding ridges over mountains as chaotic as crinkled tin foil. Every year, millions walk along it, most famously at Badaling, without any effect on its stonework.

Simatai is the most astonishing section. A 610-metre (2,000-foot) wall of rock rises like a fossilised wave with the Wall as its crest. It defies all sense, for no Mongol cavalry could possibly have climbed that ridge. The Wall teeters up a near-vertical slope, reduced at the top to a stairway no wider than a shoe, with vertiginous drops on either side.

The stone Great Wall of the Ming was completed just in time for the dynasty's fall in 1644. It never proved itself, because long before it was finished the Ming and the Mongols were trading, not fighting. When it might have come in handy for keeping out another upstart people, the Manchus from Manchuria, civil strife in China created a power vacuum. The leader of one Ming faction simply opened the gates to the Manchus, and the Wall became instantly redundant because the Manchus, like the Mongols, ruled on both sides as the Qing dynasty (1644–1911). To cap the peace process, the Mongols became part of the Manchu empire by treaty. The Wall ceased to be a barrier. Chinese colonisation proceeded apace and Mongols increasingly became strangers in their own lands.

For 150 years, no one took any notice of the Wall. It took foreigners to see, admire and record,

> "The leader of one Ming faction simply opened the gates to the Manchus, and the Wall became instantly redundant"

the first being a young artist, Lieutenant Henry Parish, who accompanied the British envoy George Macartney when he tried (and failed) to negotiate a treaty with the Manchu emperor Qianlong in 1798. Parish's painting, when turned into a much-copied engraving, presented the Wall as a glorious, pre-photographic cliché: a monumental curtain of stone reaching (it was widely assumed in the West) right across China.

Yet still there were no admirers on the ground, for the Wall runs over remote areas far from the ports where Westerners lived in the 19th century. For the first half of the 20th century, internal conflict, war and Mao's communist revolution in 1949 kept China closed. Finally, after U.S. President Richard Nixon made his famous visit in 1972 and China began to open, the tourists came, and came, and came.

Today, the Wall has risen above politics, strategy and controversy to become a proud symbol of Chinese greatness and the value of unity. It is pure heritage. ★

EXPLORE THE RICH HERITAGE OF THE LAND OF THE RISING SUN

The ancient island nation of Japan has a history that goes back thousands of years and includes some of the most dramatic and chilling events the world stage has ever seen. Find out more...

Ordering is easy. Go online at:
magazinesdirect.com
Or get it from selected supermarkets & newsagents

THE Silk Road

FIND OUT HOW THIS ANCIENT TRADING NETWORK BECAME THE WORLD'S FIRST COMMERCIAL HIGHWAY AND A CONNECTION BETWEEN CULTURES

WRITTEN BY TIM WILLIAMSON

For the average medieval European peasant, the far-off lands of Persia and China were only heard of in stories, and few could even dream of travelling there. Despite this, they might have been more familiar with the sight of the few exotic goods arriving in Europe from Eastern trade routes.

By the late Middle Ages, items such as jade, spices, tea, precious metals and silk could be found for sale in bustling European markets. Many different trade routes had developed between China and the West over the centuries, beginning as early as around 125 BCE when the Chinese Han dynasty began searching far beyond its borders. In the 19th century these routes, which stretched over thousands of kilometres and connected two continents, were nicknamed the Silk Roads after the unique export that the Western world had long coveted.

Silk was first produced in China as far back as 2700 BCE, and for a long time it was the preserve of the Chinese royal family. For this reason, the method of its production remained a closely guarded secret for centuries. However, by the 2nd century BCE the export of silk gradually became permitted. Emperor Wudi allowed silk to be traded for valuable war horses – something the Chinese military desperately needed to help defend their borders. The Yuezhi tribes with whom they traded lived in the western regions of the empire in the Fergana Valley. These exchanges formed the first building blocks of the Silk Road.

It was around this period that the Roman Republic – and later the Empire – was growing in strength and expanding its territory eastwards from the Mediterranean Sea. During military campaigns against the Parthian Empire (which today encompasses Iran, Iraq and Syria) in the 1st century BCE, the Romans observed the silk banners of their enemy and were fascinated by this unfamiliar material that was both strong yet delicate to the touch. The Roman aristocracy soon became obsessed with silk garments and created a great demand for this must-have fabric. Inevitably, these luxury products brought in a premium profit for merchants, but transporting the goods across thousands of miles of challenging terrain was no mean feat.

After leaving the Chinese capital of Chang'an – the heart of silk production in this period – travelling convoys or caravans were forced to traverse around deserts and mountains with their wares. The rough terrain beyond the safety of city walls was perfect for marauding bandits, who stalked the routes the caravans were known to take. Sections of China's Great Wall were extended to protect weak points along the roads, and armed garrisons were stationed in key towns.

Upon arriving safely at the next trading post, town or city, merchants would often sell or barter their wares rather than continuing on the journey west. On the far western Chinese border, Kashgar was one such profitable stop, where traders travelling from the Indian Peninsula, Persia and beyond would gather to buy and sell. In this way the merchants themselves didn't have to risk the long and perilous journeys, but their goods continued onwards along a chain of different owners.

Eventually, the road reached the Parthian Empire, a vast state that was neighbour to both Roman territory and the regions to the east occupying a midway point along the Silk Roads. Becoming aware of the high demand for Chinese goods in the West, the Parthians were able to raise the price on silk sold in their lands, especially to European merchants travelling from Rome and elsewhere. The Parthian capital of Ctesiphon served as a major trading hub, where goods could be exchanged before travelling across the deserts of Mesopotamia strapped to the backs of camels. Palmyra and Damascus were key stop-off points on the way to the ports of Antioch or Tyre before passage across the Mediterranean and Europe.

Of course, not all routes between the East and West were land roads. Sea routes traversing the Indian Peninsula in particular were popular with spice traders. Cinnamon, pepper, ginger, nutmeg, saffron and other goods crossed some 15,000 kilometres (9,320 miles) of sea routes between the Arabian Peninsula and as far as Japan and the islands of the Philippines.

Many of these products found their way into the Mediterranean through southern routes via

MARCO POLO

Born into a prosperous Venetian family in 1254, Marco Polo was one of the most famous explorers of the late Middle Ages. His father and uncle, Niccolò and Maffeo, both successful jewel merchants, joined a diplomatic mission to the court of the Mongol emperor Kublai Khan in 1260, arriving back in Venice in 1269. On their next journey two years later they took young Marco with them. Between 1271 and 1295 the group travelled across Persia and Asia to Khanbalik (now Beijing) and Khan's court.

Shortly after returning to Venice from his 24-year round trip, Marco was captured by Venice's rival city-state, Genoa. However, it was while in captivity that his adventures were first written down. The finished book, *The Travels of Marco Polo*, gives the earliest detailed accounts of European interactions with and impressions of Asian societies and cultures.

"The rough terrain beyond the safety of city walls was ideal for marauding bandits"

RIGHT For centuries silk was exclusively produced in China and was highly sought-after in the West

ABOVE Caravan stops, like this one discovered in Turkey, were used by travelling merchants to rest their camels and trade their wares. In the well-maintained areas of the Silk Road, there were caravan stops every 30 to 40 kilometres (18.5 to 25 miles)

中國歷史

the Red Sea, eventually entering into the bustling markets of Italian trading hubs such as Venice and Genoa. As navigation techniques improved and new hull designs produced faster ships, this route by sea became more and more popular, despite the occasional threat from pirates. As the centuries passed these 'sea roads' became even more preferable, as warring countries occasionally shut down or embargoed the flow of trade.

Back on land, travellers along the road were increasingly carrying with them ideas, philosophies and religious beliefs unheard of in the regions through which they travelled, often with the intention of converting others to their faith. Buddhism first arrived in China across the southern routes leading to India, and likewise Islam and Christianity arrived from the western routes. Soon pilgrims, missionaries, preachers and explorers were common sights on the caravan paths.

It was around the 13th century that the secret of silk production was finally smuggled back to Europe by Christian missionaries. Two Franciscan friars learned the centuries-old Chinese methods and the secret of the silkworm. It was also around this period that the famous explorer Marco Polo was trekking to and from the Mongol court in the far east of China, bringing back with him detailed accounts and stories of his experiences. Rather than the generation of huge profits, it is this mass cultural exchange over centuries that makes the Silk Roads so significant in world history. ★

A DEADLY EXPORT

The horrific bubonic plague, also known as the Black Death, killed millions of Europeans during the 14th century and is thought to have spread via trade ships and busy port towns. However, recent research has suggested that strains of the disease might have travelled even further.

Scientists studying victims of a deadly plague in 19th-century China and the European victims of the 14th-century Black Death have found a startling similarity in the DNA pattern of the two diseases. This suggests the plague not only could have travelled across the Silk Roads heading east but may have been dormant for centuries before being unleashed in another outbreak long after the original Black Death.

RIGHT Tens of millions of people died as a result of the Black Death in medieval Europe

The route to the East

Traders used several different paths to transport their precious cargo

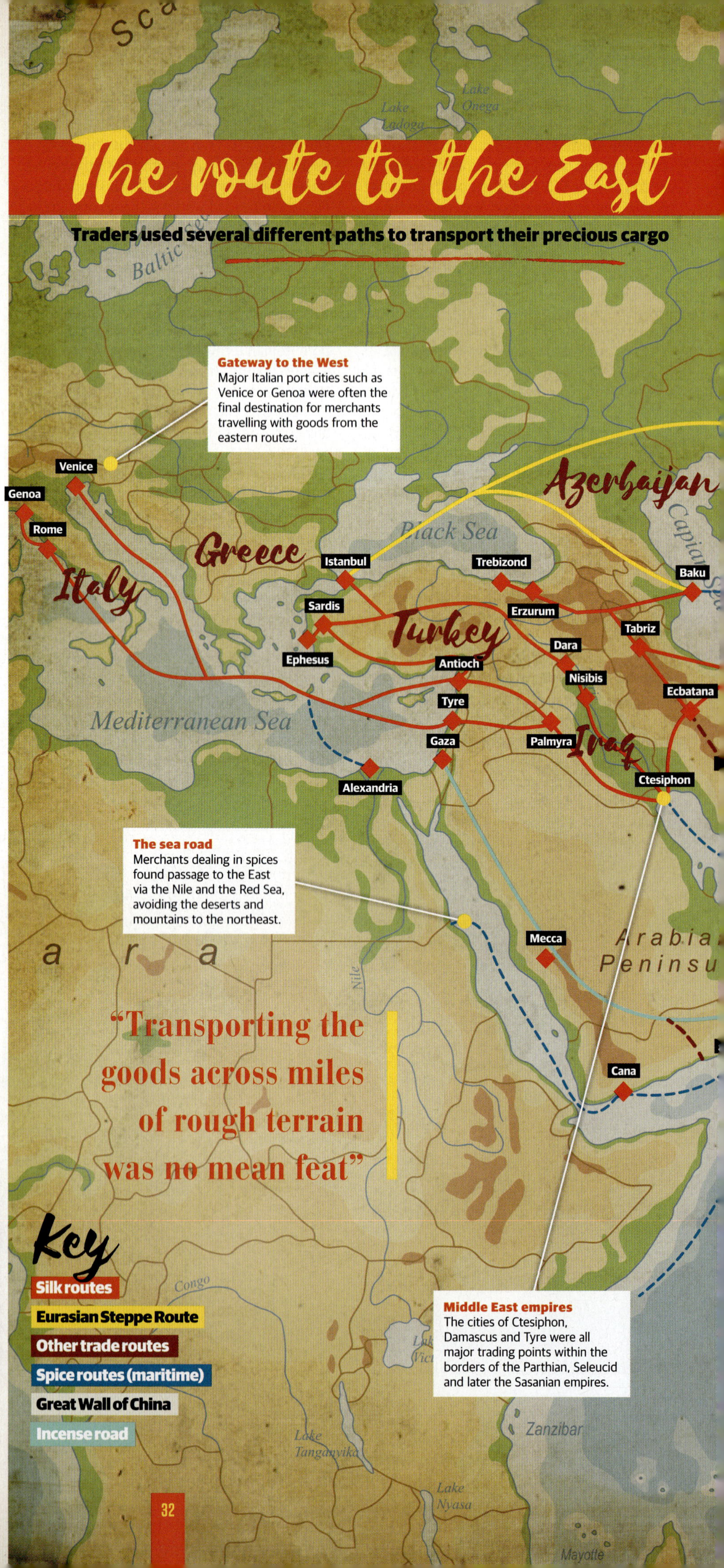

Gateway to the West
Major Italian port cities such as Venice or Genoa were often the final destination for merchants travelling with goods from the eastern routes.

The sea road
Merchants dealing in spices found passage to the East via the Nile and the Red Sea, avoiding the deserts and mountains to the northeast.

Middle East empires
The cities of Ctesiphon, Damascus and Tyre were all major trading points within the borders of the Parthian, Seleucid and later the Sasanian empires.

"Transporting the goods across miles of rough terrain was no mean feat"

Key
- Silk routes
- Eurasian Steppe Route
- Other trade routes
- Spice routes (maritime)
- Great Wall of China
- Incense road

The Three Kingdoms

220–280 CE

FOLLOWING THE COLLAPSE OF THE RULING HAN DYNASTY, THE STATES OF WEI, SHU AND WU PLUNGED INTO SIX TURBULENT DECADES OF CARNAGE AND CHAOS

The Three Kingdoms period begins with the foundation of the state of Wei in 220 CE and closes with the conquest of the state of Wu by the Jin dynasty. The years between 220-263 CE were characterised by the formation of a militarised tripartite that segregated China's central regions, while a series of brutal battles dominated the period of 263-280 CE.

ABOVE A giant bronze statue of General Guan Yu in Yuncheng, Shanxi province, north China

Key figures

155-220 CE
Coa Coa
The penultimate chancellor of the Han dynasty, Coa Coa laid the foundations for the state of Wei.

161-223 CE
Liu Bei
Despite lacking the resources and men of his rivals, Liu Bei became a prominent warlord and established the state of Shu.

179-251 CE
Sima Yi
The grandfather of future Chinese emperor Sima Yan, Sima Yi was the period's most famous general, winning many decisive battles.

182-252 CE
Sun Quan
The founder of the state of Wu in the Three Kingdoms period, Sun Quan was an expert administrator and well known for his efficiency.

236-290 CE
Sima Yan
Sima Yan brought the Three Kingdoms period to a close by defeating the Wu and became the Jin dynasty's first emperor.

BELOW A statue dedicated to Liu Bei, founder and first ruler of the state of Shu

BELOW Red incense burns at the Three Kingdoms Temple in Chengdu, China

Far from minted

When the imperial court collapsed and the Han dynasty fell, so did the imperial mint, with no new coins created. As such, in 221 CE, Cao Wei – the leader of the remnants of the Han that had since largely transformed into the state of Wei – officially declared that silk cloth and grain was the main currency. Despite this many new coins were secretly minted.

The unification bout

The states of Shu and Wu were created largely off the back of the Battle of Red Cliff, which saw Cao Cao, the penultimate chancellor of the collapsing Han dynasty, decisively defeated as he tried to re-unify China in 208 CE. The northern warlord was forced to retreat back to the north, leaving his foes Liu Bei and Sun Quan free to establish their own fiefdoms.

ABOVE The three sworn brothers (Guan Yu, Liu Bei and Zhang Fei) participating in the Yellow Turban Rebellion

Romanticised memory

The Three Kingdoms period crippled the country economically and culturally, with millions of people killed or forced to migrate out of the country, but today it's remembered largely due to its romanticisation in numerous works of later fiction. The most famous example of this is Luo Guanzhong's *Romance of the Three Kingdoms*, a novel that dramatises the lives of the feudal lords and their retainers as they vie for control.

Yellow Turban Rebellion

While 220-280 CE is the modern periodisation of the Three Kingdom period, there is actually no set period, with many Chinese historians citing different starting points. One of the most popular starting dates is the Yellow Turban Rebellion of 184 CE, a mass peasant revolt against the then ruler of the Han dynasty, Emperor Ling.

Reunified under the Jin

With the eventual fall of each of the three warring kingdoms by 280 CE, the reunification of China was instigated by the conquering Jin dynasty. The Jin would continue to rule China for another 140 years, with their control only receding in 420 CE with Emperor Gong's abdication to Liu Yu, ushering in the Liu Song dynasty, the first of the Southern dynasties.

LEFT A scene from Luo Guanzhong's *Romance of the Three Kingdoms*
RIGHT Sima Yan defeated the Wu

> "A series of battles dominated the period"

Major events

219 CE — A rebellious fall
From the Yellow Turban Rebellion of 184 CE onward, the ruling Han dynasty starts to collapse, finally disintegrating in 219 CE.

263 CE — Tripartite broken
After 43 years of existence, being established in 220 CE following the emergence of the tripartite, the state of Shu is conquered by the Wei after a brutal six-month siege.

264 CE — Cao abdicates
Sima Yan forces Cao Huan to abdicate, thereby overthrowing the Wei dynasty and establishing the Jin dynasty.

280 CE — Five-prong offensive
Sima Yan launches a massive five-prong offensive into Wu territory, defeating their military and taking their capital, Jianye.

280 CE — Reunited at last
After 60 years of turmoil, China is reunified under the dominant Jin dynasty, which proceeds to rule the country for 140 years.

The three teachings of China

HOW RELIGION AND PHILOSOPHY SHAPED BOTH ANCIENT AND MODERN CHINESE SOCIETY

WRITTEN BY BEE GINGER

Ancient Chinese society witnessed the spread of three main religions and philosophies during the nation's rich history: Confucianism, Taoism, and Buddhism. These philosophies and beliefs not only formed unique social structures but also influenced government, science, spirituality and the arts. Through these philosophies, we have been able to gain a more detailed insight into ancient Chinese society, which has been carried through the centuries and is still reflected in modern China today.

1 Taoism

Taoism (also called Daoism) developed after Confucianism. Unlike its predecessor, it was focused more on life's spiritual elements. Many of its ancient philosophy-based teachings are attributed to the philosopher Lao Tzu (or Laozi) and his writings.

Translated roughly as 'the Way', Taoists strive to do things in line with Tao and yield to the Taoist structure of harmonious natural order that connects humans to the world and extended universe. By following the 'true nature of the world' and not concerning oneself with government, society and humanistic mortality, Taoism clashes somewhat with the teachings of Confucianism. Taoists embrace nature and seek to become one with it. Their focus is on spiritual immortality and the longevity of the human body and soul. Both traditions provided ancient Chinese society with positive influences and concepts.

Taoism also focuses on the arts, literature and science by studying the natural world to create Chinese medicines. This drive for research and knowledge aided in making enormous contributions to health sciences, which later went on to be further developed. Taoists hold important beliefs in yin and yang and the unity of these opposing forces of energy: life should be lived simply and in harmony and be in balance with both nature and the universe.

Taoists believe that after death a person's immortal spirit will leave the body and join with the universe.

2 Confucianism

One of the most influential religious philosophies in the history of China was Confucianism, which became the central political philosophy of the Han dynasty. It was a somewhat complex school of thought – both a religion and a philosophy. It centred around a strict adherence to social roles, respect for the community and its values, morality and a person's inner values. Its teachings were highly conservative, imploring citizens to acknowledge their place in the social order. You may well be familiar with Confucianism's golden rule: "Do not do unto others what you would not want others to do unto you." These were the words and beliefs of the teacher and philosopher Confucius himself, who lived between 551 and 479 BCE. His teachings were recorded by his disciples over many generations into countless books, including the sacred scripture the *Lunyu* (or Analects), which is the most revered. His teachings of self-discipline, familial respect, obligation, rituals and worship of ancestors are still noticeable in the structure of modern-day Chinese society.

BELOW A woodcut engraving of Confucius teaching students

> "Taoists embrace nature and seek to become one with it"

ABOVE The Tian Tan Buddha statue in Hong Kong is popular with locals and travellers alike. The name Buddha means 'Enlightened One' in Sanskrit

BELOW A Song dynasty statue of the philosopher and father of Taoism, Lao Tzu, in Quanzhou

3 Buddhism

Buddhism was founded by Siddhartha Gautama, commonly known as Buddha, who hailed from India and is thought to have lived from 563 to 483 BCE.

The Buddhist faith concentrates on attaining deep knowledge, growth and personal development. Put simply, Buddhists believe that human life is one of suffering marred by uncertainty and trappings. Through practising spiritual learning, meditation and positive behaviour, Buddhists aim to achieve enlightenment, with the ultimate end goal being to reach Nirvana. Belief in reincarnation is another core pillar, and although it originated in India, the beliefs and practices spread to China some time around 206 BCE.

Buddhist ideas spread as trade along the Silk Road increased. Over time, some of the central doctrines were changed and altered by Chinese influences. Buddhism became popular among the ancient Chinese communities, especially as some of the practices and concepts shared similarities with those of Taoism. Buddhist monks would use these to better explain the concepts to the Chinese, which helped to circumvent the language barrier.

The arrival of Buddhism created competition with Taoism, with each striving to recruit more followers in order to achieve stronger government influence. Over time, Confucianism, Taoism and Buddhism began to merge, providing a strong basis for society, government and daily life. These values and ideas remain, and their influence can be seen in all manner of art, architecture and literature. Each of the traditions continue to be held in high regard in China.

Known collectively as the 'three teachings', Confucianism, Taoism and Buddhism hold an enduring significance in Chinese and Eastern culture. Although some of the teachings and specific beliefs have been slightly at odds with one another, they have remained unified in their influences on society, sharing a concern for respect and self-cultivation.

In modern life a person could observe all three philosophies – for example, by embracing the words of Confucius by honouring ancestors and observing the rules of social behaviour, practising Taoist exercises and breathing techniques, and completing the day with some Buddhist meditation. Even so, there is no doubt which of the three dominates China, with 244 million people (roughly 18 per cent of the population) classified as Buddhists.

10 Great Chinese Inventions

ANCIENT CHINA WAS A MELTING POT OF ADVANCED TECHNOLOGIES AND INGENIOUS INNOVATIONS

WRITTEN BY **PETER FENECH**

1 Paper

It's hard to imagine a world without paper. It's an essential resource in almost every aspect of modern life, from supermarket receipts to sensitive government documents. The history of paper is fascinating, and like many great inventions its birthplace was China. It was first crafted in Lei-Yang during the Han dynasty in 105 CE by Ts'ai Lun, a court official. While early humans used rudimentary symbols applied to cave walls, paper enabled widespread communication and record-keeping, transforming how we pass information geographically and between generations. The initial process likely involved the pulping of hemp, waste rag fibres and the bark of mulberry trees, but the Chinese refined the process further, creating textured and coated papers, even innovating insect-resistant materials and the use of plant-based types, specifically from bamboo. It may seem a modest invention, but it took a further 800 years to reach Europe, and without paper, literature, history, education and entertainment as we know it simply would not exist. You certainly wouldn't be reading this bookazine.

2 Gunpowder

As with many inventions, gunpowder was a discovery produced by the search for an unrelated item, in this case a medicine capable of extending human life. Stumbled upon by Chinese monks in the 9th century CE while experimenting with the medicinal properties of saltpetre (potassium nitrate), it didn't take long for the militaristic applications to be embraced. Gunpowder as we know it today is a blend of saltpetre, carbon (charcoal) and sulphur in a ratio of 75:15:10, although the recipe has gone through multiple revisions over the centuries. Travelling via the Middle East to Europe, the addition of a liquid to the mixture to form a paste created a more stable product, which could be ground more effectively. This safer, more reliable powder has transformed the landscape of modern warfare, leading to the development of complex weapon design, as well as the application of pyrotechnics in fireworks and even theatre.

3 Movable type printing

Just as the invention of paper had an immeasurable impact on human communication and record-keeping, so too did the printing process. Before mass printing techniques, books and complex documents had to be scribed and copied by hand, which was a time-consuming process. Next came block printing, where an entire wooden block was engraved with a page of type, inked and pressed onto paper. Then, in the 11th Century, Chinese inventor Bi Sheng (990–1051 CE) developed movable type. With this method, each character was carved into clay blocks, which could be rearranged as necessary, ink applied and paper pressed against them. This was a far less expensive option since mistakes were much easier to correct than starting a whole page block from scratch. By around 1297, inventor Wang Zhen had introduced wooden moveable type, a more durable option than Bi Sheng's fragile clay. These early printing presses paved the way for literary mass production, enabling the creation of larger books in higher volumes, quickly and cost-efficiently.

4 Compass

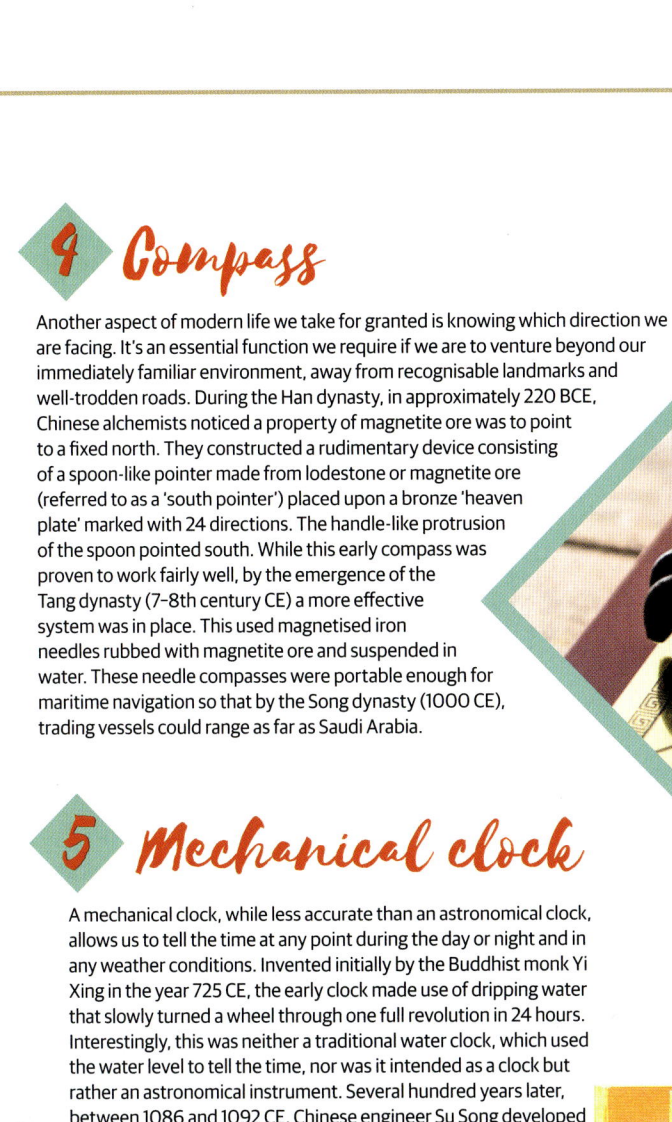

Another aspect of modern life we take for granted is knowing which direction we are facing. It's an essential function we require if we are to venture beyond our immediately familiar environment, away from recognisable landmarks and well-trodden roads. During the Han dynasty, in approximately 220 BCE, Chinese alchemists noticed a property of magnetite ore was to point to a fixed north. They constructed a rudimentary device consisting of a spoon-like pointer made from lodestone or magnetite ore (referred to as a 'south pointer') placed upon a bronze 'heaven plate' marked with 24 directions. The handle-like protrusion of the spoon pointed south. While this early compass was proven to work fairly well, by the emergence of the Tang dynasty (7-8th century CE) a more effective system was in place. This used magnetised iron needles rubbed with magnetite ore and suspended in water. These needle compasses were portable enough for maritime navigation so that by the Song dynasty (1000 CE), trading vessels could range as far as Saudi Arabia.

5 Mechanical clock

A mechanical clock, while less accurate than an astronomical clock, allows us to tell the time at any point during the day or night and in any weather conditions. Invented initially by the Buddhist monk Yi Xing in the year 725 CE, the early clock made use of dripping water that slowly turned a wheel through one full revolution in 24 hours. Interestingly, this was neither a traditional water clock, which used the water level to tell the time, nor was it intended as a clock but rather an astronomical instrument. Several hundred years later, between 1086 and 1092 CE, Chinese engineer Su Song developed a metal cog mechanism the he called his "Cosmic Engine" that more closely resembled the modern clock. It even had a chime that sounded on the hour. This time-measuring tool paved the way for the development of complex technologies, from essential navigation instruments to modern computer networks and Global Positioning Systems.

LEFT While the exact dates of some inventions are unknown, the excavation of similar technologies allow for estimations

BELOW Many great Chinese inventions moved west to Europe along the Silk Road and associated trade networks

RIGHT Many inventions in China were forwarded by cultural, spiritual or militaristic traditions and necessities

6 Alcohol

Alcohol production and consumption are widely considered to be almost universal practices across human cultures. As recently as 2013, evidence was discovered in Henan province that indicated alcoholic beverages brewed from rice, honey, grapes and hawthorn fruit were being produced in China almost 9,000 years ago through analysis of pottery from that period. By the late Shang dynasty (1600-1050 BCE) there were bone inscription records of diverse types of alcoholic drinks, including beer with an alcohol content of around five per cent. While often seen as a recreational substance, it is believed that drinking alcohol played a critical role in societal structure and politics. Ancient people drank to commune with the gods and the dead in the spirit realm, while royal houses used wine to forge political relationships. Today, the alcoholic drinks industry is worth an estimated $1,176 billion, with countries such as the U.S. leading the demand for diversification of craft beers.

7 Silk

Silk is a natural protein fibre that has found widespread use in textiles due to its attractive reflective properties and strength. Industrial silk production can be traced back to neolithic China, around the 4th millennium BCE. The earliest example of silk fabric was a child's burial shroud found in Qingtaicun near Xingyang, Henan province. Legend depicts Princess Xi Lingshi discovering that cocoons of the mulberry silkworm *Bombyx mori* could be unravelled into threads when one fell into her tea as she sat below a mulberry tree. The process of silk production began with rearing domesticated Bombyx larvae, soaking their cocoons and weaving the silk threads on a loom. For almost a thousand years China monopolised silk production before the opening of the Silk Road to the west, where it became a signature of wealth. Beyond clothing, silk has also been used for writing for its ink-absorption properties, for home decoration and even for constructing parachutes and bicycle tyres.

LEFT Innovation in China has not slowed, with the country leading in many manufacturing practices

10 Iron smelting

Despite conflicting evidence that suggests some smelting skills diffused into China from the west, the pre-existing knowledge of furnace technology the Chinese possessed certainly enabled them to develop quality iron-smelting techniques independently. The earliest examples of iron in China date from the 8th century BCE, significantly before evidence of European production. This type of iron was likely too brittle to be used for a wide variety of functions, but by the 5th century BCE annealing processes allowed for strengthened iron. By the time of the Wei dynasty (386–535 CE), metallurgist Qiwu Huaiwen had discovered how to use wrought iron and cast iron in the manufacture of steel. Private iron-making had been banned, creating a state monopoly. From this point, iron production techniques flourished and spread across the globe. Along with general furnace technology, smelting fuelled the industrial revolution in Europe, leading to the creation of many things we take for granted today, from ships to large multi-storey buildings. ★

8 Toothbrush

Having clean teeth is a cornerstone of a healthy population. One of the earliest records of a device used for dental cleaning dates from 1223 CE and was made by Japanese Zen master Dōgen Kigen, who was travelling through China. It is thought, however, that such a tool was being used as early as the Tang dynasty (619–907 CE). The humble bristle toothbrush, in a form we might recognise today, came into being in China in the 15th century. It was originally made up of a handle crafted from animal bone or bamboo with bristles made from Siberian hog hair. The hair itself, being sourced from animals inhabiting the cold northern Chinese climate, was stiff and ideally suited for use as a brush. By the time Europeans brought it to the continent, hog hair had been replaced by horse tail hair, which was softer and preferred by Western gums. By the 20th century, electric toothbrush designs had transformed dental hygiene, helping prevent widespread oral infection.

9 Umbrella

The first mention of a collapsible paper umbrella dates from 21 CE, which referenced one made for the chariot of the Emperor Wang Mang of the Xin dynasty (9–23 CE). This type of umbrella is said to have been constructed with articulated joints that enabled the material to be extended and retracted and, while this does not specifically reference a collapsible nature, such an example was found at the burial site of Wang Guang, Wang Mang's son. Brass joints dating from as far back as the 6th century BCE have also been found, meaning their use in the movement of an umbrella was certainly possible. Silk Chinese umbrellas were commonly made for the wealthy and painted as luxury fashion accessories. Chinese paper umbrellas are also an iconic feature of the Terracotta Army, found in the tomb of Emperor Qin (221–207 BCE), suggesting the umbrella was an integral part of the fabric of ancient Chinese society. Even today, quality umbrellas are associated with wealth and success.

10 GREAT CHINESE INVENTIONS

41

CHINA'S
Golden Age

WITNESS TO REVOLUTIONARY INVENTIONS, TERRITORIAL EXPANSION AND WIDESPREAD PROSPERITY, THE REIGN OF THE TANG TRANSFORMED CHINESE CULTURE AND ESTABLISHED CRUCIAL LINKS TO THE OUTSIDE WORLD

WRITTEN BY **BEE GINGER**

Preceded by the Sui dynasty, the Tang dynasty was truly a golden era in China's rich and turbulent history, for it was not only one of the greatest empires of China but also of the entire mediaeval period. Previously, China had been fragmented for nearly 400 years, with the Sui dynasty responsible for its reunification in 589 CE. Coming to power in 618 CE, the Tang went on to benefit greatly from the foundations laid by the Sui, expanding the nation's boundaries both culturally and geographically. At the height of Tang rule China's territory encompassed vast swathes of Asia, a sphere of influence that spanned from the Korean Peninsula in the east to present-day Afghanistan in the west and stretched north into the windswept steppes of Mongolia and south to the jungles of Vietnam.

In order to ensure that its newly acquired territories were ruled by competent officials,

BELOW Scenes from the life of Emperor Xuanzong and his concubine Yang Guifei, painted by Kanō Mitsunobu

soldiers. However, in time it became apparent that a permanent professional force would be needed if the Tang were to retain their grip on the lands they fought to conquer.

Taizong would oversee huge territorial gains during his illustrious tenure (his reign was so successful that studying his leadership became required reading for future regents), a string of victories that culminated in the Tang annexing the ancient Buddhist kingdom of Kucha (located in what is today the Xinjiang region in northern China) in 648 CE.

With its borders protected, the Tang administration could focus on improving the lots of its subjects. Significant agricultural innovations were developed that enhanced both the production of food and its subsequent impact on the economy. Crops like tea and cotton were introduced, the former becoming a popular beverage both at home and as a luxury export item. The textile industry benefited greatly from the introduction of cotton, and the cultivation of sugarcane brought far-reaching benefits both culinary and economic. Land reclamation followed, with farmers implementing new and improved irrigation. Greater agricultural productivity fostered a period of sustained prosperity that was essential to supporting a burgeoning population.

and allowing for the transportation of people, produce and information to spread across China. The Tang (who introduced the concept of government-regulated building codes) excavated additional canals, and nearby Yangzhou benefited exponentially from its location beside the waterway, in time transforming into the economic centre of the empire.

A period of booming prosperity was further aided by the Tang reopening the Silk Road after marching west to confront the Western Turkic Khaganate, which encompassed vast swathes of Eurasia. Emerging in the 1st century BCE, this crucial passage derived its name from the silk industry, which was first established in Han China. Stretching as far as Constantinople (modern-day Istanbul), it was a major network of trade routes, and by ensuring that merchants could once again traverse it safely the Tang breathed new life into countless industries.

The exchange of goods such as glassware, textiles, sculptures and metal works along the Silk Road made a major impression on the arts of the Tang era. Craftsmen were inspired to experiment with these new and novel techniques, producing unique designs, colours and shapes.

Of the arts, painting in particular flourished, helped in no small way by the Tang court's

"Painting in particular flourished, helped in no small way by the Tang court's patronage"

the Tang established a civil service system based on an individual's merit. The brainchild of the finest Tang emperor, Taizong (whose personal name was Li Shimin), government officials were to be selected following a series of examinations that tested their knowledge of law, literature and Confucian classics, among other subjects. The higher someone scored, the more prestigious their position would be. This gave equal opportunity to all individuals regardless of their social background or family status. Where once titles had been awarded to those with aristocratic ties or supposedly high hereditary standing, now they would have to be earned, and this meritocratic system would later become a model for future administrations.

Like any state, the empire had to be both funded and protected, and the former matter was supported by an increase in tax revenues secured by re-registering the population. As for martial considerations, an impressive standing army was created to replace the previous *fubing* (territorial soldiery) doctrine that had seen troops rotated in and out of the cities and stationed along the frontiers. The Tang had inherited this system from the Sui rulers who had preceded them, with the Tang founding a Ministry of the Army to better regulate its

Architecture and structural engineering also made great leaps. Completed in 609 CE during the twilight of the Sui, the Grand Canal, which remains the world's longest canal at 1,776 kilometres (1,104 miles), connected two of the country's major waterways in the Yangtze and Yellow rivers, thereby linking the northern and southern parts of the country together

continued patronage. The court attracted painters from across the empire, many of whom established themselves there and continued to produce revered works. Several of these artists in residence excelled not only at painting but also at calligraphy and poetry, and it was these related endeavours that became known as the 'three perfections' and were considered to be

LEFT This scroll painting depicts general Guo Ziyi (regarded as one of the greatest Tang-era commanders) accepting the allegiance of the Uyghurs

BELOW Sancai remains one of the most well-known Tang styles of decoration

ABOVE *The Diamond Sutra* of 868 CE is the earliest-dated printed book comprising both illustrations and calligraphy

ABOVE Ancient music and orchestras were revived and greatly enjoyed. They brought with them foreign dance and alternative music, which were embraced by the Tang

the ultimate in artistic achievement. Developed by the multi-talented Wang Wei, monochrome ink painting became popular. It was a style that was in stark contrast to the bold and energetic brushwork of another prominent artist named Wu Daozi, a painter hailed by one British historian as a "master of the 7th century". Another celebrated creator was the architect and artist Yan Liben, who, like Wu Daozi, loved rich and vibrant colours. Yan Liben served under Emperor Gaozong as chancellor, but he is best remembered for the *Thirteen Emperors Scroll*, a stunning painting that depicts 13 emperors from earlier dynasties.

Alongside painting, woodblock printing also flourished in the Tang era, with examples that date back to 650 CE. This form of printing is credited with assisting Buddhist monks in spreading the faith to more people by mass-producing texts, including new translations of Buddhist scripts. There were also notable advancements in the production of porcelain and ceramics, many of which are characterised by their vibrant glazes and elegant designs. The craftsmanship is exquisite, and these products were highly sought-after and exported along with silk as luxury goods the world over. Tang dynasty ceramics boast a striking combination of colours, an array known as *sancai* (three-coloured) that usually combines green, white and amber. Archaeologists have discovered that sancai was originally manufactured exclusively for the imperial elite, who placed them in tombs.

The power of the written word was another form of art that the Tang appreciated, and many poets from the era are still celebrated today for their notable contributions. Li Bai wrote of the human experience, capturing nature's beauty in his intoxicating words. His verses encapsulated profound themes with an emotional depth that conjured vivid imagery for the reader. Another revered scribe was Du Fu, who is considered a literary icon. His words are insightful, focusing more on historical events and social issues of the period.

In addition to literature, great progress was made in the field of mathematics and astrology, with mathematicians delving further into the studies of trigonometry and algebra. Several calendars were developed during this period, one of the most notable being the Xuanming calendar, a lunisolar system and the penultimate one used by the Tang.

Pivotal advancements in medicine were also made. Led by a medical scholar named Su Jing, in 659 CE a team of 23 writers finished compiling the *Tang Bencao* (Tang Materia Medica). Regarded as the first pharmacopoeia ever written, it comprises 54 volumes divided into three sections. The Tang government decreed that it should be issued throughout China to be used as the basis for medical practices.

The achievements of the Tang were many, but arguably it is the inventions of gunpowder and woodblock printing that stand above all else as symbols of the height of Tang ingenuity. Both creations would have an immeasurable impact on the world, respectively revolutionising the art of war and making the process of reproducing texts cheaper and easier, in time leading to the founding of library collections and the advent of moveable type printing. As if these discoveries were not enough, the Tang are also credited with inventing playing cards, air conditioning, gas stoves and the first clockwork escapement

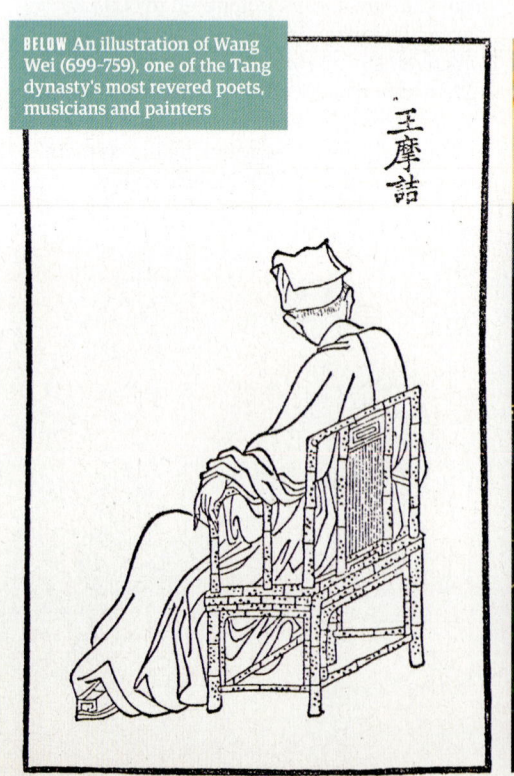

BELOW An illustration of Wang Wei (699-759), one of the Tang dynasty's most revered poets, musicians and painters

BELOW The Tang dynasty commissioned the building of the Giant Wild Goose Pagoda for the study and translation of Buddhist scripture

mechanism (responsible for moving the hands of a clock).

Practical and industrious though they may have been, the people of Tang China were also incredibly spiritual. Along with merchants, pilgrims and diplomats from central and east Asia, as well as further afield, used the Silk Road to navigate their way to China. It wasn't long before Luoyang and Chang'an, the two capitals of the time, were bustling with visitors from every corner of the world. These new arrivals brought with them fresh ideas and new cultural practices and religions that were embraced – and in some cases adapted – by the Tang.

With such a cosmopolitan mix of cultures came various faiths and religions, including Buddhism, which would in time come to reign supreme across large parts of the Asian continent, its practices gradually spread by believers along newly excavated transport links. Its influence was further bolstered by an intrepid Chinese Buddhist monk named Xuanzang. A traveller, translator and scholar, Xuanzang made a perilous 16-year pilgrimage to India to gather 657 scriptures and bring them back to China, where he worked diligently to translate them. He managed to translate 75 out of a total of 1,335 chapters, and it was these writings that helped to foster beneficial cultural connections between the two civilisations and assisted in enriching the knowledge of the Buddhist faith, thus cementing Buddhism's place in China.

Buddhist monasteries gained substantial power as the faith garnered wider attention, insinuating themselves into numerous aspects of daily life by providing lodgings for travellers and acting as school rooms and spaces for holding large gatherings. Among these influential monasteries (some of which owned large tracts of land that brought in a steady stream of money) was a particularly shrewd establishment based in Chang'an that operated the aptly named Inexhaustible Treasury, through which it accrued vast wealth in the form of money, treasures and silk donated by people who had come to repent for their sins. Although the monastery did distribute some of its horde to less fortunate counterparts, in 713 CE Emperor Xuanzong (who would preside over the sharp decline of the Tang dynasty and the beginning of the disastrous eight-year An Lushan rebellion that drastically weakened Tang rule) shuttered the doors of the treasury and ordered all of its wealth to be shared out to more Buddhist monasteries as well as Taoist abbeys. Some of the funds were set aside to pay for the repairing of bridges and halls in the city.

Although it came to dominate the religious landscape (and would do so until the 840s CE, when Emperor Wuzong, a devout Taoist, moved to persecute Buddhists, whom he viewed as a drain on society due to their tax-exempt status), Buddishm wasn't the only faith that was practised. Islam was introduced to China by Arab traders in 651 CE, and at some point during the age of the Tang the imposing Huaisheng Mosque was erected in Guangzhou. Nestorian Christianity was likewise brought inside China's borders by merchants around the same time.

The Giant Wild Goose Pagoda in Chang'an stands as an awe-inspiring testament to the Tang's inclusive approach to religion and cultural exchange. This once five-storey building was constructed in 648–649 CE during the reign of Emperor Gaozong to hold the Buddhist scriptures brought to China by the aforementioned Xuanzang. It was rebuilt in 704 CE on the orders of Empress Wu Zetian (deemed to be the only legitimate female ruler in Chinese history), who commissioned an additional five storeys to be added. Despite being reduced to seven storeys by an earthquake in 1556, it still stands today, dominating the city's now modernised skyline and attracting locals and visitors alike.

As with any dynasty, the Tang era eventually came to an end in 907. As it had done so in 755, rebellion boiled to the surface in 874 during a spell of floods and droughts that had wrought havoc across China. Spearheaded by a general called Wang Xianzhi and his fellow salt smuggler Huang Chao, the uprising saw Chang'an and Luoyong sacked and thousands of foreigners slaughtered in Guangzhou. Although the revolt was eventually crushed in 884, the Tang dynasty had been fatally wounded and would never fully recover. In 907, a warlord named Zhu Wen toppled Emperor Ai, whose father Wen had assassinated three years before. The time of the Tang was over, but no man, no matter how powerful, could ever destroy the legacy of the greatest dynasty to rule China. ★

"Buddhist monasteries gained substantial power as the faith garnered wider attention"

ABOVE These ceramic sculptures of a merchant and a camel date from the time of the Tang dynasty and are today on display at Longmen Museum in Luoyang

中國歷史

Conquering

ABOVE The Mongol steppe warriors obliterated the Chinese on the field. When they hid behind their walls, they simply tore them down

CHINA

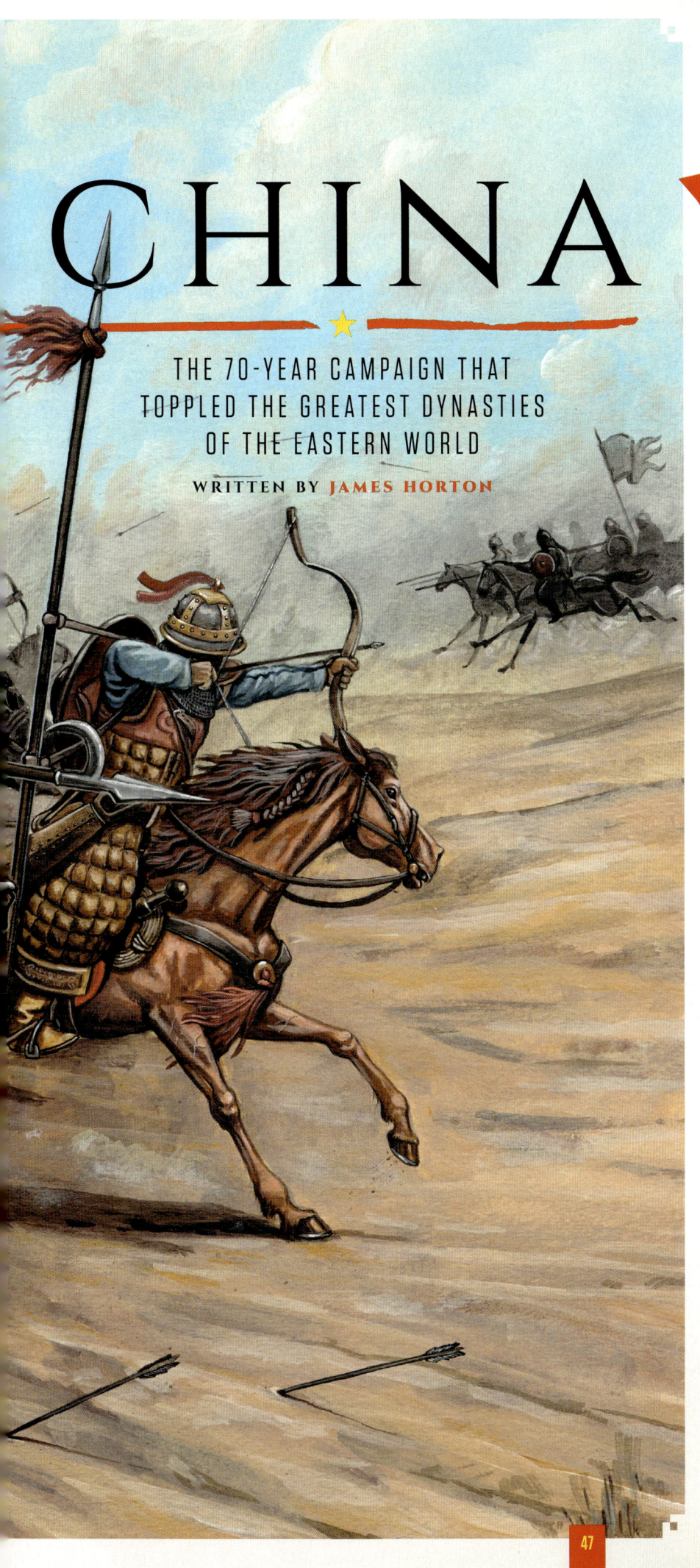

THE 70-YEAR CAMPAIGN THAT TOPPLED THE GREATEST DYNASTIES OF THE EASTERN WORLD

WRITTEN BY JAMES HORTON

In 1200 CE, mainland China was dominated by three primary powers. Oldest among these was the Song dynasty, which had once boasted dominion over a large bulk of China. The lands of the Song had since receded to the south, however, following the emergence of the Jurchen tribes of China's northeast. The Jurchen established their own dynasty – the Jin – early in the 12th century, which acted as a powerful counterweight to the Song.

Eventually, the two fell into an equilibrium just south of China's massive Yellow River. The Song dominated south China and the Jin the north. Jin dominion stretched from China's border in the northeast to a region in the northwest, which was lorded over by their vassals, the Tangut. The Tangut had formed the Western Xia dynasty in the late 10th century within the pocket of the Gansu Corridor, which enjoyed excellent trade links. As such, despite being the smallest and weakest of the three powers, the Tangut were wealthy and boasted a competent military.

The Jin were not oblivious to their dangerous northern neighbours who occupied the steppe. The lands that would soon fall under sole rule of Genghis Khan represented a considerable threat to both the Tangut and Jin, whose lands bordered the nomads. Jin emperors exploited internal fighting between clans on the steppe to prevent unification of the nomadic warriors. Yet despite their best efforts, they could not prevent a Mongol from overcoming the odds, uniting the Mongol clans and ascending to the title of Genghis Khan in 1206. Genghis had no love for the Jin dynasty and knew that the only way to maintain his forces was foreign conquest. The writing was on the wall: the invasion of China was about to begin.

It was the inferior Tangut, not the Jin, who were the Mongols' first target. Genghis sent raids into the Tangut kingdom from 1205 to 1208 under the pretext of revenge, as the Tangut had previously briefly welcomed one of his steppe rivals into their territory. The Tangut opted to pay tribute to appease the Mongols but stopped in 1209, prompting Genghis to launch his first full-scale invasion into foreign lands.

His forces invaded Western Xia and stormed towards the Tangut city of Wu-la-hai. The Tangut mustered a force of 50,000 to stop them, but although they managed to gain the upper hand in a skirmish, the defenders were soon routed as things escalated into a pitched battle. The victorious Mongols then chopped their way through the city before marching south towards the Tangut capital of Chung-Hsing. Between Genghis and the capital lay the Helan Mountains, where the Mongols came upon an imposing sight in the Kei Men fortress. The impassable fortification straddled the mountainous terrain and boasted a hefty garrison numbering in the tens of thousands behind its walls. In 1209, the Mongols were simply flummoxed by the idea of a serious siege. Kei Men's commander, Wei-Ming, repelled an initial Mongol assault, and being aware of the threat the steppe warriors posed in the open field, declined to leave his fortifications.

Genghis was forced to sit his army idly in front of the fortress for two months as he and his generals conceived a way to capture the walls. Eventually, he seemed to surrender the attempt, packing up his camp and marching his army away from the fortress in withdrawal, with his rearguard lagging behind. Wei-Ming sensed an opportunity to deliver a crushing blow on the retreating Mongols and rushed his forces from behind the walls, quickly driving them at the rearguard. Despite being initially confident of victory, it soon became apparent that the Tangut commander had fallen for Genghis' trap. As the two forces clashed, Mongol forces emerged from a sheltered hillside and engaged the Tangut rear, severing the army from the safety of its fortress. The Tangut were defeated, Wei-Ming was captured and the fortress of Kei Men surrendered shortly after the battle, allowing Genghis to continue.

The Mongols then plundered and pillaged their way to Chung-Hsing, but they were once more slowed to a grinding halt upon arrival at the capital. Equipped with defensive towers and high stone walls, the Mongols' amateur approach to siege warfare bore fruit. Unable to destroy or storm the walls, Genghis had his men turn to damming canals fed by the nearby Yellow River in an attempt to flood the city. However, the Mongols' engineering ability lagged behind the ingenuity of the idea, and the dam eventually broke. Instead of flooding the city, water rushed

ABOVE The Mongol general Samuqa swept across Jin territory in 1216 on a great raid, earning many victories

"Between Genghis and the capital lay the Helan Mountains, where the Mongols came upon an imposing sight"

BELOW Tangut mausoleums, erected to entomb the Tangut kings, still rest at the base of the Helan Mountains

into the Mongol camp. Sodden and embarrassed, Genghis was forced to move his men further back from the city walls.

Despite this reprieve the situation inside the city continued to deteriorate. The Tangut king appealed to the neighbouring Jin dynasty for help, but the Jurchen failed to send military aid to their vassal. With his lands devastated, the Tangut king eventually capitulated and agreed to switch his allegiance to Genghis, offering a daughter in marriage and providing the invaders with a tribute of falcons, camels and textiles.

Genghis had achieved victory over the Tangut by January 1210, but he would lead another massive invading force into China by summer 1212. After raiding the border lands of Jin territory in 1211, Genghis marched his full force into their domain the following year. The campaign started well but was abruptly suspended after the Great Khan was struck in the leg by an arrow.

The Jin recaptured much of their lost territory as the Khan's forces fell back to their side of the border for the winter, but the horde would return the following spring. One of Genghis' famous generals, Muqali, captured the Jin's northern capital as the Khan's main force moved towards the central capital, Zhongdu. As the Mongol forces loomed on the horizon, the Jin emperor's court in Zhongdu became restless. The emperor was assassinated and a regency established in his place, but this regent was himself soon murdered. The whole affair achieved little but to weaken the fractured Jin yet further. With their enemy in disarray and the ruling court pinned within the walls of their capital, Genghis left a meagre force at the gates of the city and sent the rest of his forces across Jin territory to plunder.

The army reunified for a final siege of Zhongdu in spring 1214. Their new weapons punctured the Jin capital's walls, but Genghis' men were unable to storm the breaches. The Jin ruling court, after ignoring the pleas of the Tangut just over four years prior, had found themselves in an almost identical position. Succumbing to the mounting pressure, the new emperor, Jin Xuanzong, surrendered in June, offering a bride to Genghis and paying tribute in the form of jewellery, horses, slaves and silk.

Although the Jin had capitulated, the emperor had avoided relinquishing his official title in the peace talks. After the Mongols had returned north with their booty, Xuanzong wasted little time and swiftly moved his court south of the Yellow River to the city of Kaifeng, establishing it as his capital. This flight angered Genghis, who wheeled his army around and marched them back into Jin territory, returning there himself in 1215.

The former capital of Zhongdu did not escape the Mongols' wrath on their second invasion. This time the Chinese were patiently starved

BELOW The Jin Emperor Aizong took his own life so that he could not be forced to submit to the Mongols

BELOW Tolui's men suffered from frostbite and starvation as they laboured through the Qinling Mountains

THE JOURNEY OF TOLUI

How Genghis Khan's fourth son earned a crushing victory through luck and ruthless strategy

In 1231, Genghis Khan's fourth son, Tolui, had set off on an epic march to outflank his unsuspecting Chinese enemy – the Jin. Tolui marched 30,000 men into the freezing Qinling Mountains, forcing his army to suffer the hardships of the punishing cold with only meagre supplies of food. Yet they successfully emerged in December 1231 at the southern border of Jin territory. The Chinese army was startled to find a Mongol host emerging from the mountains and frantically called their armies from the north to face them. Tolui, unprepared for a pitched battle, was forced to withdraw with the Jin hot on his heels.

The winter weather came to Tolui's aid, as heavy rainfall reportedly clouded the vision of the Chinese soldiers and allowed his force to avoid engagement. The Jin army doggedly chased the Mongols as the weather worsened and the rain became snow. Wanting to deteriorate his enemy's position yet further, Tolui ordered the destruction of all supplies in the mountain villages he passed, denying the enemy their resources. After four days of pursuit the Jin soldiers were low on both energy and morale, encouraging Tolui to turn and fight. The Mongols fell upon the exhausted Jin and inflicted heavy casualties on their pursuers, sending them into flight.

Tolui was allowed to complete his journey uncontested and reconnect his forces with the general Subutai, whose army had been able to move south with little resistance thanks to Tolui.

into submission, and Genghis' army unleashed their frustrations on the inhabitants once they surrendered. Rape, mass murder and all manner of brutalities were committed as the Mongols tore the city to pieces over the course of an entire month.

The Jin power base was buckling, yet inexplicably they continued to wage war on multiple fronts. As they attempted to fight off the Mongols they also made forays into southern Song territory. This is a testament to the deep well of manpower that was available to the Jin and their bitter rivalry with their southern neighbours. The Song, for their part, were happy for the Mongols to wage war on the Jin, the foreshadowing of the Tangut and Jin fates somehow not making an impression on them.

By 1217, Genghis Khan had been pulled away from China to fight elsewhere, leaving command in the hands of his general Muqali. From 1217 to 1223 Muqali led a combined force of Mongol cavalry, Khitan forces from China's northeast and Jurchen defectors against the Jin. Muqali was also relying on Tangut troops to bolster his forces. The Tangut were initially reluctant to send soldiers but agreed to do so after an angered raid committed by the Mongols. They served Muqali for well over half a decade as he engaged in a laboured offensive of sieges.

By 1223, Muqali's forces had taken most Jin territories north of the Yellow River, but the death of a Tangut commander discouraged the Mongol vassals and they soon abandoned the campaign. Muqali died in the spring, declaring on his deathbed that he was proud never to have tasted defeat. After some key cities south of the Yellow River were recaptured by the Jin they began peace talks with the Tangut and Song.

> "Rape, mass murder and all manner of brutalities were committed as the Mongols tore the city to pieces"

RED COATS
The militia outlaws who rose from the ashes of northern China's scorched fields to claim their own territory

The war between Genghis Khan's Mongols and northern China's Jin dynasty across the 1210s and 1220s took a severe toll on the population, who found themselves the most brutally punished party of the protracted conflict. The Great Khan's armies wreaked havoc on their homes, striking fear into the peasantry and townsfolk who recoiled in dismay at the rampaging hordes. As their lands descended into chaos and lawlessness took hold, some sensed which way the winds were blowing and cast their support behind the Mongols. Others opted to form local militias to protect their families, while some rose up in rebellion and formed their own independent forces.

One of the most famous of these were the Red Coats, who petitioned the neighbouring Song dynasty for supplies in exchange for their loyalty. The Song agreed to supply the militia, but although the red in their name matched the 'fire' colour of the Song court, the Red Coats were anything but subservient. Instead of acting at the behest of the Song, the Red Coats used their supplies to wrestle control of the Shandong Peninsula from the waning Jin. The Mongols had paved the way for the ascension of the bandit Red Coats, and it served them well. The rebels would prove a thorn in the Jin's side during the years between Genghis and his son Ögedei's invasions.

BELOW Ögedei assumed the role of Great Khan after Genghis died in 1227 and led the Mongols to victory over the Jin

ABOVE Lawlessness and banditry became commonplace as the Jin were unable to police or protect their lands

It may have appeared that peace was finally approaching mainland China, but Genghis would be back. The Great Khan was in his mid-60s by 1226 when the Mongols mustered a massive force to crush the rebellious Tangut once and for all. Genghis had recently fallen from his horse during a hunt, but the ageing conqueror endured to march his men into battle outside the Tangut capital. Genghis waited for the Yellow River to freeze before crossing with his army and smashing the Tangut forces, sealing their fate. This was the Great Khan's final military victory. Genghis died soon after the battle in 1227 – possibly from lingering damage from the horse fall – but his death was kept a secret while the siege of the capital was taking place. Once the city had submitted the Mongols ferociously ripped it to pieces and slaughtered the inhabitants, eradicating the Tangut state.

The Tangut territory was incorporated into the Mongol Empire, but it would fall to Genghis' third son Ögedei to bring the Jin to heel. Ögedei was around 40 years old when

ABOVE The Jin dynasty possessed considerable economic and military power before its destruction by the Mongols

he was named Great Khan, and along with his brothers he enjoyed personal dominion over a portion of Genghis' empire. Ögedei had inherited the conquered lands of China and sought to expand his personal territory, bringing his father's wish of a Mongol-ruled unified China closer to fruition.

Together with his younger brother Tolui and Genghis' long-serving and famous general Subutai – who had recently been campaigning on the fringes of Europe – Ögedei led his forces against the Jin in 1230. The Jin were still mostly hemmed in south of the Yellow River, but they had managed to recapture several towns in the interim years between major Mongol offences. Ögedei's forces first successfully besieged the stubborn city of Feng-Hsiang, which had been a thorn in Muqali's side during his years commanding the Mongol armies. Using a strategy favoured by his father, the new Khan next divided his forces into three in order to march on the capital of Kaifeng from different directions.

The Mongol armies reunited in early 1232 and clashed with a massive Jin host numbering perhaps 100,000 outside Kaifeng's city gates. This defiant stand proved futile, as the Mongols once more displayed their superiority in pitched battles and crushed the opposition. Ögedei's forces settled into a siege in April as the Jin desperately pleaded to the Song for help. But as with the Tangut, the mutual distrust and dislike between the powers of China ran deep and the dynasties remained divided.

Subutai was left in charge of the siege. He made an attempt at negotiating the city's surrender, but his envoys were killed. He was therefore forced to attack the city, which proved especially difficult as the Jin employed gunpowder weapons. Gunpowder was not a new invention, but its use in firearm precursors and in primitive explosives was novel to the startled Mongol soldiers.

The Jurchen soldiers employed weapons known as 'fire lances', which resembled spears with an additional tubing attached to them. The tube could be stuffed with gunpowder and ignited, sending flames spewing outward over a few metres. Yet more dangerous were the primitive bombs that exploded after being ignited by a fuse. The Jin soldiers tossed these over the battlements and lowered them on chains

ABOVE Gunpowder was used in many forms of weaponry, from fire arrows and lances to primitive explosives

into sheltered trenches dug by the Mongols. The explosions tore the enemy soldiers to pieces and set the ground ablaze, teaching the Mongols a harsh lesson about the potential devastation and usefulness of gunpowder weapons.

Subutai kept applying pressure on the Kaifeng defences, and towards the end of the summer plague broke out in the city. Sensing all was lost, the emperor and his entourage fled and attempted to establish a new capital elsewhere. Abandoned by their ruler, the defenders lost heart, and before long they surrendered to the Mongols. The forces of Kaifeng showered Subutai and his army with gifts and tribute in an effort to save the population, which yielded the desired effect. The Mongols plundered, but they refrained from sacking the city, much to the population's relief.

The Jin were stubborn in relinquishing power, though, and still held hope of restoring their fortunes from yet another new capital. However, this was not to be, as the Song dynasty made a deal with the Mongols to send an additional 20,000 troops as reinforcements to help destroy their old foe. The last Jin holdout was taken in February 1234, with the emperor opting to hang himself rather than fall prey to the Mongols. Ögedei absorbed the Jin territory into his domain, completing the conquest of northern China. The Great Khan likely harboured ambitions to begin an invasion against the Song in the near future, but bizarrely it was the southern Chinese dynasty who tossed the fledgling niceties between the two empires aside first.

Later in 1234, the Song launched a surprise attack into Ögedei's domain, capturing Kaifeng. The former capital of the Jin had once been the nexus of the Song Empire, and they were probably glad to have it back in their hands. However, this feeling of elation didn't last long, as the Mongols promptly recaptured the city. The provocative actions of the Song may appear brazen given that over the previous 25 years the Mongols had annihilated the Tangut and destroyed the Jin, but they initially appeared justified in their belief that they could avoid a similar fate.

Southern China was a new type of territory unlike any other theatre of war the Mongols had encountered. The oppressive heat showed the steppe warriors no mercy and the mountainous terrain that filled the landscape was incompatible with their fluid, cavalry-based fighting style. In addition, Song cities were connected by an interweaving series of rivers that meant dominance on the water would prove essential for starving key cities and fortifications into submission.

As such, the conquest of southern China would require a serious investment of manpower, but Ögedei instead turned his attention to the west during the latter years of his rule. His forces did manage to capture the critical city of Xiangyang in 1236, but Song forces soon overwhelmed the garrison tasked with guarding it and recaptured the city.

BELOW Many Chinese towns were offered a choice by the Mongols: surrender or die. Those who resisted were slaughtered or sold into slavery

RIGHT The Silk Road - a massive trading route that stretched from Asia to Europe - ran through Tangut territory, providing them with excellent trade networks

RIGHT This ornate Mongol helmet is made of iron and sports a dramatic depiction of a roaring dragon

Ögedei died in 1241 from the effects of alcoholism at the age of 55. Due to political turmoil his successor, his son Güyük, wasn't coronated until 1246. Güyük also appeared to favour western expansion over making a concerted drive further into southern China, but he died in 1248 before he had the chance to launch any serious campaigns. The rank of Great Khan then switched from Genghis' third son Ögedei's line to his fourth son, Tolui's. Tolui's son Möngke Khan came to power in 1251, and he placed his younger brother Kublai in control of northern China.

Kublai felt a strong affinity for China. As a child he had been nursed by a Tangut, and Chinese advisors featured prominently in his inner court. At this stage Kublai had limited military pedigree, but he swiftly began honing his battle skills by launching a campaign against the Dali Kingdom, which sat on the Song's western border. Dali swiftly capitulated and Kublai and Möngke later launched a joint invasion against the Song. They split their hordes and marched down opposite flanks of

ABOVE Genghis Khan's fourth son, Tolui, helped his brother Ögedei depose the Jin dynasty

CONQUERING CHINA

ASSIMILATION
Morphing foes into subservient allies was one of the Mongols' greatest strengths

The Mongols were nothing if not adaptable. They were masters of steppe warfare, but as Genghis Khan's horde spread out from Mongolia, they were found to be novices in many elements of medieval warfare. However, one way they accelerated their learning and manpower was by assimilating conquered foes into their ranks. It is safe to say that without the incorporation of Chinese soldiers into the Mongolian army, it would have been incredibly difficult – perhaps even impossible – for the Mongols to have conquered China.

In the early years of Mongol invasion into north China, Chinese engineers were both captured and voluntarily defected to their cause, quickly helping the Mongol armies to grow accustomed to siege warfare. As the war continued and more Chinese continued to defect, many were placed at the vanguard of the Mongol armies. By assuming the most dangerous positions at the front of sieges, the Mongol generals hoped to keep their steppe warriors safe in exchange for the lives of expendable Chinese troops.

Yet more value came from the Chinese thanks to their knowledge of weaponry. After the fall of Kaifeng, the Mongols absorbed those who could educate them on gunpowder's use in weapons, adding another lethal element to their arsenal. By Kublai's era the Mongols in the army were actually outnumbered by their allies and conquered forces, highlighting just how prominent Chinese soldiers were in the Mongol conquest of China.

ABOVE The Chinese were pioneers in gunpowder weaponry and passed this knowledge onto the Mongols

ABOVE The child emperor Zhao Bing was the last crowned ruler of the Song dynasty

Song territory, earning ground in many hard-fought engagements.

However, Möngke died while on the campaign in 1259, inciting discourse throughout the ruling family. Both Kublai and his younger brother Ariq Böke had themselves declared Great Khan, forcing Kublai to make a truce with the Song while he turned his attention north to settle affairs with his sibling.

Ariq surrendered to Kublai in 1264, allowing the undisputed Great Khan to properly invest in the last great Mongol conquest – that of subjugating southern China. His major offensive started off successfully as his army won a large engagement and captured a fleet of ships in 1265. The Mongols next set their sights on Xiangyang, the same city Ögedei's forces had briefly captured in the 1230s. Kublai would have likely rued his predecessor's failure to hold the fortification, as Xiangyang sat on the banks of the Han River and was essential for dominating the waterways of Song territory.

The Song understood that holding the city was critical to their war effort and so invested heavily in ensuring that it was kept well supplied with food and weaponry. Xiangyang would endure the siege for over five years, and it would take expertise from across the Mongol's vast empire to eventually take it.

By the early 1270s the Great Khan's army was a chimera of different nationalities and battle styles, and it was this diversity of skill sets that allowed him to capture Xiangyang. Korean marines helped the newly constructed Mongolian naval warships to impose a blockade on the Han River, and in late 1272 Persian engineers designed a powerful trebuchet that could shatter the city's walls with 300-kilogram (661-pound) boulders. The northern Chinese

ABOVE The fortifications at the Song city of Xiangyang were formidable and resisted the Mongols for over five years

BELOW The capture of Xiangyang gave the Mongols control of the Han and Yangtze rivers, making it easy for them to penetrate southern Song heartlands

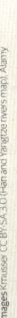

"Kublai ruled over China as emperor of the newly established Yuan dynasty"

lent their knowledge too, as crude gunpowder-based explosives could be loaded into these devastating war machines.

Xiangyang fell in 1273, and with it the will to continue fighting across many towns and cities of the Song Empire. Surrender and defections became commonplace, with many believing a Mongol victory was now inevitable and some actually welcoming the rule of Kublai.

With the Yangtze and Han rivers now firmly under his control, Kublai mustered a gargantuan force of 200,000 to march on the capital of Hangzhou. In an echo of the Jin, the realisation that their capital was threatened turned the Song court against one another. Prominent members jostled for power, achieving little and encouraging defections of their commanders to Kublai's side. A massive Song army did manage to assemble just outside the capital, but after being bombarded by the Mongol's catapults their loyalty began to waver and many defected to the Mongol's side. Accepting that resistance was futile, the Song empress capitulated in early 1276, but some defiant members of the court stubbornly refused to surrender. They hurried to crown a new emperor, Duanzong - who was only six at the time - and fled. Sadly, the Song's 17th emperor didn't sit the throne for long, with Duanzong dying in 1278 at the age of just eight. His younger brother, Zhao Bing, was promptly elevated to the rank of emperor. He would be the last emperor of the Song dynasty.

The Song made their last stand off the coast of Guangdong, where they'd anchored and bound together roughly 1,000 ships to prevent retreat. Despite withstanding the Mongol navy initially, in March 1279 the Mongols launched a vicious assault on the fleet's centre. One of the emperor's advisors watched the enemy close on them with mounting horror and eventually resolved to grab Zhao Bing in his arms. He then leapt overboard, killing them both. In that moment it was over: Kublai Khan had become the undisputed master of all China.

The Mongols were the first foreign conquerors to ever dominate China. It had taken them over 70 years to bring their new subjects to heel, and in that time the Mongol Empire had grown and fragmented, the army had changed dramatically and even the ruling khanate had evolved. Kublai ruled over China as emperor of the newly established Yuan dynasty and embraced the Chinese way of life, but it was still a Mongol who sat on the throne. The steppe nomads had entered the 13th century as China's bothersome northern neighbours, yet they would leave it as supreme overlords of the entire state. ★

THE RED TURBAN Rebellion

HOW A BUDDHIST SECT LED TO THE OVERTHROW OF CHINA'S MONGOL OVERLORDS AND THE RISE OF THE MING DYNASTY

WRITTEN BY EDOARDO ALBERT

Floods, famine, pestilence. For the hard-pressed peasants of Yuan China, ruled over by the domineering descendants of the Mongol conquerors who had established themselves as overlords of the land, the series of natural calamities indicated one thing: their Mongol rulers had lost the Mandate of Heaven. With the Mandate of Heaven withdrawn, rebellion became not just possible but legitimate: Heaven itself asked of them to remove their unjust emperor and replace him with a new ruler.

But the Yuan dynasty, descended through Kublai Khan from Genghis Khan himself, was not about to simply shuffle back to Mongolia. There would be 17 years of conflict before a new emperor was able to found a lasting dynasty.

The conditions for this long transition had been laid earlier in the political weakness and infighting of the last Yuan emperors and the range of natural disasters that afflicted China in the 1340s and 1350s. The first phase of natural disasters culminated in the 1344 flood of the Yellow River. The river itself, sometimes called 'China's Sorrow' for the devastation inflicted by its floods, is an essential part of China's wealth, its waters providing irrigation for vast areas of agriculture. But because it carries huge amounts of silt, the river lays down deposits on its river bed wherever the stream runs slowly, raising the underlying level and, roughly every 100 years, causing the Yellow River to break through the levees and seek a new path to the sea. But the flatness of the North China Plain, while ideal for agriculture, means that these new channels can be hundreds of kilometres apart: in historical times, the Yellow River has flowed into the sea both north and south of the Shandong Peninsula. The 1344 flood moved the river's mouth to south of the peninsula, where it remained until the middle of the 19th century.

The response of the Yuan regime to the flood of 1344 caused them as much political damage as the flood itself. To try to prevent future floods, the emperor forced huge teams of Han Chinese peasants to raise new embankments. But this forced labour, rather than securing the regime against future floods, served simply to push more people into following the various rebel groups that were springing up around China. Of these, the most important and the most successful was the White Lotus Society.

Originally a Buddhist sect, the White Lotus adapted to persecution by the Yuan dynasty by broadening both its religious base – bringing elements of Daoism, Manichaeism and folk religion into its belief system – and its social base, opening out membership and, crucially, leadership to secular Chinese. As such, it became a focus of resistance against the corrupt rule of the Yuan.

The White Lotus planned to begin an open rebellion in 1351, but the putative leader of the rebellion, Han Shantong, was betrayed and executed by the Yuan. However, the White Lotus united around his son, Han Lin'er, proclaiming him the legitimate heir to the Song dynasty that the Mongols had overthrown under the title 'Little Prince of Radiance'. Contemporary records have been either lost or suppressed, so not much is known about Han Lin'er, but what is clear is that one of his generals, Zhu Yuanzhang, quickly became an important part of the movement supporting the 'Little Prince of Radiance', his ability outweighing his humble birth.

While the response of the Yuan to these mounting threats was hampered by political infighting and rivalry, the same

THE RED TURBAN REBELLION

ABOVE The Great Wall was largely built during the time of the Ming dynasty, which took control of China following the rebellion

ABOVE *The Yellow River Breaches its Course* by Ma Yuan (1160-1225)

THE WHITE LOTUS

The Buddhist secret society that overthrew the Mongol Empire

Buddhist sects had provided the focus for opposition to the later Yuan dynasty, but since most were limited to professed monks the regime had managed to suppress them. The White Lotus Society was a different beast all together. Its doctrine, that the Maitreya, the Buddha Who is to Come, would arrive and overthrow the Yuan dynasty, gave it huge eschatological appeal. With the Maitreya's arrival, the order of life would be restored following its decay under the Mongols who had dominated China for the last century.

Just as important as the coming of this divine figure was the social innovation that allowed the White Lotus Society to accept secular leaders alongside religious ones. With its spread into wider society – the Society even allowed women to join its ranks – the White Lotus became a force to be reckoned and a strong opponent of the Yuan loyalists.

The White Lotus broadened its popular appeal further by incorporating aspects of Daoism, Manichaeism and Chinese folk religion into its stew of beliefs, making itself a belief system that could accommodate almost anyone among the Han Chinese. It was from the White Lotus Society that the Red Turbans emerged.

BELOW A Ming-era depiction of the White Lotus Society meeting to prepare for the arrival of the Maitreya, the Buddha who will put the world to rights

was true of the rebels. About the only thing that united them initially was their headwear: red turbans, to distinguish themselves from forces loyal to the Yuan dynasty. Thus the revolt became known as the Red Turban Rebellion.

As with other turbulent periods in Chinese history, the revolt soon devolved into a contest between rival warlords, each one controlling part of China's huge area and its resources. The Yuan dynasty had effectively sabotaged its own chances of winning the struggle because of Emperor Toghon Temür's decision to sack his most effective general, Toqto'a, and then later allow him to be assassinated.

General Toqto'a, who was also a notable historian, was extremely popular among his troops; if he had commanded it, they would have followed his standard rather than that of the emperor's. But Toqto'a accepted his sacking rather than rebel. However, many of his soldiers, disgusted by the treatment of their beloved general, deserted to the various rebel forces rather than continuing to fight for the emperor. Toghon Temür himself seemed to lose interest in the struggle, nominating his son to reign after him but doing little to halt the disintegration of his regime.

Meanwhile, Red Turban warlords were establishing their own fiefs over various parts of

> "The revolt devolved into a contest between warlords, each one controlling part of China"

China and jockeying for the necessary position that would enable them to strike the final blow against the Yuan while still keeping an eye open for a knife in the back from a rival warlord.

As the power of the Yuan waned, the Red Turban warlords gradually realised that the Yuan emperor could be put to one side while they decided among themselves who would finally remove him and become emperor in his place. In this messy conflict, with up to a dozen or so warlords in competition, there were nevertheless only a small number who ever looked capable of seizing power. The first two serious contenders were Zhang Shicheng (1321-1367) and Fang Guozhen (1319-1374), both of whose careers had started with smuggling and piracy.

Fang Guozhen, a pirate whose main business income was salt smuggling (a very profitable enterprise when salt was the only effective food preservative and the government taxed it), established his superiority at sea, but he proved unable to effectively govern the coastal strip that he controlled.

For his part, Zhang Shicheng gained control of some of the richest and most-populated parts of China, from the coast south of the Shandong Peninsula and covering a wide swathe of the rich agricultural plain inland from the coast. However, according to later historians, having gained mastery of these rich lands Zhang and his entourage decided to indulge themselves on the fruit of their spoils rather than attempt to govern effectively or move against rivals. Effective administration in China depended on an educated class of professional bureaucrats: without their support, it was all but impossible to run an effective administration.

For a while, Chen Youliang (1320-1363) looked the warlord most likely to consolidate control over the rival leaders and oust the Yuan. Playing for an opportunity, he would ally himself with other rebel factions only to betray them. A skilled but brutal general, Chen Youliang built up a strong army and brought more and more territory under his control until, in 1360, he felt strong enough to declare himself emperor of nothing less than a revival of the Han dynasty that had ruled from 202 BCE to 220 CE.

Such a claim betokened a breathtaking ambition, but Chen Youliang relied almost entirely upon military might to back up his vaulting claims. His lofty ambitions came crashing down at the Battle of Poyang Lake in 1363. While Chinese history is generally taken

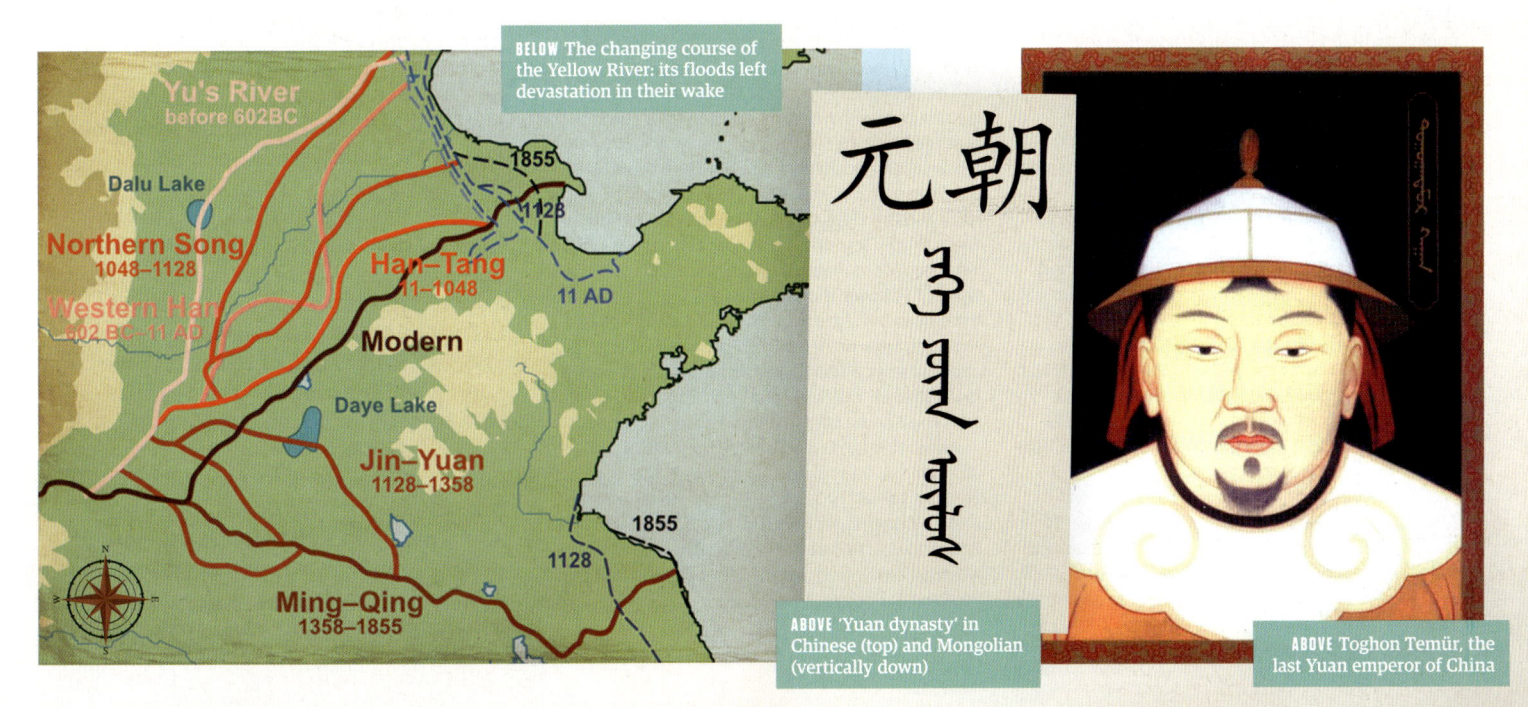

THE LIFE OF ZHU YUANZHANG
The man who went from starving orphan to emperor of China

Some rulers may have clawed their way to power from humbler beginnings, but not many started life as Zhu Yuanzhang did. Born on 21 October 1328 to a peasant family about 160 kilometres (99 miles) northwest of Nanjing, his parents were so poor that they had to give away some of Zhu's older brothers and sisters since they could not feed them. Despite this, the family still fell victim to the famine in 1344 that resulted from the flooding of the Yellow River: all died save 16-year-old Zhu.

In a China riven by floods, famine and conflict, the prospects for a 16-year-old orphan were poor. To avoid starvation, Zhu took refuge in a local Buddhist monastery as a novice monk. But the monastery, desperately poor itself, could not afford to support him, and soon Zhu found himself on the road, eking out the most meagre of existences as a wandering beggar. Having survived three years like this, Zhu returned to the monastery, learning to read and write.

ABOVE A portrait of Zhu Yuanzhang when he had ascended to the throne having left his days of starvation far behind

In 1353, he joined a rebel Red Turban force led by Guo Zixing, rapidly rising to second in command and marrying Guo's daughter. When Guo Zixing died in 1355, Zhu took over command and, a year later, seized control of Nanjing, making it the power base from which he gradually conquered the country.

BELOW The changing course of the Yellow River: its floods left devastation in their wake

ABOVE 'Yuan dynasty' in Chinese (top) and Mongolian (vertically down)

ABOVE Toghon Temür, the last Yuan emperor of China

ABOVE The Ming Xiaoling Mausoleum, final resting place of the Hongwu Emperor

ABOVE Some idea of the scale of Lake Poyang is given in this picture. The bridge, Poyang Lake No.2 Bridge, is over 5.5km (3.4mi) long

THE BATTLE OF LAKE POYANG
The largest naval engagement in history was a battle like no other

The Battle of Lake Poyang was the largest naval engagement in Chinese history, as well as the biggest naval battle in terms of numbers of men taking part in world history. And it happened on a lake. Albeit, Lake Poyang is a big lake: its size depends on the season, wet or dry, but in this time period it typically covered 3,500 square kilometres (1,351 square miles).

In 1363, Chen Youliang learned that his rival Zhu Yuanzhang was engaged on the southern borders of his territory. Taking the chance, Chen launched a naval assault on Zhu's fortress city, Nanchang, which was then on the shores of Lake Poyang. To do so, Chen assembled a force of 300,000 men manning an armada of ships, with the largest, tower ships, being armoured assault vessels. However, the defenders of Nanchang held out for two months before a messenger got through the siege to tell Zhu Yuanzhang what was happening.

In response, Zhu's fleet of 100,000 men on 1,000 ships advanced into Lake Poyang. Eager for a decisive battle, Chen Youliang ended the siege and sailed his fleet out into the lake. On 30 August 1363, the fleets met. While Chen's fleet had the advantage in men and ships, the lake's water levels had declined through the dry season: the tower ships, with their deep hulls, could barely move.

The battle lasted four days and, after nearly coming to grief himself on the first day, Zhu realised that the low water levels gave his smaller ships an advantage over Chen's fleet, bunched together in the deep water channels. On the second day, Zhu launched fire ships that, blown by a favourable wind, drifted into the tightly packed vessels of Chen Youliang. More than 100 ships were sunk. The battle was not yet over though, with the third day used by both sides for regrouping. Chen Youliang still had the advantage in men and ships, an advantage that endured after a fourth, inconclusive day of battle. Zhu withdrew his fleet, but Chen Youliang was still contained in the lake with his escape blocked.

A month later, Chen Youliang made his break-out attempt. His fleet fought its way past the land forts blocking the entry into the Yangtze River only to find Zhu waiting for him. The two fleets engaged in desperate battle but the whole affair was decided when an arrow from one of Zhu's archers hit Chen Youliang in the eye, killing him.

to be a record of land battles, with little naval history to speak of, this leaves out the pivotal encounter on the waters of Lake Poyang, China's largest lake. The battle is also reckoned the largest in naval history in terms of the number of men who took part, with some estimates suggesting as many as 850,000 sailors, soldiers and marines were involved in the fighting.

The battle pitted Chen Youliang's supporters against Zhu Yuanzhang's men. The latter had come a long way from the days when he was too poor to pay the pittance required for him to continue within the Buddhist monastery that had been his first recourse against starvation.

Zhu Yuanzhang had taken on military command of the Red Turban faction that had arisen from the White Lotus Society and, following the betrayal and death of its original leader, Han Shantong, he had gradually expanded his power base while continuing to profess loyalty to Han Shantong's son and heir, Han Lin'er. In 1356, Zhu Yuanzhang took control of the city of Nanjing, which became his capital and power base. Unlike the other warlords, Zhu Yuanzhang made it a point of policy to govern his territory well, which had the effect of attracting many incomers to Nanjing, attracted by its stability among the violence and corruption prevalent in the lands controlled by the other warlords. Such was Nanjing's reputation for safety and good government that its population swelled tenfold in the decade following Zhu Yuanzhang's conquest.

THE RED TURBAN REBELLION

ABOVE Following the expulsion of the Mongol Yuan dynasty, the Hongwu emperor and his Ming successors were determined to stop the Mongols returning, building a massive wall to ensure that they did not

ABOVE A portrait of Emperor Zhu Yuanzhang

"Chen Youliang sent his tower ships, vessels that could hold 2,000 troops, to attack Zhu's fortress at Nanching"

With the Yuan making no effort to dislodge the rebels, Zhu Yuanzhang set about forming an administration that could turn him from a warlord into an emperor, although he still publicly proclaimed his allegiance to Han Lin'er as the emperor of a renewed Song dynasty. But by taking the title Duke of Wu, Zhu Yuanzhang began to advance up the ladder of nobility towards the throne. With many of the most talented administrators in China coming into his service, Zhu Yuanzhang was slowly assembling a team that would be able to control the country.

However, in order to do so, he had first to remove his dangerous (and more powerful) rival to the east, Chen Youliang. The realisation was mutual, and it was Chen Youliang who precipitated the decisive battle by sending his armoured tower ships, vast vessels that could hold 2,000 troops as well as having separate holds for cavalry and an armoured superstructure, to attack Zhu's fortress at Nanchang. Despite the size of Youliang's fleet the garrison at Nanchang held out and sent a messenger to Zhu asking for his help lest they fall. The result was the Battle of Poyang Lake, which over four days (30 August to 2 September) saw a tactical defeat of Chen Youliang's forces, followed by their rout on 4 October, when Chen Youliang was killed.

With Chen Youliang out of the way, Zhu Yuanzhang turned his attention to Zhang Shicheng's kingdom, laying siege to its capital, Suzhou, and capturing it in 1367 after ten months of besieging it. With the heavens clearly favouring Zhu Yuanzhang, the remaining warlords decided that surrender was the better part of valour and placed themselves under his sovereignty. There was, however, the small matter of Han Lin'er, the putative emperor of a renewed Song dynasty in whose service Zhu Yuanzhang had first risen to prominence. No doubt, Zhu Yuanzhang would have served under Han Lin'er if an unfortunate accident had not befallen the would-be emperor in 1366 or 1367, in which Han Lin'er drowned in a pond. With the titular claimant out of the way, Zhu Yuanzhang accepted the Mandate of Heaven and proclaimed himself emperor on 20 January 1368, taking the name Hongwu (vastly martial). As emperor, he founded the Ming dynasty that would rule China until 1644.

With all the rival warlords out of the way, the Hongwu Emperor turned his attention to the rump state still under the control of the Yuan in the north of China, marching north in 1368. Rather than give battle, the Yuan abandoned their capital (present-day Beijing) and retreated into Mongolia. By 1381, the emperor's forces had brought the entire country to heel. After 89 years of foreign domination the Chinese ruled China again. ★

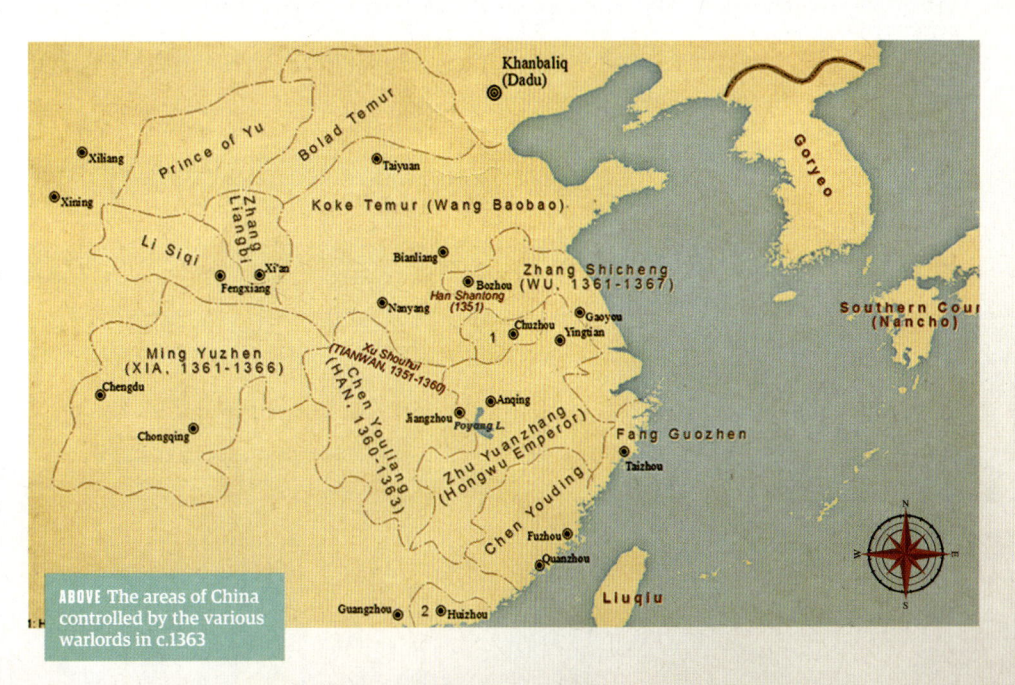

ABOVE The areas of China controlled by the various warlords in c.1363

中國歷史

THE MERCILESS
Ming

IN THE FACE OF MONGOL OPPRESSION, A YOUNG BEGGAR WOULD RISE TO BECOME THE FOUNDER OF ONE OF CHINA'S GREATEST IMPERIAL FAMILIES

WRITTEN BY **APRIL MADDEN**

ABOVE The incredible Forbidden City was built to be the Ming dynasty's imperial palace

THE MING DYNASTY

The invaders were everywhere he looked. Swaggering Mongol conquerors, rich with Chinese silver and fat with Chinese rice, stinking of horse sweat and fermented milk. The young beggar glared at them and spat. His grandfather had fought them when they came – fought and lost, for they were strong, and there were too many of them, under the banner of their Great Khan who wanted to eat the world. The old man was in his grave now, starved in a famine caused by their greed. His whole family were. Only Zhu Yuanzhang was left. He had gone to a monastery after they died – he was just a boy, and desperate. But the Mongols' grasping hands shamelessly clawed even at the Buddha's pockets too, and the monks couldn't afford another mouth to feed. Once he'd made enough, tramping from town to little backwater town, he would return there, take his vows, learn to read and write, honour the Buddha and dwell in his light and peace.

The beggar boy Zhu Yuanzhang never got his wish. He did return to Huangjue Temple, and he learned how to read and write. But he never became a monk. Destiny had a far greater plan for Zhu Yuanzhang, and it was a soldier's path his feet found themselves upon. He may have started life as the son of a poor peasant farmer in what is now Zhongli District in 1328, but he ended it nearly 70 years later in Nanjing Imperial Palace as the Hongwu Emperor, founder of the Ming dynasty. He had reigned for 30 years and restored China to the rule of its ethnic majority, the Han, having driven out the usurping Mongol invaders and claimed the Mandate of Heaven. He had overhauled corrupt court structures, protected the peasantry, improved farming, reduced the power and wealth of many aristocrats and encouraged religious tolerance among the multi-faith peoples of China. He had also purged swathes of high-ranking officials, founded a notorious secret police (the Embroidered Uniform Guard), limited the jobs people could do based on their family history, constantly tinkered with the imperial examinations of the civil service, banned haircuts and names that he didn't like and presided over massacres that cut down en masse anyone who opposed his rule.

The Hongwu Emperor carried out his bloody, capricious reforms in the name of erasing every last trace of the Mongol 'barbarians' from whom he had taken back China's governance, but in practice he also pursued personal vendettas and uncontested power like any other conquering antihero. His peasant superstition caught up with him briefly in 1380 when lightning struck the imperial palace and he believed it to be heaven's wrath, and for a while the persecution of his enemies ceased, but by the last decade of his reign the Hongwu Emperor was back to his murderous ways.

ABOVE Zhu Yuanzhang, the Hongwu Emperor and founder of the Ming dynasty, freed the country from Mongol rule

BELOW The Yongle-era Treasure Fleet projected Chinese soft power to nations that China had never encountered before

"He had reigned for 30 years and restored China to the rule of its ethnic majority"

BELOW The Yongle Emperor was a son of Yuanzhang and usurped his nephew Yunwun's throne, considering him weak

A dynasty that's founded in blood will continue in the same gushing vein when its first transfer of power occurs, and that's exactly what happened to the Ming. When the Hongwu Emperor died on 24 June 1398, the doctors who had attended him were put to death, and over 30 of the old man's concubines were sacrificed in the revival of an ancient imperial rite that China had long left behind. The old emperor had outlived his eldest son Zhu Biao and left instructions that his heir was to be Zhu Biao's eldest son. By the time of the Hongwu Emperor's death, however, Biao's firstborn son was dead, and the heir presumptive was the next oldest, Zhu Yunwen, known to posterity as the Jianwen Emperor.

Yunwen was regarded by his uncles (Biao's brothers) as a soft touch, and by their lights, he was. His regnant name means "establishing civility", and this idealistic Confucian scholar intended to do just that, attempting to limit the influence of his warlike uncles and usher in an era of peace and prosperity. It's been suggested that the Hongwu Emperor's last purges were aimed at reducing threats to his grandson's reign. If this is the case, he failed; the Jianwen Emperor ruled for just four years. The biggest threat to Yunwen was his uncle Zhu Di, Prince of Yan, who prosecuted a civil war against him and, in 1402, was responsible for burning down the imperial palace. The Jianwen Emperor was presumed to have died in the flames, and Zhu Di took his place as the Yongle Emperor. He even tried to wipe all mention of his peacemaking nephew from the historical record.

With Nanjing's imperial palace a smoking ruin, the Yongle Emperor ruled instead from Beijing, ordering the construction of the iconic palace complex of the Forbidden City. He persecuted the Confucian scholars of his late nephew's faction while favouring academics of his own from the elite imperial Hanlin Academy, who during his reign completed the *Yongle Dadian*, a vast encyclopaedia of a type known in China as leishu, which consist of anthologies and compilations of literary works. To avoid accusations of usurpation and regicide, he styled himself as a Buddhist 'sage-king', pursuing cordial relations with Tibetan abbots and claiming visions of guidance from holy bodhisattvas. He ramped up construction on China's Great Wall to keep the Mongols out, a task that subsequent Ming emperors and generals followed him in. But Di didn't just look inward. He tasked his favourite court eunuch, Zheng He, with the admiralty of the Treasure Fleet. Zheng He established favourable trade relations with nations as far away as Africa and the Middle East through a combination of 'gifts' and impressive displays of vast naval power. Sometimes Di followed this up with force: after Zheng He had visited Vietnam, the self-appointed hammer of Buddha laid waste to the multicultural country, burning all texts except Buddhist scrolls. But his main enemy was the hated Mongols, and Di died in 1424 on a campaign against his father's foes in the Gobi Desert. It's said he fell into melancholy when his army couldn't catch up to the swift Mongol horses and died of a broken heart.

One of the first tasks his son enacted on ascending the throne was to free the imprisoned survivors of a purge Di had ordered of his concubines and their eunuch guardians. The Yongle Emperor took after his father, and his son, the Hongxi Emperor, spent most of his short reign undoing his father's worst excesses.

The story of the Ming continued to seesaw between war and peace, violence and scholarship. Some rulers even embodied both of these characteristics. Zhu Qizhen, son of Zhanji, ruled first as the Zhengtong Emperor and presided over the height of Ming prosperity and refinement. Captured by the old enemy, the Mongols, on an ill-fated raid in 1449, the stricken populace replaced him on the Dragon Throne with his brother Qiyu, the Jingtai Emperor. Having talked his captor into freeing him, Qizhen returned to China only to find himself under house arrest in the Forbidden City. When his childless brother fell ill, Qizhen launched a coup and returned to the throne as the Tianshun Emperor in 1457.

Despite the violence of its early decades, in the West we use the term 'Ming dynasty' as shorthand for something rare and precious, thanks to the porcelain produced in the years of the 15th century during and after Qizhen's rule. These beautiful artefacts are the reason that we call porcelain 'china', and it took Europeans until the 18th century to learn the chemical secret of its light, fine quality. Despite being iconically Chinese, the other secret of Ming dynasty porcelain, its glorious blue colour, is cobalt oxide from what is now modern-day Iran, an international trade likely set up by Zheng He's Treasure Fleet missions.

With the nation stabilised under a now-established dynasty and protected from aggression by its Great Wall and diplomatic relationships with other nations, China in the later Ming era was free to develop its arts, culture, and sciences. As economic conditions improved and a burgeoning middle class of merchants and one-time peasant farmers – now landowners – swelled, artists and poets found high demand for their work at home, while artisans like potters and cloisonné enamellers also had access to markets abroad.

The good times couldn't last. Just as the Ming had thrown off the yoke of the Mongol oppressors, so the Qing dynasty rose to do the same. The Qing were part of a northern Chinese ethnic minority called the Manchu (or Jurchen) with cultural and diplomatic links to both Mongolia and Korea. Oppressed by their Han overlords, the Manchu raised a manifesto called the *Seven Grievances* in 1618. Sowing dissent among the Han majority, Nurhaci, khan of the Later Jin, raised an army of ethnic Jurchen and Han defectors against the Ming and embarked on decades of guerilla warfare. One of his rabble-rousers was Li Zicheng, the so-called Dashing King. Zicheng had a brief taste of imperial power when his rebel army took Beijing in 1644 and Zhu Youjian, the Chongzhen Emperor, hanged himself in the Forbidden City grounds. The Ming dynasty was at an end. Zicheng attempted to found his own imperial line, the Shun dynasty, but died soon after, shortly followed by his ill-fated brother and nephew, who claimed to reign after him. In practice, they did not. The next true emperor was the Tianming Emperor, Taizu of Qing: Nurhaci. ★

BELOW When Beijing forces fell to the Manchu rebels, the last Ming emperor killed himself in the palace grounds

BELOW Ming porcelain is the era's most iconic artefact and represents a flowering of Chinese craft and international trade

"The Ming continued to seesaw between war and peace, violence and scholarship. Some rulers even embodied both of these"

The Porcelain Tower of Nanjing

THE CONSTRUCTION, DESTRUCTION AND REVIVAL OF A MEDIEVAL WONDER

In early 15th-century China, the Yongle Emperor of the Ming dynasty ordered the construction of a towering monument to honour his mother. The Porcelain Tower was a grand pagoda built in the city of Nanjing – the imperial capital at the time – as part of the grand Bao'en Buddhist Temple complex.

The tower was constructed from white porcelain bricks, which would have glistened in the sunlight, and adorned with vibrant glazed designs of animals, flowers and landscapes in greens, yellows and browns. Historians studying the remnants suggest that the glazed porcelain bricks were made by highly skilled workers, but sadly the methods used to make them have been lost to history.

Some of the largest bricks were more than 50 centimetres (20 inches) thick and weighed as much as 150 kilograms (331 pounds) each, with the coloured glazes staying bright for centuries. Nowadays, workers trying to replicate these porcelain slabs struggle to make anything larger than five centimetres (two inches) thick and their colours fade after just a decade.

The tower was widely regarded as the most beautiful pagoda in China, and it became renowned as one of the seven wonders of the medieval world, featuring in the records of Westerners who travelled to the region. This porcelain pagoda was also one of the tallest buildings in the area (possibly in all of China) until it was almost completely reduced to rubble during the Taiping Rebellion in 1856.

Did you know?
The top four tiers of the pagoda were destroyed by a lightning strike in 1801.

> "Sadly the methods used to make the bricks have been lost"

Stairway
A 184-step spiral staircase in the middle of the pagoda led visitors up to the top of the tower, which, according to some historical documents, may have been the tallest building in China at the time, at over 79 metres (259 feet) high.

Expert craftsmanship
The porcelain bricks were larger than anything we are able to recreate with modern methods today. Unfortunately, the techniques used to create the originals have been lost to history.

Elegant decor
All nine storeys were decorated with glazed tiles, pottery designs and bells, and they were each illuminated with oil lamps at night. The pagoda was also topped with a gold pineapple-shaped sculpture.

REBUILDING THE WONDER

Today, the old and new stand side by side at the Porcelain Tower Heritage Park. The reconstructed tower (made from steel girders and glass rather than porcelain) overlooks the museum housing the original blocks of the Nanjing Tower door.

The new high-tech replica provides an interactive experience, as visitors are encouraged to use a smartphone to scan QR codes for more information about the site. The incredible interior of the new building immortalises the historical and cultural significance of the original medieval tower in mesmerising displays of sound and light, including a room of thousands of light bulbs that change colour. The new tower also offers 360-degree views of the city as it overlooks a landscape of rivers and architecture.

ABOVE Businessman Wang Jianlin reportedly funded the replica's construction with a donation of 1bn yuan (£109.5/$138.9 million)

中國歷史

66

Zheng He
CHINA'S GREATEST EXPLORER

DISCOVER THE SEVEN GREAT VOYAGES OF ONE OF THE MOST IMPRESSIVE ADVENTURERS IN HISTORY

WRITTEN BY **JOSH WEST**

ABOVE The Yongle Emperor started many impressive projects, including the construction of the Forbidden City

ABOVE One of Zheng He's sailing charts, showing India towards the top and Ceylon and Africa below

Zheng He was a Chinese Muslim soldier, diplomat and admiral, and he is remembered as the greatest explorer in Chinese history. Captured and castrated at the age of ten, he quickly rose in status within the court of the Yongle Emperor thanks to his military and intellectual skills. For 20 years in the early 15th century he led seven voyages of discovery around the Indian Ocean, travelling as far as Arabia and East Africa. These voyages spread Chinese influence and culture throughout the region and cemented China's hold over much of Southeast Asia. They also planted the seed for the Western world's obsession with the riches and tales of the Far East.

BIRTH & EARLY LIFE

Zheng He was born Ma Sanbao in c.1371 in the Yunnan province of China. Ma was raised in the Hui community – Chinese Muslims descended from Mongol-Turkish migrants. The surname Ma comes from the Chinese rendition of Mohammed, and the family was descended from an early Mongol governor of Yunnan.

Yunnan province was the last Mongol stronghold in China after their Yuan dynasty had been overthrown by the Ming dynasty in 1368. In 1381, Ming armies reconquered the province and expelled or killed the Mongol administrators, including Ma's father.

According to Edward Dreyer in his work *Zheng He: China and the Oceans in the Early Ming Dynasty*, Ma was discovered by a Ming general and taken prisoner. Like all male prisoners his age, Ma was subjected to the brutal mutilation that is castration and sent into the army as an orderly. After years of military training, in 1390 Ma was sent to Beijing to serve Zhu Di, Prince of Yan and fourth son of the Hongwu Emperor, founder of the Ming dynasty. It was at this time that his name was changed to Ma He.

MILITARY SERVICE

Ma had already distinguished himself as a junior officer, and he proved his worth to his new master after joining him on his first successful campaign against the Mongols in 1390. Ma quickly earned Zhu Di's respect through his military successes, and under the prince's patronage he received a full education in literacy and languages not normally given to eunuchs.

Ma quickly became influential at the prince's court, not least because of his unusual height. One contemporary described Ma as "seven chi [193 centimetres/76 inches] high, cheeks and a forehead that was high, glaring eyes, teeth that were well-shaped as shells, and a voice that was as loud as a bell." This strength was put to the test in 1399 when he joined Zhu Di in a war against the prince's nephew.

In 1398, the Hongwu Emperor was succeeded by his grandson, the Jianwen Emperor. The new emperor had attempted to strip his uncle of his powers and Zhu Di rebelled against him. Ma was one of Zhu Di's greatest commanders and accompanied him into the capital Nanjing in 1402, where he exiled his nephew and was declared the Yongle Emperor.

CHINESE EXPANSION

As one of the new emperor's most faithful servants, Ma was made grand director of the palace servants, the equivalent to a modern-day chief of staff. In 1404, the emperor also changed Ma He's name to Zheng He in honour of his distinguished service in Beijing and Nanjing. Zheng means 'proper' or 'correct' and is associated with the government, while He means 'peace' or 'a river'.

The new emperor had enormous plans for glorifying his kingdom. He restored the war-ravaged economy, moved the capital to Beijing and began construction of the Forbidden City. He also planned to restore China's position as the major maritime and cultural power in the East. China had been a naval power for 300 years, with sea-borne commerce stemming

BELOW Zheng He had been a close aid and servant to the future Yongle Emperor

"The sheer scale of his fleet was incredible: 317 ships carried around 27,800 men"

The Ming Voyages
The trade, tribute and exploration routes of Zheng He

Nanjing
The great capital of Nanjing was the origin of all of Zheng He's treasure voyages.

Hormuz
Venturing further than ever before, the treasure fleet finally reached Hormuz during Zheng He's fourth voyage.

Aden
Considered the crossroads of Europe, Asia and Africa, Zheng He stopped at Aden three times throughout his seven expeditions.

Calicut
Calicut, located in southern India, was the final destination of Zheng He's first three voyages.

Champa
Zheng He and his fleet were welcomed by the King of Champa. They traded blue and white Ming porcelains for rare woods.

Malindi
After exploring the eastern coast of Africa, Zheng He finally reached Malindi on his fourth journey.

Malacca
A strategic port for Zheng He, Malacca quickly became a tributary state of China.

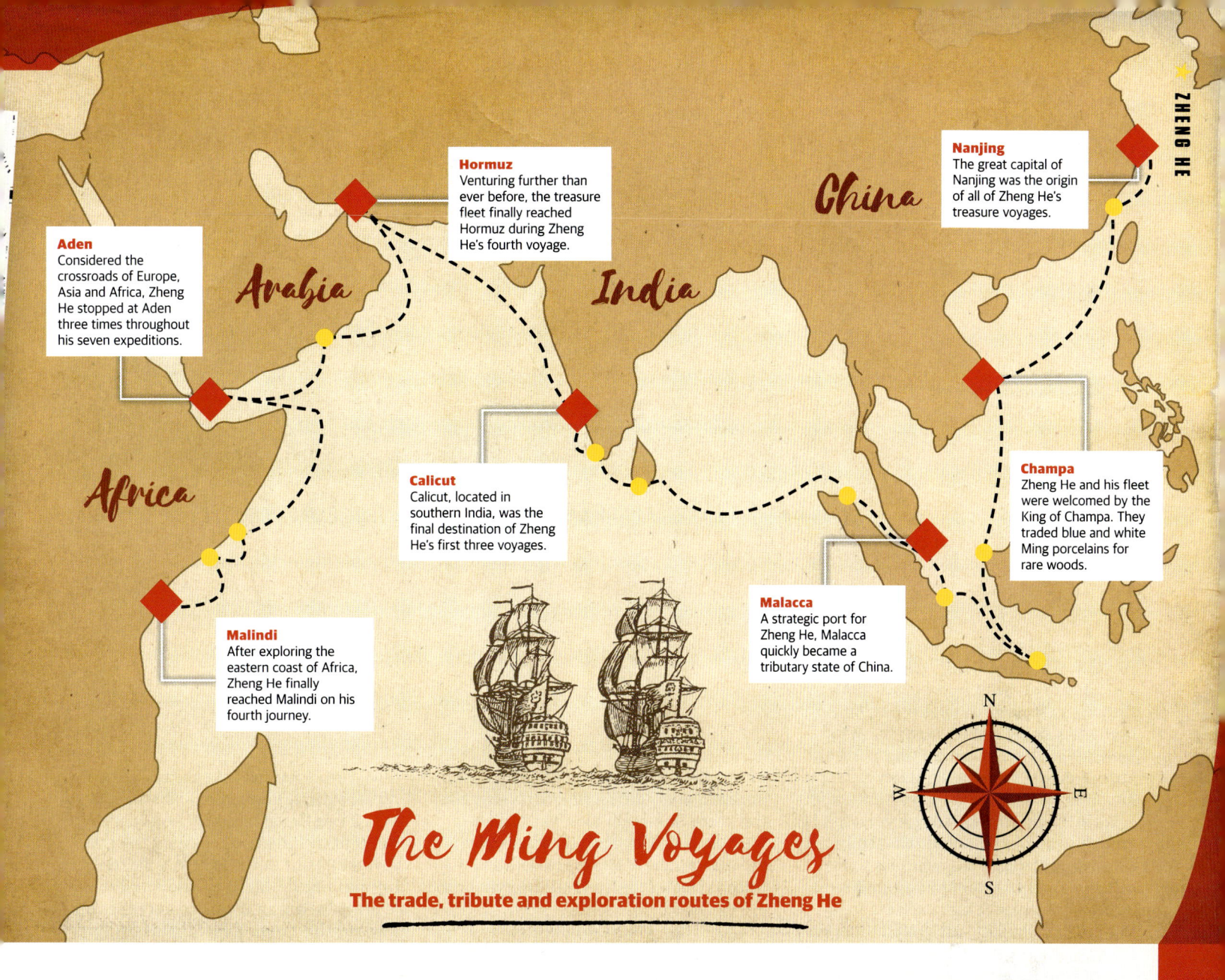

ABOVE Of the 250 vessels that made up Zheng He's fleet, 63 of them are believed to have been massive treasure ships

from the Chinese people's demand for spices, aromatics and other goods.

Traditionally, the imperial court had been the beneficiary of tribute from the smaller states around Southeast Asia. This tribute not only gave protection to minor states but was also a sign that the emperor was indeed the Son of Heaven and the world's most powerful ruler. This tradition had lapsed under the Mongol Yuan, but the emperor was determined to display his divine providence. Accordingly, he commissioned the construction of 3,500 ships, all overseen by Zheng He.

In 1405, Zheng He was named zhèngshi (chief envoy) to the emperor and grand admiral of an enormous fleet of ships. For the next 20 years it was Zheng He's mission to travel what was known as the Western Ocean to spread Chinese influence, secure naval dominance and gain tribute for the emperor.

EARLY VOYAGES

Zheng He's first voyage left China in 1405, and the sheer scale of his fleet was incredible: 317 ships carried around 27,800 men. These wooden vessels were the largest the world had seen and would see for another 500 years. The 62 treasure ships (baochuan) that led the fleet and carried the treasure bound for foreign rulers were recorded as being 127 metres (417 feet) long and had nine sails (Christopher Colombus' Santa Maria was only 19 metres/62 feet long). It would not be until the iron-hulled steamers of the 19th century that ships were built so large again.

The huge vessels were equipped with state-of-the-art water-tight compartments, magnetic compasses and paper maps. So many linguists were required for the voyage that a whole language institute was created in Nanjing.

After leaving Nanjing, Zheng He's fleet visited the small states of Southeast Asia, including Vietnam, Thailand, Malacca and Java. He then headed to India, visiting Calicut on the Malabar Coast and Sri Lanka. Zheng He would lead a delegation to the local ruler and present messages of peace and goodwill. Large and plentiful gifts would then be presented – including silk, tea, painted scrolls and fine Ming porcelain – before inviting the ruler to pay tribute to the emperor. This first expedition returned to China in 1407.

Zheng He's second voyage (1408-09) followed much the same route. For his third, Zheng He

MEASURING UP

How Zheng He's treasure ship compared to other famous vessels

Zheng He Treasure Ship
Years 1405-33 ♦ Length 127m (417ft)
Width 55m (180ft) ♦ Masts 6 ♦ Crew 2,800 (estimated)

Santa Maria
Years Unknown-1492 ♦ Length 19m (62ft)
Width 5.5m (18ft) ♦ Masts 3 ♦ Crew 40

---

sailed beyond India's ports and all the way to Hormuz on the Persian Gulf, where his Islamic heritage proved useful, before travelling all the way to Samudera on the southern tip of Sumatra. Zheng He was merely following pre-established sea routes, but what made his voyages different was the diplomacy and trade he conducted along the way.

When Zheng He's expert diplomacy failed, his formidable army and navy awed local rulers into submission. Zheng He had numerous scrapes on these voyages. On his first, he encountered a group of notorious Sumatran pirates, led by Che'en Tsuri, who had been disrupting trade on the Malacca Straight. Zheng He attacked and defeated them, killing over 5,000. Likewise, on his second voyage, King Alagonakkara of Sri Lanka attempted to raid the treasure boats; Zheng He captured him and took him to the Yongle Emperor as a prisoner. Settling these local disputes worked towards the emperor's goal of China being seen as the chief power in the East.

LATER EXPEDITIONS

Zheng He's fourth voyage (1413-15) was his most ambitious. After cruising Southeast Asia and India, he continued to Hormuz before dividing the fleet; one detachment sailed down Arabia to Dhofar and Aden, while another proceeded to Mecca and into Egypt via the Red Sea. The fleet then sailed down the east African coast, visiting Mogadishu, Malindi and even as far down as Mozambique. Zheng He returned to the Yongle court with no less than 30 ambassadors to pay tribute to the emperor.

Having secured these new sea routes, Zheng He's fifth (1417-19) and sixth (1421-24) voyages followed the same pattern, with the latter voyage returning all the diplomats home. Just as important as the Chinese goods Zheng He took to these places were the gifts and culture he brought back. He returned from his trips to Africa with ostriches, zebras, rhinos, lions and camels to glorify the Yongle court. The giraffe that Zheng He brought back from Malindi in 1415 was thought by the court to be a qilin, a mystical creature of Chinese folklore, and was taken as proof of the Mandate of Heaven on the emperor's reign.

DEATH OF ZHENG HE

In September 1424, as Zheng He was returning from his sixth voyage, the Yongle Emperor died. He was succeeded by the Hongxi Emperor (1424-26), who swiftly put an end to the costly naval expeditions. The money the emperor poured into them was deemed to be needed for war with the Mongols and rebuilding of the Great Wall. Zheng He was instead named commander of the garrison at Nanjing in 1425.

Hongxi's successor, the Xuande Emperor (1426-35) was likewise against the voyages. First was the cost, and he was reported to have said, "Some far-off countries pay their tribute to me at much expense and difficulties, all of which are not my own wish." Second, and more importantly, were his Confucian principles, which had disappeared from the imperial court under the Yongle Emperor. Xuande believed these voyages were against the isolationist values laid down by his dynasty's founder, the Hongwu Emperor, as well as the Confucian beliefs that had governed Chinese political thought for centuries.

However, Zheng He was dispatched on one last voyage of discovery in 1431. The ageing admiral sailed along his familiar routes around Southeast Asia, India, Sri Lanka, the Persian Gulf, the Red Sea and down the east coast of Africa. When sailing back to China in spring 1433, Zheng He died suddenly near Calicut, one of the ports he'd visited on his first great voyage 20 years earlier. Historians are conflicted between whether Zheng He was buried at sea or returned to Nanjing and laid to rest there. Either way a tomb was built for him in the city that still stands today.

AFTERMATH & LEGACY

Upon Zheng He's death, the Xuande Emperor passed the Haijin edict, a ban on sea trading and exploration that lasted in different forms

> "He returned from his trips to Africa with ostriches, zebras, rhinos, lions and camels"

ABOVE A reconstruction of one of Zheng He's treasure ships

Mayflower
Years c.1609-1624 ◆ **Length** 27m (88.6ft)
Width 2.6m (8.5ft) ◆ **Masts** 3 ◆ **Crew** 30

HMS Victory
Years 1765-1831 ◆ **Length** 69m (226.4ft)
Width 15.8m (51.8ft) ◆ **Masts** 3 ◆ **Crew** 821

Titanic
Years 1911-12 ◆ **Length** 269m (882.5ft)
Width 28.2m (92.5ft) ◆ **Masts** N/A ◆ **Crew** 900

until the 1820s. Alongside this isolation, the Confucian monks that ran the Ming court attempted to minimise Zheng He's achievements or even wipe them from the record altogether. All the explorer's records were destroyed and his colossal ships were left to rot. Chinese craftsmen soon lost the skills needed to build such enormous vessels, and ships that size were not seen again for four centuries. It was only in the last century that Zheng He and his voyages were rediscovered and celebrated by historians.

However, these historians are split as to the success and legacy of Zheng He's great missions and whether they were even necessary. Some argue the voyages performed little purpose other than to fan the Yongle Emperor's vanity. Historian Gang Deng argues they were in fact a manhunt for the emperor's nephew, the Jianwen Emperor, calling them "the largest-scale manhunt on water in history". Meanwhile, Mark Cartwright argues "the original aim of the voyages - to secure foreign tribute - was largely unsuccessful outside of Southeast Asia". The cost of these voyages dwarfed the returns the imperial court received, and the foreign states Zheng He visited were unwilling to accept that China was the centre of the world.

While Zheng He did not establish a vast commercial empire like Columbus or James Cook, his missions helped to expand China's political influence beyond Southeast Asia. In addition, his voyages inspired swathes of Chinese emigration, as well as fostering good relations between China, its neighbours and the Islamic world. His spreading of Chinese culture and treasure across the Indian Ocean also fostered a fascination with the Far East.

Zheng He should be remembered alongside Marco Polo and Columbus as one of the greatest explorers in the Age of Exploration. Thanks to his naval prowess his immense fleet travelled vast distances and his expert diplomacy spread Chinese culture to countless other societies. As he himself wrote on a tablet in Fujian province before his final voyage, "We have traversed more than one hundred thousand li [27,000 nautical miles] of immense waterspaces and have beheld in the ocean huge waves like mountains, and we have set eyes on barbarian regions far away hidden in a blue transparency of light vapours, while our sails, loftily unfurled like clouds day and night, continued their course as rapidly as a star." ★

ABOVE Zheng He's mission was twofold: find new trading partners and spread word of the emperor's power

RIGHT There are monuments to Zheng He all around Southeast Asia

中國歷史

Hong Kong Vice
THE FIRST OPIUM WAR

A CHASTENING DEFEAT AT THE HANDS OF WESTERN OPPONENTS DETERMINED TO MAINTAIN A GRIP ON A LUCRATIVE TRADE NETWORK DOOMED THE QING DYNASTY AND GAVE RISE TO A MAGNIFICENT COASTAL CITY

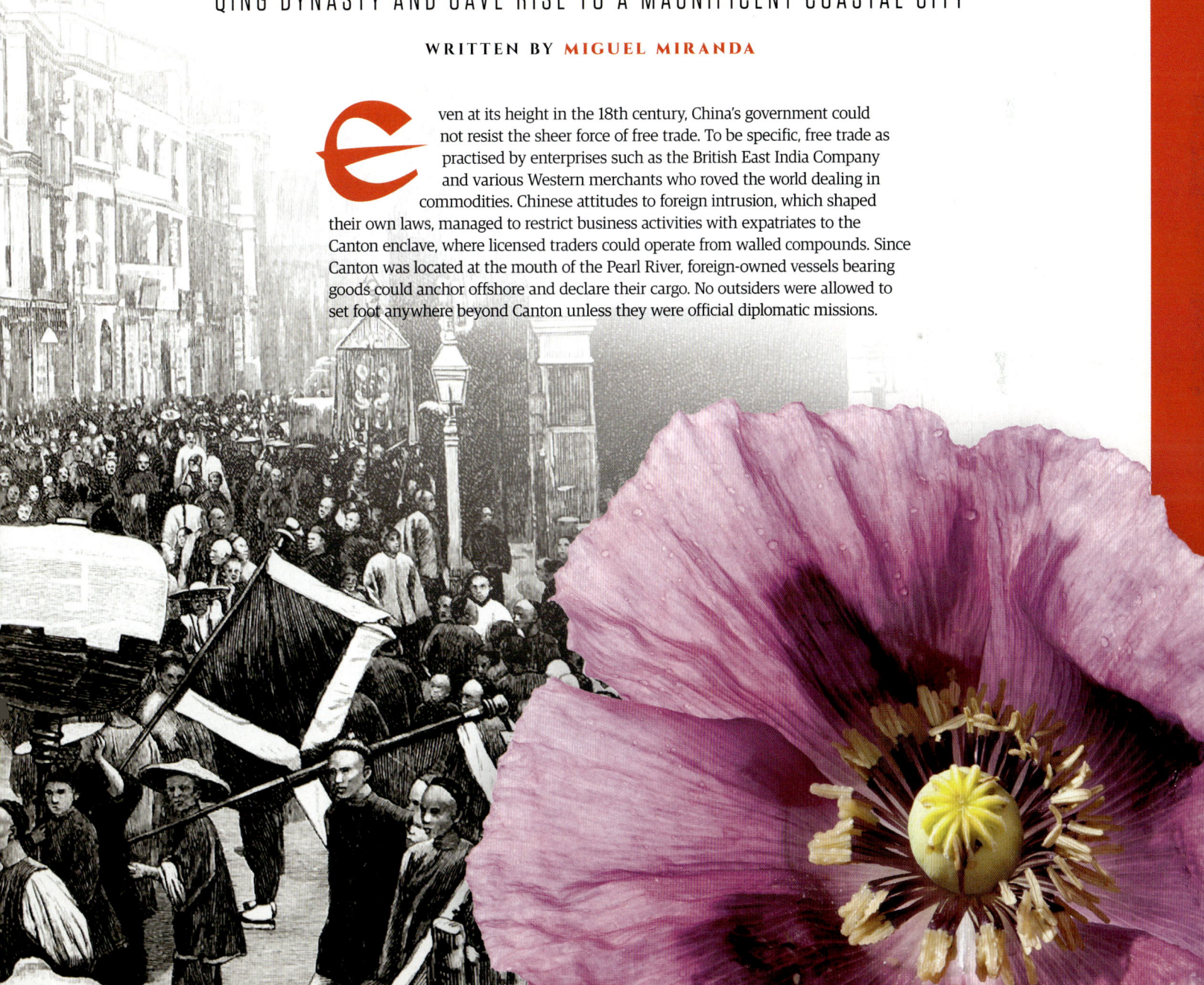

WRITTEN BY **MIGUEL MIRANDA**

Even at its height in the 18th century, China's government could not resist the sheer force of free trade. To be specific, free trade as practised by enterprises such as the British East India Company and various Western merchants who roved the world dealing in commodities. Chinese attitudes to foreign intrusion, which shaped their own laws, managed to restrict business activities with expatriates to the Canton enclave, where licensed traders could operate from walled compounds. Since Canton was located at the mouth of the Pearl River, foreign-owned vessels bearing goods could anchor offshore and declare their cargo. No outsiders were allowed to set foot anywhere beyond Canton unless they were official diplomatic missions.

中國歷史

By 1830, just a decade and a half since the Battle of Waterloo, a tantalising commerce in byproducts from the flowering plant *Papaver somniferum* flourished between the foothills of the Himalayas and China's southern coasts. A new lifestyle had swept China's guarded port cities by then. Men of all classes enjoyed their narcotic vice in parlours and backrooms where they smoked gummy balls extracted from the poppy bulb, which produced a soothing effect and had some medicinal properties.

Packaged in wooden chests and delivered by steamers across the Bay of Bengal, through the Singapore Strait and unloaded at Canton, a multitude of dens and venues purchased the opium and fed it to their clients. The Qing had outlawed opium use in 1820, but their efforts were to no avail as customs officials and mandarins were susceptible to corruption. Profits from opium sales kept rising as volumes imported doubled each year.

By 1838, the imperial court in Peking was so outraged by the narcotics epidemic it decided to take action. Another impetus was the effect on the government's finances. Indian opium was being purchased in bulk with silver, the preferred medium of exchange between China and Britain. As the amount of silver being paid to British merchants grew, a worrisome trade deficit strained the government's balance sheet. China, long an economic powerhouse that had enjoyed surpluses from exporting ceramics and silk, was now losing its revenues due an illicit import. Lin Zexu was appointed to rectify Canton's out-of-control port situation. A canny bureaucrat with a talent for spectacle, Lin had chests of confiscated opium spoilt and then thrown from the Canton wharf. Bringing troops with him, he so intimidated the British Superintendent of Trade, Captain Charles Elliot, that the Canton expatriates gave up more than 20,000 chests of opium. The demonstration sent shock waves. Having gotten used to pliable Chinese officials and almost no meddling in their affairs, these same merchants soon wrote home and demanded an official response.

Lin refused to be swayed by the outrage of foreign 'barbarians' and the sting of lost revenues left the British merchant community aghast and vengeful.

ROAD TO WAR

It was the aristocratic Foreign Secretary Lord Palmerston who concocted an adventure for the British Navy on the premise of upholding free trade. Of course, with the benefit of hindsight, Palmerston's rhetoric and writing on the matter seems laced with irony. China had been willing to trade with Europe but only as an exporter. Its culture and society had little use for foreign-made goods. But what Palmerston truly advocated was free trade that enhanced the British Empire's access to the Chinese market, whose size was measured by its awesome population of nearly half a billion subjects ruled by the Qing dynasty.

"The disparity in firepower made Chinese commanders commit suicide"

The onset of war exposed the Qing's creeping weaknesses. On paper, Peking had the resources to field a million reservists at once. After all, the Qing dynasty was built on a martial foundation by the Manchus, fierce horsemen whose conquering spirit expanded their empire into Central Asia, with the whole Tibetan plateau reduced to a protectorate. In fact, the extent of the Qing dynasty's reach in 1839 was greater than China's present borders.

By the 19th century, however, administrative problems and an insular world view reduced the mighty Qing armed forces to a paper tiger. A class of patriotic generals and officers commanded a rabble who had neither enough weapons nor uniforms. Firearms had arrived in Asia by the 16th century and saw widespread use. For a brief period, Japan mass-produced copies of Portuguese muskets that became known as Tanegashimas after the place where they were discovered. In China, government-owned foundries and mills manufactured cannons and rifles in serious quantities despite the Qing's rejection of foreign technology.

Facing the token presence of the Royal Navy in late 1839 were feeble coastal defences, small armies waiting in their forts and cannon-armed riverine junks. The first major naval engagement, on 29 October 1839, set the pace of the war. With Canton blockaded by just two

ABOVE British soldiers numbered less than 20,000 but were superior fighters

ABOVE The Chinese fought a losing battle on water

British warships, a frigate and a sloop with 18 cannons, a fleet of 29 war junks sailed down the Pearl River to meet them. The Chinese didn't hesitate to engage the British vessels only to be crippled en masse. Later on, the disparity in firepower made Chinese commanders commit suicide rather than accept defeat and relay such news to their superiors. In November the same British ships guarding Canton devastated another Chinese assault by war junks.

Once Canton was in British hands and the safety of the foreign merchants was guaranteed, a long impasse followed between the warring nations. While the press at home railed against the bizarre circumstances that led to the conflict, there was no great mobilisation undertaken as the British Empire faced off against the world's most populous country. Neither were industries tasked with churning out ships and material to furnish whole divisions. Indeed, on the British side the total manpower that fought the First Opium War numbered less than 20,000.

IRON SHIPS VERSUS WOODEN JUNKS

For the Qing government, this was the first occasion when its sovereignty was violated by a foreign invader arriving by sea. This was significant. In historical terms, China was never under threat from naval fleets. Yet in 1840 it bore the full brunt of a hostile British expedition combining Royal Navy and East India Company steamers. Commanding the fleet was Rear Admiral George Elliot, who had at his disposal three battleships, eight frigates, eight sloops and 36 transports. The fleet carried a ground force of 3,600 British soldiers and Indian sepoys mustered in Singapore. Here was a strange yet menacing hybrid of a European military operating alongside the paramilitaries maintained by the East India Company, a rare example of public-private cooperation in 19th-century world politics.

Since the war never involved immense set-piece battles or savage massacres, the rest of it can be summed up as exercises in blackmail. With the metropolis of Guangzhou located north of Canton being threatened by Admiral Elliot's expedition, an agreement was reached in Chuenpi where the island of Hong Kong was ceded to the British. This was negotiated by the same Superintendent Elliot who earlier allowed Commissioner Lin to seize chests of opium. But his personal views upheld the vested interests of the merchants in Canton. However, upon Lord Palmerston's urging, greater demands needed to be made on the Chinese and this prolonged the war for another year and a half.

The Qing court never settled matters with diplomacy because the actions of certain British officials and the Royal Navy were deemed piratical and undeserving of recognition. From late 1841 onwards, the British held on to Canton and launched attacks on Shanghai. A great distance separates the two cities and the fact that the Royal Navy's ships were unmolested in their transit shows the Qing's weakness. A last feeble attempt at resistance was met outside Nanking in the summer of 1842. Like before, stout citadels sought to halt the invading warships' progress and deliver a decisive blow. Of course, this did not happen. British gunnery and Chinese incompetence were insurmountable; never wanting for arms and men, the Qing still failed to protect their homeland. Fearing the prospect of foreign troops marching toward the capital, Emperor Daoguang allowed his ministers to negotiate peace in Nanking. Representing the British was the explorer and ex-East India Company man Henry Pottinger, whom Lord Palmerston trusted to execute Britain's will.

Since Pottinger was in a position to impose terms, the Nanking conference proved a brief one and was concluded aboard the H.M.S. Cornwallis. As Palmerston intended the year before, Chinese indemnities were broadened to opening cantonments in the port cities of Amoy, Foochow, Ningpo and Shanghai. It helped that the Canton business community, including those responsible for opium trafficking, were familiar with these locations. Yet the final blow took the greatest toll on the Qing dynasty. A grand sum of 22 million silver dollars was to be paid to Britain, with the first tranche worth 6 million paid before the year was out. Failure to deliver the sums meant the resulting debt produced interest. The Qing paid in full to the detriment of the state's foreign exchange, thereby accelerating economic decline. But the true prize of the First Opium War was Hong Kong.

Within a handful of years, well-appointed British residences were erected on its waterfront facing Kowloon, which was added along with the 'New Territories' in 1898 when a 99-year lease for the entire area was wrangled from the ailing Qing dynasty.

BELOW In the First Opium War, Chinese naval junks were at a disadvantage against the Royal Navy

ABOVE The Qing military had better manpower and firearms but its lack of preparedness and poor leadership doomed it

THE HELPLESS EMPEROR

The Qing dynasty that ruled China and other territories from 1644 until 1911 was a vast administration that underpinned a massive economic machine. With its large population and immense public works, China at the time boasted a self-sufficient economy that relied little on imports. This in turn drove British, European and even North American merchants to find novel products they could sell for Chinese silver, like opium.

At the pinnacle of the Qing state was a sovereign with unchecked powers, and in 1819 the new Emperor Daoguang, still youthful in his middle age, assumed the throne in Peking. Under his authority were countless ministers who dedicated their lives to public service. But Emperor Daoguang was at a complete loss when dealing with European merchants. A thriving opium trade drained the finances of the state and left a drug epidemic in its wake.

The Qing dynasty may have been powerful, but it was also myopic and unaware of its own limitations. This became apparent in the events leading to the First Opium War. Once hostilities began, British forces managed to defeat the Qing military in just three years. After the conflict few meaningful reforms were undertaken to help modernise China's failing institutions.

Towards the end of Daoguang's reign the once impregnable Qing state was in dire financial straits and had bits of its territory annexed by imperialists. A civil war soon engulfed the southern provinces and the Taiping Rebellion that lasted from 1850 until 1864 killed as many Chinese as all the casualties in WWI. For these reasons, Emperor Daoguang's reign was a disastrous one.

ABOVE For all their power and privilege, Chinese emperors during the Qing era lived cloistered lives in the splendour of their palaces

BELOW The signing and sealing of the Treaty of Nanking on 29 August 1842

With Hong Kong open for business, junks began crowding its harbour as far as the eye could see. Demand for warehouses and other vital infrastructure attracted thousands of Chinese labourers, who were all too happy to be leaving impoverished villages and farm work for dependable living wages. A sorry aspect of Hong Kong's expatriate society was to assign spacious residences for Europeans while the Chinese — including the island's original inhabitants — had no choice but to fend for themselves in slums.

ISLAND TREASURE

The decades of rapid urbanisation took a toll on public health, and it wasn't until bubonic plague struck Hong Kong in 1894 that a more concerted effort at addressing social ills and better living conditions was undertaken. Despite the outbreak the city kept growing, and by 1900 it was estimated the population had reached 300,000.

An unsavoury aspect of Hong Kong's origin story is the unrestricted opium trade. It's beyond doubt the Treaty of Nanking was a boon for opium smugglers, who now had multiple ports in which to receive their merchandise. Despite having a police force among its first vital institutions and British laws upheld throughout the island, Hong Kong's underworld was born the moment the island passed to foreign rule. The personal governance of Pottinger, who negotiated with Qing officials at Nanking, did little to save Hong Kong from becoming a prime destination in the maritime opium route to China. Even when illicit poppy cultivation flourished in certain provinces of the Republic of China (1911-1946), narcotics kept arriving in Hong Kong until the mid-20th century.

The legacy of the First Opium War is a terrible one. The Qing dynasty's decline had begun in earnest and its effect on generations of Chinese cannot be understated. Once Asia's greatest empire, unsullied by colonialism, China was now ripe for exploitation. If the First Opium War was so onerous, the humiliations of the Second Opium War left deep scars in a nation reeling from the Taiping civil war that lasted from 1850 until 1864. While the fanatical Taipings carved a path of destruction in central and southern China, a joint Anglo-French army marched on Peking and burned down the Imperial Palace. Of course, the expectations were the same: China must capitulate to Europe's strongest countries or else.

To put China's decline in perspective, we should recall it fought a losing war against Japan in 1895, where it lost the Korean Peninsula and Formosa (now Taiwan), and the Qing dynasty collapsed by 1912 after the revolt led by Sun Yat-sen. The civil war that followed reduced the fledgling Chinese republic to a patchwork of territories and the country's troubles worsened as Japan tried annexing ever greater swathes of its territory.

This long decline, or century of humiliation, as it has become known in China, so haunts the nation's current leadership that it now promotes a brand of nationalism that holds China's needs to be inviolate, its territory sacrosanct and its ascension to becoming a world power unstoppable. The ideas that formed this world view stem from the bitter lessons of the First Opium War.

Meanwhile, in Hong Kong, the cultural and legal antipathy for the drugs trade endures today. There is no graver bookend to the heritage of laissez-faire drug trafficking unleashed by British merchants than the modern Hong Kong police's own listed penalties for plying the trade. The harshest reads: *"Any person who cultivates any plant of the genus cannabis or the opium poppy shall be liable upon conviction to a fine of HK$100,000 and imprisonment for 15 years."* ★

"The expectations were the same: China must capitulate to Europe or else"

LORD PALMERSTON

Rather than spend his life managing the Temple family's estates in Northern Ireland, Henry John Temple assumed the title of 3rd Viscount Palmerston and committed himself to politics. Once appointed Foreign Secretary, Lord Palmerston was involved in whatever global events impacted the British Empire's maritime trade.

A contentious matter in the historiography surrounding the Opium Wars was Lord Palmerston's susceptibility to lobbyists. Evidence of moneyed influences using their connections in vital government offices to press for war against China exists. It was Lord Palmerston who kept urging the British Navy to not reach a settlement with the Chinese, thereby prolonging the First Opium War.

Lord Palmerston never set foot in China, nor did he bother arranging conferences with the Qing emperor to normalise diplomatic ties. But the backwater port of Hong Kong prospered and Lord Palmerston went on to become a formidable Prime Minister in the Victorian era.

BELOW Henry Pottinger was the man the British entrusted to handle negotiations after the war with China was won

JOURNEY THROUGH THE EMPIRE OF HISTORY'S MOST FAMOUS WARLORD

Traverse the harsh lands of the Mongols, meet the ruthless commanders who fought their way to forging a medieval superpower, and marvel at the ingenuity of a nomadic people who tamed the world.

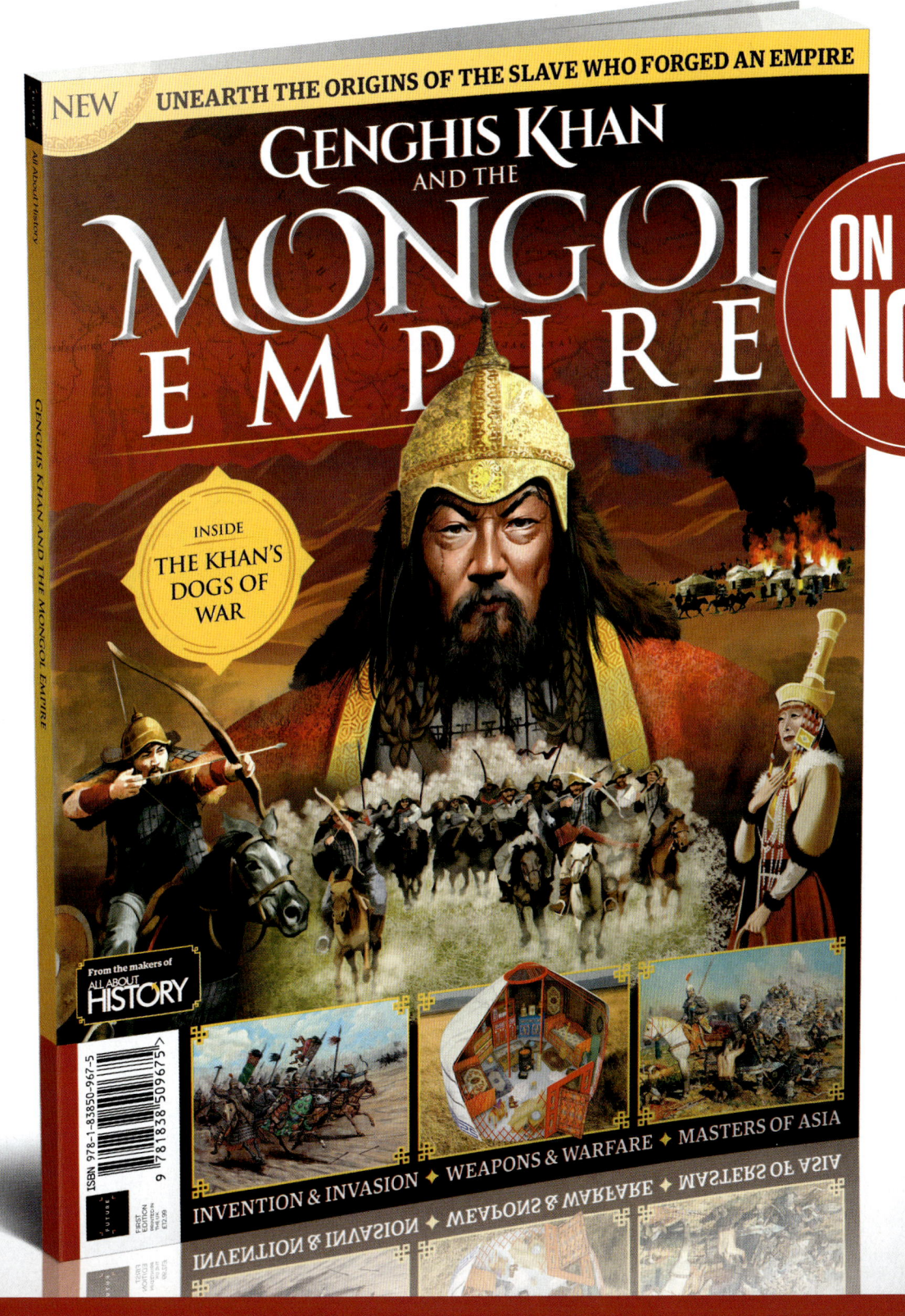

ON SALE NOW

Ordering is easy. Go online at:
magazinesdirect.com
Or get it from selected supermarkets & newsagents

中國歷史

THE TAIPING
Rebellion

HOW ONE MAN'S FEVER-INDUCED VISION TRIGGERED THE BLOODIEST CIVIL WAR IN HUMAN HISTORY

WRITTEN BY **NEIL CROSSLEY**

ABOVE The walls of Jinling, a suburb of Tianjing, are breached by forces loyal to the Qing dynasty

History is filled with incidences of people driven by religious epiphanies to incite rebellions and revolutions. One of the most extraordinary examples of this is the Taiping Rebellion.

Over the course of 14 years, from 1850 to 1864, a radical political and religious upheaval ravaged 17 Chinese provinces and resulted in the deaths of over 20 million people. The uprising was the most devastating event in 19th-century China and the bloodiest civil war in human history.

VOLATILE TIMES

Nineteenth-century China was an unstable place, one ruled by the Manchu-led Qing dynasty. Since the collapse of the Ming dynasty in 1644 the population had trebled from 150 million to 450 million. This burgeoning populace was forced to contend with famines, natural disasters and economic turmoil. On top of this, farmers were heavily overtaxed, rents rose dramatically, and peasants began to desert their lands in droves.

The Manchu-led government succumbed to the temptations of corruption, leading to a rise in anti-government sentiments that were at their strongest in southern regions of China, particularly within the Hakka community. It was here, in the village of Guangdong, where the seeds of the Taiping Rebellion would be sown by a former schoolteacher named Hong Xiuquan.

CELESTIAL VISIONS

Born into a Hakka family, Hong's ambition was to become a scholar-official in the civil service, but in 1837 his hopes were shattered when he failed the imperial examination for the third time. Hong suffered a nervous breakdown and sank into a brief state of delirium. While recovering he experienced a series of visions of heaven that convinced him that he was the younger brother of Jesus Christ and that he had been sent to rid China of demon worship.

In 1843, Hong failed his imperial examination for the fourth and final time. Around this time he was handed a pamphlet by an American missionary. "Follow the Christian God," he told Hong, "and you will reach the highest glory."

Hong believed the pamphlets held the key to interpreting his visions. He began preaching an early form of communism blended with Old Testament doctrine that stressed the importance of sharing property. He was soon attracting followers, and in 1844, one of these followers, Feng Yunshan, established the God Worshipping Society. This would become a dynamic new Chinese religion known as Taiping Christianity.

Hong's promise of free land attracted tens of thousands of disciples, and by 1849 the movement had expanded into four areas of China. Hong annointed himself as the Taiping King and decreed that his followers should not "commit adultery or be licentious", cast "amorous glances", harbour lustful thoughts, smoke opium or sing "libidinous songs". The punishment for not obeying these rules ranged from a beating to being beheaded.

THE REBELLION BEGINS

In 1850, the Qing Government attempted to suppress the Taiping, efforts that were met by the Taiping adopting guerilla tactics. Before long the soon-to-be rebels were buying gunpowder in bulk and organising into military units. The fuse had been lit.

On 11 January 1851, in the city of Jintian in Guangxi, Hong declared a new dynasty, the Taiping Tianguo, or Heavenly Kingdom of Great Peace. Hong's forces numbered 60,000 at the time but his ranks would swell to over a million.

It was late 1851 when a Taiping army first engaged the Qing military in a large-scale clash of arms. The Taiping emerged victorious, and later that year they seized the city of Yongan. In early 1853, Taiping forces marched north, recruiting as they went, and in March they reached Nanjing, which they took by force.

Hong proclaimed that the city would be the capital of his Heavenly Kingdom and renamed in Tianjing. He and his Taiping soldiers then set out to cleanse it of what they called Manchu "demons". Manchu men and women were executed, burned and expelled from the city.

That same year, Hong stepped down from active control of the Taiping forces to live in luxury inside his palace. He would now rule entirely by written proclamations.

> "Hong experienced a series of visions of heaven that convinced him he was the younger brother of Jesus Christ"

ABOVE Hong Xiuquan dreamed that he had a heavenly father who wore a black dragon robe and a wide-brimmed hat and sported a golden beard

ADVANCING NORTH

In May 1853, the Taiping military set out on the Northern Expedition. Their objective was to capture Beijing, but they were unprepared for the severity of winter in northern China and met fierce resistance from the Qing. In early 1856, the Qing army forced the weakened Taiping army back to Tianjing.

The Taiping were further weakened by internal power struggles. Hong often clashed with one of his lieutenants, Yang Xiuqing, and decided to have Yang and his followers massacred. Hong instructed two of his most trusted military leaders – Taiping general Wei Changhui and Hakka leader Qin Rigang – to kill Yang and his followers.

THE TIANJING INCIDENT

On 1 September 1856, Wei Changhui arrived in Tianjing with 3,000 troops. He and Qin stormed Yang's palace and slaughtered Yang and his family. Six thousand of Yang's followers still remained in Tianjing, so Hong and his generals set a trap. Hong pretended to arrest Wei and Qin and invited Yang's followers to watch as the two were beaten inside a hall. Once most of Yang's followers were in place the beatings were stopped and Yang's followers found themselves imprisoned. The following morning they were all systematically slaughtered. Over the next three months Yang's remaining supporters were mercilessly hunted down and slaughtered.

Things did not end well for Wei and Qin, however. In October 1856, respected Taiping commander Shi Dakai – who had planned one of the Taiping's most strategically brilliant victories in 1855 when he defeated the Qing's elite Xiang marines led by Zeng Guofan – arrived in Taiping and castigated Wei for the excessive bloodshed. Unwilling to accept Shi's accusation, Wei and Qin plotted to assassinate Shi, who learned of their plans and fled. Frustrated in their attempt to silence Shi, Wei and Qin stormed Shi's mansion and slaughtered his family and retinue. It would prove to be a fatal decision for both.

A vengeful Shi returned to Tianjing with 10,000 soldiers and demanded the heads of the men who'd murdered his family. Hong promptly ordered his bodyguards to kill Wei. Qin fled but was lured back to Tianjing and put to death. Fearing a similar fate at the hands of an increasingly paranoid Hong, Shi led his army out of Tianjing in 1857.

The Tianjing Incident proved to be the beginning of the end for the rebellion. The surviving leaders lost popular support in the wake of the bloodshed and the severely rattled Taiping troops who had once been fanatical in their devotion to the cause suffered a loss of morale and a string of defeats on the battlefield.

A GLOBAL RESPONSE

The ripples from the Taiping Rebellion were felt across the globe. In a piece for the *New York Tribune* in 1853, Karl Marx predicted that the uprising would spell the end of the British Empire's predatory capitalism and would "throw the spark into the overloaded mine of the present industrial system".

The Taiping Rebellion was hailed by 19th-century revolutionaries as evidence that radical global change was afoot. As American writer and historian Stephen R. Platt put it in his 2012 book, *Autumn in the Heavenly Kingdom: China, the West, and the Epic Story of the Taiping Civil War*, the Taiping uprising "seemed a remarkable parallel: the downtrodden people of China, oppressed by their Manchu overlords, had, it seemed, risen up to demand satisfaction. . . . Here was evidence that the empire on the other end of the world was now connected to the economic and political systems of the West."

In the U.S., the quasi-Christian nature of the Taiping uprising was perceived by many as a golden opportunity to transform China into a Christian nation.

Economically, it promised huge potential. *The New York Times* argued that the U.S. should recognise the Taiping rebels and trade with

> "A vengeful Shi returned to Tianjing with 10,000 soldiers and demanded the heads of the men who'd murdered his family"

BELOW Taiping fighters take aim. Some estimates put the total death toll of the rebellion at 30 million – one-twentieth of the population

ABOVE Charles 'Chinese' Gordon refused huge financial rewards for his superb service in China

LEFT Qing forces chase the Taiping out of Yuzhuang. One of their commanders, Shi Dakai, was executed by slow slicing in 1863 in return for his men being spared

them, as they occupied China's most productive tea- and silk-producing zones.

In Britain, the rebellion was monitored with alarm. As Platt points out, the U.S. and China were key cogs in the London-centred globalisation of the day. The British took it upon themselves to meddle, and the man chosen to help spearhead this intervention was Charles 'Chinese' Gordon.

ALLIED AMBITIONS

In 1860, Gordon was posted to China as part of the Allied Expeditionary Force that was fighting the Second Opium War. He was disappointed to be informed upon his arrival that he'd missed the last of the fighting, but his journey to the Far East would not be in vain.

Enlisting in the Anglo-French force sent to China to help the Qing restore order, Gordon joined the staff of General Charles William Dunbar Staveley, who would later appoint Gordon commander of the Ever Victorious Army, a 3,500-strong peasant force of mercenaries led by European officers.

The first Chinese army to receive training in European methods, in time the EVA became a formidable adversary, and it would play an instrumental role in ending the Taiping Rebellion.

Gordon, who had initially sympathised with the Taipings' cause before witnessing the brutal treatment of China's peasants by the rebels (Hong wrongly believed that all of the West welcomed the rebellion), instilled discipline into his men and led them into battle carrying only a walking stick. He even designed their uniform of green turban, jacket and trousers and black boots.

THE DREAM DIES

Prior to Gordon's rise to command of the EVA, in June 1861 the Taiping had advanced on Shanghai. Two months later, a 20,000-strong Taiping army took the Pudong district of the city but was pushed back by the Qing and their Western allies.

In September 1862, the Taiping made a second assault, this time with 80,000 men, but they were once more repelled by troops under the leadership of an American soldier of fortune called Frederick Townsend Ward, who had been pivotal in teaching the Chinese how to deploy Western tactics. By November the Taiping abandoned any hopes of seizing the city.

Bolstered by Western leadership and weaponry, the Qing forces reorganised and began to reconquer areas occupied by the Taiping. The Ever Victorious Army enjoyed a string of victories (Gordon would win 33 battles in a row during his time in China and receive promotions from both a grateful Emperor Muzong and the British Army). However, they were not alone in confronting Hong's hordes.

Established by the aforementioned Zeng Guofan in the early 1850s with the help of funding from the nobility of the province of Hunan, the Xiang Army had been fighting the Taiping rebels for over a decade by the time it laid siege to their capital of Tianjing in May 1862. The siege lasted two years, and by early 1864 the food situation was so perilous that Hong commanded his citizens to eat weeds.

In May 1864, Hong was found dead. Poisoning was suspected, but it's unclear whether he took his own life or was assassinated. Either way, his death portended the doom of his movement.

The former Heavenly King was buried in a yellow-silk shroud and laid to rest nearby to the former Ming Imperial Palace. He was replaced by his son, Hong Tianguifu, who had the misfortune of witnessing the fall of Tianjing a month after his father's passing.

The Xiang soldiers unleashed a wave of violence upon the inhabitants of the city, committing mass rape and murder, torching buildings and looting anything of value. Some of the Taiping reportedly gathered into crowds and sacrificed themselves. When the carnage finally ended on 14 July 1864, between 200,000 and 300,000 people lay dead. The rebellion was over, but its legacy would live on.

THE REBELS' LEGACY

The 14-year struggle for dominion over China claimed more than 20 million lives, equivalent to around one-tenth of the population. The Qing Government had prevailed, but it was fatally weakened. The rebellion had galvanised huge support and tapped into mass disaffection. It had also unleashed forces that would result in a revolution in 1911 that would pave the way for the rise of communism and of Mao. Hong's hazy dreams of the divine had spelled hell on Earth and irreversibly altered China's destiny.

China Transforms: The Second Opium War

ALREADY WEAKENED BY THE FIRST OPIUM WAR, QING CHINA'S CONTINUED EFFORTS TO STIFLE THE ILLICIT DRUGS TRADE STOOD NO CHANCE AGAINST THE WEST

WRITTEN BY **MICHAEL E. HASKEW**

Opium addiction gripped China in the mid-19th century. Chasing the dragon, as some called it in reference to the wisps of intoxicating smoke that curled from the user's pipe, had become a debilitating addiction for millions. However, the efforts of the Daoguang Emperor to stem the damaging tide had merely been met with hostility.

Chinese attempts to control the opium trade had precipitated the First Opium War of 1839-42. Simply put, Britain had gone to war to protect the lucrative opium trade of the East India Company, which was a quasi-government conglomerate that wielded considerable influence over international trade. In the case of China, a growing imbalance of exports and the refusal of its government to allow other economic activity had actually fuelled the British opium trade.

China's defeat in the First Opium War was a severe blow to the prestige of the Qing dynasty, as the Treaty of Nanking resulted in the cession of Hong Kong Island, while the ports of Canton, Shanghai, Fuzhou, Amoy, and Ningbo were opened to European commerce. The opium trade continued to flourish as the Chinese were compelled to loosen restrictions. The entire affair contributed to the beginning of a period historically known as China's 'century of humiliation'.

Still, China was reluctant to comply with the terms of the Treaty of Nanking, and in the wake of the First Opium War, the Taiping Rebellion, a civil war fuelled by religious strife that lasted 14 years and resulted in the deaths of over 20 million people, preoccupied the government.

At the same time, Britain and other Western nations interested in opening China's lucrative markets to trade (with the help of the most favourable clauses contained in the Treaty of Nanking and other agreements) became disgruntled with the Chinese Government's obvious reluctance to comply with earlier accords. Britain seized the opportunity to lead a coalition of Western nations including France, the United States and Imperial Russia in pressuring the Qing emperor for greater concessions.

Britain made excessive demands on the Chinese, including the full legalisation of the opium trade, the discontinuation of certain tariffs and duties, the appointment of a British legation and resident ambassador in the Chinese capital of Peking (Beijing), further territorial concessions, and the opening of the interior of China to Western travel via the great Yangtze River. The last point was particularly problematic for the Chinese as Christian missionaries and Western merchants would be allowed to move freely throughout their vast country.

In October 1856, Chinese customs agents seized the British-flagged cargo vessel *Arrow* and arrested its Chinese crew. When British demands for the release of the prisoners and an official apology were not immediately forthcoming, Sir John Bowring, governor of Hong Kong, threatened military action. The prisoners were freed, but the absence of an apology brought a British warship to the mouth of the Pearl River and a barrage of shells that fell on the forts guarding the approaches to Canton.

Chinese recalcitrance only increased, and by the end of the year violence against Europeans living in China and the destruction of property brought

ABOVE Chinese customs agents seize the cargo ship *Arrow*, precipitating the Second Opium War

> "Britain had gone to war to protect the opium trade of the East India Company, a quasi-government conglomerate"

ABOVE British and French forces fight the Qing Chinese for control of Canton in December 1857

outcries for further British armed intervention. The murder of French missionary priest Auguste Chapdelaine also brought his country into the burgeoning conflict.

Though immediate British action was postponed due to the diversion of troops initially bound for China to quell the Indian Mutiny of 1857–59, sufficient reinforcements had arrived by the end of 1857. Canton was subjected to artillery bombardment, and British and French troops stormed the city, capturing Chinese diplomat Ye Mingchen and imprisoning him in India, where he later died. When British and French demands for direct negotiations with the Qing emperor were rebuffed, the Europeans sent forces further up the Pearl River, where they shelled the Taku Forts guarding the approaches to Peking at the mouth of the Peiho River.

With their capital threatened, the Chinese agreed to parlay at Tientsin, and a treaty was signed there on 26 June 1858. The whole event was a thorough embarrassment for China. War reparations were to be paid, more Western nations would be allowed to establish legations in Peking, and all of the other original aims of the Europeans would be achieved.

Even so, a persistent faction in the Qing Government persuaded the emperor to continue resisting. Britain and France responded with roughly 17,000 troops and more than 170 naval vessels. In the summer of 1860, these forces neutralised the Taku Forts and captured Tientsin. Negotiations were fruitless, and the Chinese seized the British delegation. Several of these prisoners were tortured and later died.

BELOW British and Chinese negotiators part company after discussions during the Second Opium War

Meanwhile, the Europeans defeated Chinese forces at Chang-kia-wan and Palikao on the outskirts of Peking. In October 1860, Anglo-French troops burned the emperor's summer palace in retribution for the hostage situation at Tientsin. Artillery was drawn up in preparation for the bombardment of Peking itself. By then, the Chinese had had enough. The emperor was spirited out of the capital, and his brother, Prince Gong, led the ensuing negotiations.

The Convention of Peking was signed in October 1860. China ceded the Kowloon Peninsula (mainland territory near Hong Kong Island) to Britain, and the other British demands were also met. France and the U.S. reaped trade benefits through the treaty as well, while property confiscated from French missionaries was to be returned. As for Russia, it received a sizable portion of territory in the province of Manchuria.

The ramifications of the war were far-reaching. Many historians see the subsequent century of exploitation as the catalyst for the spread of anti-Western sentiment throughout China that culminated in the rise of Mao Zedong. ★

中國歷史

THE BOXER
Rebellion

WHY DECADES OF WESTERN IMPERIALISM, THE DECLINE OF THE QING DYNASTY AND FEARS THAT THE TRADITIONS AND HERITAGE OF THE PEOPLE WERE IN JEOPARDY SPARKED AN ANTI-FOREIGN UPRISING

WRITTEN BY **MICHAEL E. HASKEW**

For more than 200 years the Qing dynasty had ruled China – a country that was to Westerners a vast, mysterious land that seemed to beckon the entrepreneurial, adventurous and ambitious from Europe and America to explore, discover and sometimes exploit. As early as 1793 Emperor Qianlong told Lord Macartney, a British envoy, that China possessed "all things" and neither needed nor desired trade with the industrialising West.

Nevertheless, within half a century the Chinese had suffered defeat in the Opium Wars, exploited first by Britain and later Russia, France, and the United States to open China to trade. As Western influence grew, China's natural resources were plundered while the people watched the steady imperialist encroachment, seemingly powerless to stem the tide.

> "To this day the debate rages as to where real culpability lies"

Along with European and American incursions came the cultural shock of Western civilisation, particularly the introduction of the Christian church. While some Western observers decried the exploitation of the Chinese, others adopted a more paternal perspective. Conversion to Christianity would be positive, they reasoned.

The Chinese were presented as being incapable of managing their own affairs in the modern world. European and American 'benefactors' would assist. In 1884, France was victorious in a brief war with China and took control of Indochina (later Vietnam). A decade later Japan, which had by then embraced industrialisation, decisively defeated China in the Sino-Japanese War of 1894–95, seizing control of the Korean Peninsula and assuming trade concessions similar to those of the Western powers.

To exacerbate matters, floods, droughts and famines wracked the land, compounding the woes of the Chinese peasant class. In the midst of the upheaval created by grinding poverty in northeastern China rose the Society of the Righteous and Harmonious Fists, a secretive association that practised martial arts and intense physical exercise in the belief that it would make them impervious to injury from the bullets of Western guns. Observers of their regimented exercise routines were reminded of 'shadow boxing' and referred to the society's members as 'Boxers'.

Their perception of the erosion of Chinese culture, society and political autonomy inevitably drove the Boxers to militancy. In defence of their way of life, the Boxers became violent, anti-Western and anti-Christian while fostering divided loyalties even within the hierarchy of the ruling Qing dynasty. The Boxer Rebellion raged across the countryside from November 1899 until September 1901 and erupted in the streets of the capital of Beijing and the port city of Tientsin. The Boxers burned churches, threatened the economic interests of Europe and the United States in China, murdered Westerners and killed their own people who had converted from the traditional religion to Christianity. Dowager Empress Tz'u-Hzi restrained the army from suppressing the Boxers as violence escalated in Shandong and Zhili provinces and went a step further with a declaration of war against any foreign nation with diplomatic or economic ties to China. By the time the Eight-Nation Alliance of Britain, Russia, France, Germany, the United States, Italy and Austria-Hungary had put down the rebellion thousands had died – the majority of them innocent Chinese.

The clash of cultures was inevitable, and violence was its predictable by-product. To this day the debate rages as to where real culpability lies. Western imperialism and its lust for power was, without doubt, a contributing factor, as were the series of man-made and natural disasters that had befallen the Chinese people in the decades preceding the Boxer Rebellion. The ineffective leadership of the Qing rulers as their capacity to govern steadily declined, and the militancy of the Boxers bolstered by their disregard for life and property, all played a part. Ultimately the Boxer Rebellion was the furious release of pent-up rage against the burgeoning Western philosophy of a 'better way' that offered a convenient excuse to exercise imperialism in China.

At times the most salient point in an evaluation of the Boxer Rebellion, its causes and its wretched aftermath is overlooked. Western historians tend to consider the crisis through the prism of Western values and the eyes of those immersed in Western culture. But the Chinese people had developed and lived in a complex society with its own value system and its own perspective on the world long before the first Europeans set foot on the Asian continent. Ultimately both sides were guilty of judging the other culture's way of life through their own cultural values, which led to misunderstanding and conflict.

THE SIEGE OF BEIJING

Captain John T. Myers of the U.S. Marines surveyed the situation along the Tartar Wall enclosing the Legations quarter of Beijing, where 2,800 international civilians, diplomats, Chinese Christian converts and Western soldiers had taken refuge from the estimated 80,000-strong force of Boxers and elements of the Chinese Army bent on their destruction.

LEFT Ts'u-Hsi, who was effectively ruler of China for almost 50 years, opposed the Westernisation of her country

RIGHT This propaganda cartoon depicts the Eight-Nation Alliance as vicious dogs bringing down the weary Chinese Empire

THE BOXER REBELLION

中國歷史

ABOVE A depiction of the soldiers and civilians fighting the Boxers in the Legations quarter in Beijing

"The men all feel they are in a trap and simply await the hour of execution," wrote Myers. The situation did indeed appear bleak. Sporadic combat inflicted casualties and sapped the strength of the British, American, Japanese, French, German, Italian, Austrian and Russian defenders. An international relief force under British Vice Admiral Edward Seymour had already been thwarted by stiff Chinese resistance and had turned back to the port of Tientsin with heavy casualties.

Rather than overwhelming the handful of Western troops that numbered no more than 900, the Boxers laid siege to the Legation district, an area only 3.2 kilometres (two miles) long and 1.6 kilometres (one mile) wide. Another band of refugees was marooned at Beitang 4.8 kilometres (three miles) away, where 43 French and Italian soldiers, 33 priests and nuns and about 3,000 Chinese converts had sought refuge in the church.

The Siege of the International Legations had begun on 20 June 1900, and British minister Sir Claude MacDonald had taken command of the Western forces with American diplomat Herbert Squiers as his deputy. Ronglu, the Chinese commander, actually opposed the Boxer movement, which possibly explained his reluctance to mount an overwhelming assault. Nevertheless, the situation within the Legation district rapidly became desperate. Boxers initially tried to burn the defenders out. Then they attacked the Fu, a large palace that dominated the area, but were thrown back by Japanese marines.

The Germans were driven from the Tartar Wall on 30 June, leaving the Americans temporarily alone. Reinforced, Captain Myers led 26 British, 15 American and 15 Russian soldiers in a night attack that surprised the Chinese, ejected them from the wall and saved the Westerners from annihilation.

On 4 August a powerful Western force known as the Eight-Nation Alliance marched from Tientsin. General Sir Alfred Gaselee led its 3,000 British Commonwealth soldiers and was nominally in charge of the entire 20,000-man army. The route to Beijing stretched 160 kilometres (100 miles) through hostile countryside. Searing heat took its toll, and many soldiers were incapacitated or died of heat exhaustion.

A day after its march began, the Western army defeated the Chinese at Beicang, and on 6 August the Chinese were again defeated at Yangcun. A week later the relief force arrived outside Beijing. British, American, Russian and Japanese contingents were each ordered to assault one of the city gates, and early on 14 August Russian cannon tore open the Tung Pein gate, which was actually assigned to the Americans. Thirty Chinese were dead, and the Russians lost 26 killed and over 100 wounded in the ensuing melee, which lasted for several hours. The Japanese also met stiff resistance. Meanwhile, the Americans moved roughly 200 metres (655 feet) south of their assigned gate and scaled the city's nine-metre (30-foot) outer wall, entering Beijing and moving quickly towards the Legation district.

The British found their assigned gate virtually undefended and waded through a canal to reach the Legations quarter. As they raised the 55-day siege at 2.30 p.m., the British were warmly welcomed by the rescued civilians, many of them donning their best clothes to greet their liberators. The Americans fought their way to the district, arriving two hours later. Remnants of the Boxer force still controlled parts of Beijing but were driven off the next day. The Americans lost seven killed and 29 wounded in that engagement. Beitang was relieved on 16 August, and Dowager Empress Tz'u-Hsi and her ministers fled Beijing, taking refuge in the city of Xi'an.

The battle for Beijing broke the back of the Boxers, and the movement waned. On 7 September 1901 the signing of the Peking (Beijing) Protocol formalised terms for keeping the peace. Raising the Siege of the International Legations cost the Eight-Nation Alliance 60 dead and over 200 wounded. Another 55 soldiers died and 135 were wounded as they awaited rescue. Dozens of civilians were killed or wounded, while exact casualty figures among the Boxers and Chinese troops are unknown but are believed to have been heavy. ★

"The battle for Beijing broke the back of the Boxers, and the movement waned"

ABOVE U.S. Marine Captain John T. Myers helped rebuff Boxer attacks on the Legations quarter

---

FAILURE OF THE SEYMOUR EXPEDITION

Chinese forces defeated the initial attempt to protect Western interests from the marauding Boxers in Beijing

BELOW Seymour Expedition soldiers return to Tientsin with their dead and wounded

On 10 June 1900, more than a week before the Boxers laid siege to the Legations in Beijing, British Admiral Edward Seymour departed the port of Tientsin with 2,000 troops, including contingents from Britain, Japan, Germany, Russia, Italy, France, Austria and the United States. Their mission was to protect Western diplomats in the capital city along with civilians and sympathetic Chinese, including hundreds who had converted to Christianity, from the wrath of the Boxers. Moving by rail, the expedition was attacked twice on 14 June but continued to advance slowly.

Four days later at Langfang, south of Beijing, the Chinese attempted to trap the Western force. Although hundreds of Boxers and Chinese Muslim troops were killed, their fanaticism was disconcerting and Seymour ordered a general retirement to Tientsin. Following the course of the Hai River, the Westerners were continually harassed. Casualties mounted, ammunition was low and food and water supplies were depleted.

On 23 June the beleaguered Seymour Expedition luckily found supplies at the abandoned Xigu fort, and a messenger reached Tientsin with an urgent request for support. Within hours, 2,000 Western troops were en route to Xigu. On the 26 June Seymour's ill-fated expedition, with 62 dead and 232 wounded, limped back into the city under escort.

中國歷史

THE BOXER REBELLION
Timeline
1899-1901

AS VIOLENCE ESCALATES IN CHINA, WESTERN NATIONS TAKE MILITARY ACTION AGAINST THE BOXERS, RAISING THE SIEGE OF THE INTERNATIONAL LEGATIONS

Battle of Senluo Temple
Despite divided loyalties in the Chinese Government, Qing troops defeat the Boxers in a pitched battle at the Senluo Temple. Executions of Boxer leaders follow. However, unrest continues to spread across northern China.

---

1 NOVEMBER 1897 — **18 OCTOBER 1899** — **2 NOVEMBER 1899** — **30 MAY 1900**

Juye Incident
A mob of Chinese radicals murders two German Roman Catholic missionaries in Juye, Shandong province. The incident is a harbinger of the violence to come with the Boxer Rebellion.

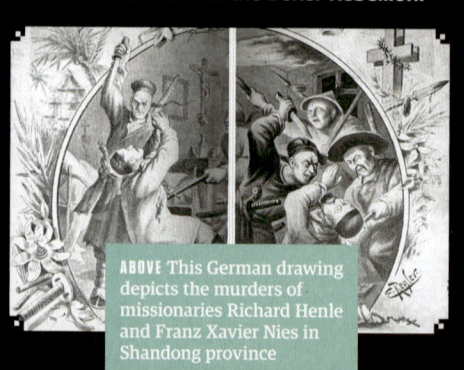

ABOVE This German drawing depicts the murders of missionaries Richard Henle and Franz Xavier Nies in Shandong province

Rebellion begins
Amid a wave of anti-Western violence, the Society of the Righteous and Harmonious Fists initiates the uprising dubbed the Boxer Rebellion. After 22 months of unrest the revolt is put down.

LEFT Houses and other structures near the American Legation in Beijing burn furiously after being set on fire by Boxers

MacDonald calls for assistance
Aware of the growing hostility of the Boxers, British minister Sir Claude MacDonald calls for a defence force to protect the legations in Beijing. Chinese authorities allow 400 foreign troops into the city.

RIGHT This drawing of a dapper Sir Claude MacDonald appeared in *Vanity Fair*

THE BOXER REBELLION

BELOW The executions of Boxers are carried out publicly in retribution and as a warning to others who might dissent

Tz'u-Hsi decrees war

A day after the Boxers lay siege to the International Legations quarter in Beijing, Dowager Empress Tz'u-Hsi declares war on all foreigners in China, revealing her support for the uprising.

ABOVE In this German cartoon Dowager Empress Tz'u-Hsi deposes Emperor Guangxu and holds the European powers at bay

Victory in Beijing

After heavy fighting, troops of the Eight-Nation Alliance defeat the Boxers and raise the 55-day Siege of the International Legations in Beijing. The Boxer movement rapidly disintegrates after the defeat.

LEFT American and Japanese troops launch an attack against Boxers during the fight to raise the Siege of the International Legations in Beijing

> "A day after the Boxers lay siege to the International Legations in Beijing, Dowager Empress Tz'u-Hsi declares war on all foreigners in China"

10 JUNE 1900 — **21 JUNE 1900** — **14 AUGUST 1900** — **7 SEPTEMBER 1901**

Seymour expedition marches

A relief expedition of just over 2,000 international troops under Vice Admiral Edward Seymour sets out towards Beijing only to come to grief against stiff resistance from the Boxers.

LEFT Sir Edward Seymour turned his expedition back to Tientsin as casualties mounted in the face of opposition by the Boxers

Boxer Protocol signed

The signing of the Boxer Protocol formally ends the rebellion and imposes harsh terms, including reparations of more than $330 million (approximately £260 million) on the Chinese. Several nations later return their payments to China.

ABOVE Months after the fighting has essentially ended Western and Chinese diplomats gather to sign the Boxer Protocol

THE BOXER REBELLION
Heroes & Leaders

NOTABLE FIGURES EMERGED IN BATTLE, IN THE CHURCH AND IN THE HALLS OF GOVERNMENT DURING MONTHS OF CULTURAL STRIFE AND ARMED CONFLICT

Xu Jingcheng
1845-1900
CHINA

Xu Jingcheng was a major political figure and served as a diplomatic envoy to several European countries during a political career that spanned more than three decades. He was a key advocate of modernisation in China and supported the Hundred Days' Reforms, which resulted in improvements in infrastructure such as railways and other public works.

As a young diplomat Xu gained an understanding of European industrialisation during the late 19th century and authored an encyclopaedia of foreign ships and naval vessels while advocating the modernisation of the Qing Government's navy. In 1890 he returned to Beijing and rose to a post among the top six ministers of the Chinese Government.

Sometime during his diplomatic sojourn, Xu converted to Roman Catholicism. As the Boxer Rebellion took shape at the turn of the 20th century he spoke openly against the violence and breaches of international law that he realised would bring retribution from Western powers. His Christian faith made Xu a target of suspicion and ridicule among the Boxers, as well as those in the Qing Government who supported them.

As the unrest of the Boxer Rebellion spread to Beijing from the northern Shandong province, Xu was one of six liberal members of the court that issued a petition to Dowager Empress Tz'u-Hsi seeking a diplomatic solution to the uprising and opposing any further support for the Boxers. The empress was enraged by its language and decreed that Xu and the other ministers should be put to death for "building subversive thought" and "wilfully and absurdly petitioning the imperial court".

Xu was beheaded on 28 July 1900 at the Caishikou Execution Grounds in Beijing, and his severed head was displayed as a warning to others. His protégé, Lou Tseng-Tsiang, later served as a diplomat and became a Catholic priest and missionary as well as Chinese prime minister.

RIGHT An influential diplomat during the rebellion, Xu Jingcheng's beliefs cost him his life

Dong Fuxiang
1839-1908
CHINA

One of the most highly respected military units among the enemies of the Eight-Nation Alliance during the Boxer Rebellion was known as the Kansu Braves, Chinese Hui Muslim soldiers who were led by the non-Muslim General Dong Fuxiang. Dong was born in western Gansu province in 1839. He joined the Qing army, rising rapidly through the ranks and successfully leading his Muslim troops in suppressing the Dungan Revolt in 1895. Vehemently anti-foreign in his beliefs, he led 10,000 soldiers to Beijing three years later in preparation for war against Westerners in support of the Boxer Rebellion. As the Qing court escaped from an embattled Beijing, Dong's soldiers provided an escort to the city of Xi'an. Although he became a national hero in China, Dong was exiled to Gansu after the Boxer Rebellion failed. He died in 1908 at the age of 69.

ABOVE Dong Fuxiang commanded the Kansu Braves during the Boxer Rebellion and gained lasting fame in China

> "He joined the Qing army, rising rapidly through the ranks and successfully leading his Muslim troops in suppressing the Dungan Revolt in 1895"

Corporal Calvin P. Titus
1879-1966
UNITED STATES

On 14 August 1900, the 14th Infantry Regiment of the U.S. Army was hotly engaged with Boxers along the outer wall of the Chinese capital of Beijing. With his command pinned down at the Tung Pien gate, Colonel Aaron Daggett asked for volunteers to scale the adjacent nine-metre (30-foot) wall and lay down suppressing fire.

A 19-year-old corporal named Calvin P. Titus from Oklahoma stepped forward and said, "I'll try, sir!" While others gasped, Titus, who went on to graduate from the U.S. Military Academy at West Point in 1905 and later became a chaplain assistant and ordained minister, used the cracks and jagged edges of the bricks to work his way upwards and was the first to reach the top. Others followed. Titus later received the Medal of Honor from President Theodore Roosevelt. He retired from the U.S. Army with the rank of lieutenant colonel after 32 years of service and died at the age of 86 on 27 May 1966.

ABOVE Calvin P. Titus received the Medal of Honor during West Point's centennial celebration in 1902

> "Halliday killed four Boxers but was severely wounded, a bullet tearing through his shoulder. Unable to move forward, he ordered the marines to continue the advance"

Captain Lewis Halliday
1870-1966
BRITISH EMPIRE

When the British Legation in Beijing was assaulted by marauding Boxers on 24 June 1900 and several buildings were set ablaze, 30-year-old Captain Halliday led 20 Royal Marines in an attempt to drive the attackers back. Opening a hole in the Legation wall, Halliday's command met heavy enemy fire. Halliday killed four Boxers but was severely wounded, a bullet tearing through his shoulder. Unable to move forward, he ordered the marines to continue the advance. Alone, he walked back to an aid station.

Halliday received the Victoria Cross and was promoted to brevet major. He recovered from his wound and continued in the service, attaining the rank of general and holding the post of adjutant general Royal Marines from 1927 until his retirement in 1930. He was also appointed knight commander of the Order of the Bath. Halliday died at the age of 95 in Dorking, Surrey, on 9 March 1966.

ABOVE In this 1964 photo, 93-year-old Lewis Halliday, a recipient of the Victoria Cross, attends a state function

Qiu Jin
1875-1907
CHINA

An acclaimed heroine of the Chinese people, Qiu Jin was a poet, feminist and revolutionary whose perspective on the future of China and the role of women in the country was partially shaped by the events of the Boxer Rebellion. Born in Xiamen in 1875, she grew to advocate the overthrow of the Qing dynasty and wrote poetry referencing the anti-Western uprising and the future of China.

In 1903, Qiu became a resident of Beijing and later that year she left her husband and two children to study in Japan. The profound effect of the Boxer Rebellion and continuing unrest in China motivated her to oppose many of the country's ancient customs that denigrated women. In 1905, she joined the Triads, a secret society committed to revolution. She subsequently became principal of the Datong School in Shaoxing, where revolutionaries were regularly trained. In July 1907, she was arrested, tortured and then beheaded at the age of 31.

RIGHT Revolutionary poet Qiu Jin is revered in China and memorialised in a museum in Shaoxing

The Last Dynasty

THE REPUBLIC OF CHINA ROSE FROM THE ASHES OF THE BRIEF BUT BRUTAL REVOLUTION OF 1911

WRITTEN BY **MICHAEL E. HASKEW**

The decades-long downward spiral of the Qing dynasty reached its climax with the revolution of 1911. European influence, steadily growing after the humiliating Chinese defeats in the Opium Wars, internal strife of the Taiping Rebellion, the divisive Boxer Rebellion at the turn of the 20th century, and belated attempts at reform had created a powder keg that only needed a spark to explode.

The last real opportunity to retain Qing power passed with the death of Empress Tz'u-Hsi and her politically inept nephew, the Guangxu Emperor, in the autumn of 1908. When the throne was inherited by two-year-old Puyi, destined to be the 11th and final Qing emperor, the regency that assumed nominal power proved ineffective.

All the while there were stirrings of political change and potential constitutional reforms, but the decline was irreversible. Through military victories in the 1894–95 Sino-Japanese War and the defeat of Imperial Russia in the Russo-Japanese War of 1904–05, Japan had begun to assert primacy in East Asia, including territorial gains on the Asian continent.

Although constitutional reforms were attempted, it was all too little too late. By 1911, millions of Chinese activists, domestic and expatriate, had begun to advocate, fund and openly speak on behalf of political change. Among these leaders was Sun Yat-sen, a committed nationalist who had succeeded in uniting several factions that supported a republican government into the Revolutionary Alliance. Other activists included Kang Youwei and Liang Qichao, proponents of constitutional monarchy. Much of the revolutionary discourse had emanated from the south of China, and simmering revolutionary ambitions had fomented at least seven small insurrections in the years just prior to the open rebellion of 1911.

Two incidents contributed to the uprising that finally removed the Qing dynasty. In April 1911, government intervention in a railroad project in the Sichuan province of central China raised the ire of investors and violence resulted. Even worse,

ABOVE Qing Prince Tchuen sits with his children Pu Chieh (left) and future emperor Puyi (right) in 1907

> "By 1911, millions of Chinese activists had begun to advocate political change"

ABOVE General Yuan Shikai served as president of the newly established Republic of China after Sun Yat-sen's resignation

ABOVE Empress Tz'u-Hsi is shown with an entourage shortly before her death in 1908

in October a republican-leaning army unit posted at Wuchang mutinied, capturing the local arsenal and government buildings. The revolt grew like a brushfire as violence broke out in cities across the vastness of China. In a desperate attempt to retain their positions, leaders of the Qing court regency agreed to numerous reforms that would virtually ensure the formation of a constitutional monarchy. Statesman and army general Yuan Shikai was called out of retirement to serve as prime minister.

However, because of Shikai's hesitation to act decisively to enact reforms, along with a groundswell of support for the Revolutionary Alliance from no fewer than 14 provinces that were then up in arms, the situation called for Sun Yat-sen, who returned to China from a fundraising tour in the United States to meet with the provisional government established in the city of Nanking. Sun was quickly elected provisional president of the newly proclaimed Republic of China, and in December Yuan was persuaded to negotiate.

The child emperor Puyi was forced to abdicate the throne on 12 February 1912 in favour of a government led by Yuan. Sun resigned the presidency as a unifying gesture, and presidential authority was consolidated in Yuan, assuring the cooperation of the Chinese military with the fledgling government. Yet although the Qing dynasty had been stripped of its authority, there were troubling days ahead.

Ironically, the swiftness of the republic's establishment and the relative lack of opposition to it may perhaps be construed as detrimental. The ebb of Qing influence created a lack of leadership in some provinces of China, while the new republican government was unable to bring the immense nation together under a centralised government. Consequently, the wave of real reform that had been anticipated fell far short of full implementation and created significant disenchantment with the apparent result of the revolution. Local warlords seized actual power in some areas of China and virtually ignored the central government, first at Nanking and then relocated to Peking in April 1912.

The international response to the revolution was one of wariness, particularly among those countries with substantial investment at risk. However, in a somewhat remarkable show of restraint given historical precedent, foreign countries remained neutral. Perhaps it was the expectation of republican government that convinced Western leaders not to intervene. The U.S. officially recognised the Republic of China in 1913, and other nations followed in succession.

As the goal of national unity proved elusive, the succeeding decades brought more turbulence. One witness to the 1911 Revolution was young nationalist Mao Zedong, whose subsequent adoption of Marxist-Leninist political theory served as the catalyst for continuing upheaval, eventually leading to civil war with nationalist forces under Chiang Kai-shek and the birth of the communist People's Republic of China in 1949. ★

ABOVE Sun Yat-sen was a political leader of the Revolutionary Alliance during the 1911 revolution

THE CHINESE Civil War Timeline
1926-1949

CHINA TEARS ITSELF APART IN A BLOODY CONFLICT THAT LEADS TO THE ESTABLISHMENT OF COMMUNIST RULE AND THE CREATION OF AN INDEPENDENT TAIWAN

中國歷史

Communists & nationalists
The Republic of China is increasingly politically split between the Kuomintang (KMT) Nationalist government, the Chinese Communist Party (CCP), regional warlords and the original republican Beiyang Government. However, the KMT and CCP initially cooperate with the assistance of the Soviet Union in an attempt to unify the country.

1920s

---

9 JULY 1926 – 29 DECEMBER 1928

Northern Expedition
KMT Generalissimo Chiang Kai-shek leads a military expedition against the Beiyang Government and warlords in order to unify China. The KMT takes control of the whole country, with Chiang proclaiming his aim to "build an independent, free nation".

LEFT Nationalist soldiers guard a pile of weapons after the KMT capture of Shanghai

---

12 APRIL 1927

Shanghai massacre
Chiang Kai-shek and conservatives within the KMT conduct a violent suppression of CCP organisations in Shanghai. Thousands of communists are killed and cooperation between the CCP and KMT ends. The Chinese Civil War begins when the CCP launches several uprisings to regain power.

ABOVE Gunmen shoot at windows near Station Square, Shanghai

RIGHT KMT soldiers swear an oath to Chiang Kai-shek, c.1930

1927-37

Ten-year civil war
China descends into a decade-long period of civil strife between the CCP and KMT. The Nationalists launch several German-inspired encirclement campaigns aimed at destroying the burgeoning Communist People's Liberation Army (PLA). The first four campaigns all fail but the fifth succeeds with assistance from Nazi Germany.

> "Consisting of 100,000 soldiers and led by Mao Zedong, a communist host travels 6,000 miles over mountains and rivers"

BELOW Luding Bridge became an important propaganda event for the CCP and the story of the battle is taught in Chinese elementary schools

Battle of Luding Bridge

A key moment of the Long March occurred on Luding Bridge, a 100-metre-long (328-foot) structure made of chains and wooden planks. It's the only reliable crossing over the Dadu River in any direction for hundreds of kilometres. Just 22 PLA soldiers cross the bridge and defeat the pro-KMT forces on the other side under heavy fire. Their success allows the PLA to cross by 2 June 1935.

Chinese Communist Revolution

The CCP and KMT resume the civil war after defeating the Japanese. Although the KMT has greater material, numerical and territorial strength, the CCP has many secret headquarters built in former Japanese-occupied territories during WWII. The Soviet Union gives aid to the communists while the United States assists the nationalists.

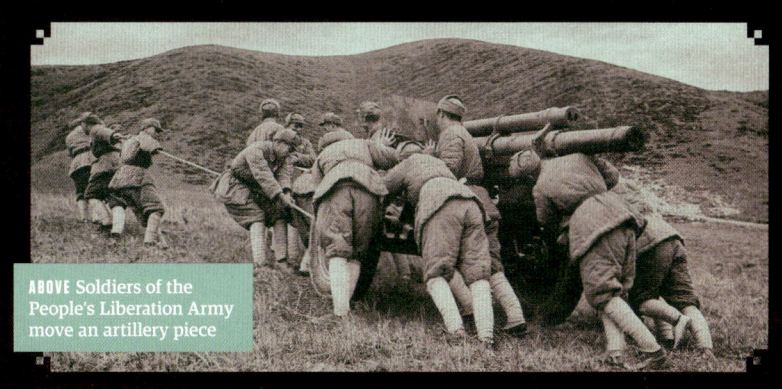

ABOVE KMT soldiers who support President Sun Yat-sen display their machine guns, c.1922. Sun had overthrown the Qing imperial dynasty and was succeeded by Chiang Kai-shek

ABOVE Soldiers of the People's Liberation Army move an artillery piece

---

16 OCTOBER 1934 – 22 OCTOBER 1935 | **29 MAY 1935** | **1937-45** | **1945-1950**

The Long March

PLA forces conduct an epic withdrawal from southeast to northwest China. Consisting of 100,000 soldiers and led by Mao Zedong, a communist host travels 9,600 kilometres (6,000 miles) over mountains and rivers. About 26,000 survive the journey to reach Yan'an, and the march establishes Mao as the effective leader of the CCP.

ABOVE Mao Zedong pictured during the Long March

Sino-Japanese War

Japan invades China, which forces the CCP to join the KMT in an uneasy alliance to defeat the invaders. The conflict becomes part of WWII, with Japan capturing many parts of the country. Tens of millions die and the Japanese win major victories, but China eventually regains all of its lost territories.

ABOVE Japanese infantrymen fire at a town close to Wuhan, Hubei province, October 1938

Map of China — Civil War campaigns

Labels on map:
- Liaoshen campaign — 4
- Battle of Kalgan — 3
- Pingjin campaign — 6
- Huaihai campaign — 5
- Shanghai massacre — 1
- Battle of Luding Bridge — 2
- The Great Retreat — 7

1945-49

Operation Beleaguer

Fifty-thousand American troops fight communist forces during the revolution while they repatriate over 600,000 Japanese and Koreans following WWII. The U.S. is markedly less successful at negotiating a peace treaty between the KMT and CCP.

ABOVE American soldiers march through Qingdao, Shandong province, c.1948

10-20 OCTOBER 1946

3 Battle of Kalgan

Nationalist forces besiege the communists during a mediatory ceasefire between the KMT and CCP. The nationalists take the city of Kalgan, which is symbolically important for the CCP, and destroy it. This action is regarded as a political mistake by the KMT.

ABOVE Students evacuate Kalgan during the battle

4 Liaoshen campaign

The communists launch the first of three campaigns against the nationalists. Numerous defeats are inflicted on the nationalists and northeast China is captured. It's the first time that the communists have a strategic numerical advantage over the KMT.

ABOVE Communist-type 97 Chi-Ha tanks advance into Shenyang during the Liaoshen campaign

7 The Great Retreat

The remnants of the KMT's government and armed forces retreat to the island of Taiwan. This includes approximately 2 million soldiers and many refugees. The measure is only meant to be temporary, but Chiang Kai-shek turns Taiwan into a country independent from the Chinese mainland. It officially remains the last bastion of the original Republic of China.

LEFT Taiwan's economy grows and its American support is cemented when President Dwight D. Eisenhower visits President Chiang Kai-shek in 1960

6 Pingjin campaign

Over 64 days, communist forces end nationalist dominance in the North China Plain. This vast territory eventually comes under CCP control and includes the KMT surrender of Beiping (Beijing) and Tianjin.

LEFT & RIGHT The People's Liberation Army enters Beiping

12 SEPTEMBER – 2 NOVEMBER 1948 | **6 NOVEMBER 1948 – 10 JANUARY 1949** | **29 NOVEMBER 1948 – 31 JANUARY 1949** | **1 OCTOBER 1949** | **DECEMBER 1949**

Huaihai campaign

A major communist offensive is launched against the KMT's headquarters in the city of Xuzhou. The city falls after being encircled and the communists occupy the territories north of the Yangtze River.

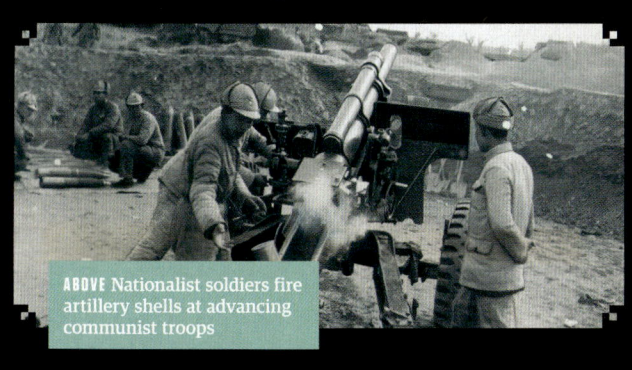

ABOVE Nationalist soldiers fire artillery shells at advancing communist troops

5 Communist victory

Mao Zedong, who is now the Chairman of the CCP, announces the proclamation of the new People's Republic of China in Tiananmen Square. Beiping replaces Nanking as the Chinese capital. The proclamation is followed by the first public military parade of the PLA and a new Chinese flag is unveiled.

ABOVE Chairman Mao reads out the proclamation

THE CHINESE CIVIL WAR

THE CHINESE CIVIL WAR
Heroes & Leaders

POLITICIANS, IDEOLOGUES AND MILITARY COMMANDERS ALL PLAYED A CRUCIAL ROLE IN THE STRUGGLE TO DETERMINE CHINA'S FUTURE

Zhou Enlai
AN INDISPENSABLE COUNSELLOR, ZHOU WAS MAO'S RIGHT-HAND MAN

1898-1976
PEOPLE'S REPUBLIC OF CHINA

Perhaps no member of the Communist Party was as astute and versatile as Zhou Enlai, an intellectual and professional soldier who handled the thorniest problems besetting the Red Army. Like Zhu De, he served for a brief period in the Whampoa Military Academy that was established with the help of foreign advisers. This same institution became Chiang Kai-shek's springboard to power in the mid-1920s. After the Kuomintang's (KMT) violent purge of communist sympathisers Zhou defected and joined Mao in the thriving Jiangxi Soviet that resisted the KMT's annihilation campaigns in the 1930s. Having survived the Long March, Zhou's role only grew under Mao's direction. He was both adviser and diplomat and enjoyed the respect of the KMT's own generals. When the communists finally won the civil war in 1949 Zhou was elevated to the premiership of China. This made his role comparable to a prime minister serving in the cabinet of a lifelong autocrat – that is, Chairman Mao. Unfortunately, even Zhou's adroit diplomatic skills and intellect could not avert the economic and social disasters caused by Mao's tyranny in the following decades.

Mao Zedong
ZEALOUS AND UNYIELDING, THE FUTURE RULER OF CHINA WAS A FIGUREHEAD FOR A STRUGGLING REBELLION

1893-1976
PEOPLE'S REPUBLIC OF CHINA

With little practical experience in subversive activities before he joined the Chinese Communist Party in 1921, Mao endured failure after failure trying to further the cause. A measured success came about with the founding of the Jiangxi Soviet in 1931, but this remote enclave was abandoned in October 1934 as his besieged army started their Long March to escape certain annihilation. The lasting impact of this shambolic retreat that almost wiped out the Red Army was to elevate Mao's leadership over the entire Communist Party and buy them valuable time. Being surrounded by capable advisors and colleagues was one of Mao's understated advantages. In Zhu De and Lin Biao he had unquestioning commanders who imparted valuable knowledge on all aspects of warfare. Mao's own writings on the topic may be authoritative but he would not have achieved this without the hardships and bloody lessons gleaned from decades spent fighting – and mostly evading – Chiang's nationalists. When the Communist Party won the civil war in 1949 a huge geopolitical shift occurred, with Mao as its architect. Of course, in the ensuing decades he orchestrated catastrophic policies such as the Great Leap Forward that led to mass famine and economic stagnation.

Lin Biao
THE ARCHITECT OF CHAIRMAN MAO'S PERSONALITY CULT, HIS DEATH BECAME A LONG-KEPT COMMUNIST PARTY SECRET

1907-1971
PEOPLE'S REPUBLIC OF CHINA

Another alumnus of Whampoa Military Academy who served under Chiang Kai-shek, Lin Biao defected to the communists in 1927 and served in the Jiangxi Soviet. His war record during the next 20 years was impeccable. It was his leadership of the 8th Route Army that allowed it to scale up with Soviet assistance in the years 1945-49. When the communists won the civil war the PLA's numbers had swelled to millions and short conquests of Tibet and Xinjiang ensued, further increasing China's territory. Lin became very close to Chairman Mao in the 1950s and was considered a sycophant by detractors in the Communist Party. *The Little Red Book* (officially titled *The Quotations of Chairman Mao*) was a massive propaganda campaign believed to have been engineered by Lin. For all his talent and loyalty, Lin met an ignominious end. In 1971 he fled China aboard a plane that disappeared under mysterious circumstances. His role in an aborted coup against an aging Chairman Mao was believed to be the reason for his attempted escape.

Zhu De
A SKILLED GENERAL, HIS ASTUTE LEADERSHIP STEADIED THE RED ARMY

1886-1976
PEOPLE'S REPUBLIC OF CHINA

Were it not for Zhu De's professionalism and fortitude, Mao's attempts at founding a soviet enclave in the Jinggangshan wilderness would have failed. It was Zhu De, who was serving as an instructor at the prestigious Whampoa Military Academy, who led the failed putschists in Nanchang on an arduous march towards Jiangxi, where he knew a fledgling communist encampment was growing. If Mao and Zhu had not become partners, with the latter subordinate to the former, then the Chinese Red Army would not have formed. Mao, unlike Zhu, never had any formal military training aside from a brief spell of conscription. Zhu's conduct during the KMT's annihilation campaigns and the Long March were just as exemplary. His character was indomitable and his thinking always clear-headed even when danger was close by. In the first months of the Long March, which lasted from October 1934 until October 1935, the continuous battles and aerial bombardments killed more than half of the Red Army. That Zhu and other commanders survived is miraculous. Mao's loyal general is now memorialized among the 'Ten Great Marshals of the PLA'.

Peng Dehuai

WITH A REPUTATION AS A GREAT MARSHAL, PENG DISTINGUISHED HIMSELF THROUGH 25 YEARS OF WAR

1898-1974
PEOPLE'S REPUBLIC OF CHINA

Peng was another Red Army stalwart who remained loyal through crushing defeats and desperate losses. Possessing the same taciturn resolve and unquestioning obedience of his superior, Zhu De, his later career was spent moulding the PLA into the world's largest military. Having joined the communists in his youth, it was not until the Second Sino-Japanese War that he rose to prominence. With Mao agreeing to a nominal alliance with the KMT, Peng was a deputy commander who saw extensive combat against the Japanese in northwest China. After the civil war that was concluded in 1949 Peng was next involved with commanding China's overwhelming response to the UN and South Korean forces that had overrun North Korea. The years of attrition along the 48th parallel may have killed as many as 3 million Chinese soldiers, but it also showed the tenacity and discipline of the PLA under its commanders. Before he was ostracised during the Cultural Revolution, Peng's main preoccupation was the establishment of clandestine factories and infrastructure in China's 'third front'.

Deng Xiaoping

A MINOR FIGURE IN THE RED ARMY, DENG'S EVENTUAL RISE TO POWER LAID THE FOUNDATIONS OF MODERN CHINA

1904-1997
PEOPLE'S REPUBLIC OF CHINA

Few members of the Communist Party served the cause with as much devotion and fervour as Deng Xiaoping, who joined at 23 and began organising cadres to establish soviets, or self-sufficient enclaves. Like the rest of his compatriots in the Red Army he was toughened by the years spent battling the KMT and the struggle against Japan. Deng survived the Long March and the decade spent in the canyons of Shaanxi under Mao Zedong until the communists finally won the civil war in 1949. A cruel fate awaited Deng and his family in the turbulent 1960s when he ran afoul of the Cultural Revolution. Stripped of his title and condemned to hard labour, Deng toiled for years in a government factory before he was rehabilitated and forced back into national politics. Deng is revered in China today as a reforming leader who mended ties with the United States in the late 1970s. It is Deng's success at 'opening up' China's economy that is further celebrated rather than his role in enforcing the violent crackdown on pro-democracy activists in 1989. When he passed away in 1997 his legacy was enshrined in the Chinese Communist Party's annals.

Chiang Kai-shek

A DITHERING STRONGMAN AND AN UNRELIABLE ALLY AT BEST, CHIANG'S INDECISIVENESS COST HIM HIS COUNTRY

1887-1975 REPUBLIC OF CHINA

A true son of the 1911 revolution that swept away the ailing Qing dynasty, Chiang was an ardent soldier but a poor strategist. His close relationship with China's great modernising patriot, Dr. Sun Yat-sen, elevated him to the upper echelons of the KMT. By the time he adopted the title Generalissimo and launched the Northern Expedition to subdue China's stubborn warlords, Chiang was the toast of the world. The Soviet Union, rather than the United States, was his most eager benefactor at the time; before he married, Chiang received training from both Japan and the Soviet Union. But the dismal results of the Northern Expedition revealed his less-stellar qualities. When faced with daunting adversity Chiang always found the best course was a sudden escape – he exiled himself to Japan in 1927 for a respite, leaving his homeland without a head of state until his return. While he proved a staunch opponent of the communists, whose numbers he decimated with annihilation campaigns from 1930 until 1935, the same willingness to abandon a lost cause drove him away from the Chinese mainland in 1949. Chiang spent the rest of his life as Taiwan's resident dictator, his wish to reconquer the mainland unfulfilled.

General George C. Marshall

THE WWII GENERAL FAILED TO CRAFT A VIABLE STRATEGY FOR ASIA IN THE POST-WAR ORDER

1880-1959
U.S.

Unlike other great powers, the United States never had cruel designs on China other than to secure a dependable Asian ally. But this modest role grew problematic in WWII as President Roosevelt and then President Truman could not fully commit to the KMT with vast quantities of material when the European theatre was the Allies' priority. After the defeat of Japan the renowned General Marshall, already celebrated as a visionary and hero, was given a delicate assignment by Truman: to go to China and forge a lasting peace between the communists and the nationalists. Backing up Marshall's presence were 100,000 advisers, technicians, and marines tasked with keeping the peace. The Soviets, on the other hand, having entrenched themselves in Manchuria, were seen as spoilers who may or may not encourage the communists to attack. To thwart this possibility, Marshall made personal contact with Mao or liaised via Zhou Enlai. Despite his best efforts and the open support of Chiang Kai-shek and the Communist Party's own leadership, Marshall could not build a coalition government in China and when he departed in 1947 the civil war ran its inevitable course.

Japan

INTOXICATED BY VISIONS OF IMPERIAL CONQUEST, JAPAN'S FANATICAL MILITARISTS LAUNCHED A GENOCIDAL CAMPAIGN TO SUBDUE CHINA AND PLUNDER ITS RESOURCES

WRITTEN BY MIGUEL MIRANDA

Only a peculiar madness could inspire the aspiration to carve up East Asia. For Japan's generals and statesmen, however, this was imperative to create a world empire, even when it was unfeasible.

How far within a hostile country could an army of occupation travel before it became bogged down? How many soldiers, bullets, tanks, ships and planes would it take? What about the untold millions to be checked by a permanent garrison? And what of the risk of sanctions, of Western interference? None of these quibbles seem to have shaken the Imperial Japanese Army's resolve as it set about fulfilling an ancient dream in the late 1930s but where this dream originated is hard to discern. What historians now refer to as the Second Sino-Japanese War is commonly overshadowed by the events after 1941. Not even its excesses and brutality caused too much alarm among the Great Powers - not until modern times at least.

DREAMS OF AN EMPIRE

There once was a dream among the fighting men of Japan, whose tireless martial vigour mired their nation in endless civil war. It was a dream of boundless empire acquired by merciless brute force. In the last decade of the 16th century, the warlord Toyotomi Hideyoshi launched two campaigns to conquer the Korean Peninsula. Once a foothold on the Asian mainland was established, his legions of Samurai and musketmen would then march on Peking and subsequently rule China.

Both endeavours were spectacular failures and Hideyoshi died soon after his last debacle. Japan closed its doors and outlawed its guns. Christian missionaries were expelled throughout the realm. Then, after 250 years of domestic peace and isolation, an American naval squadron would force Japan to accept free trade - a rude awakening for the complacent Tokugawa shogunate. By 1889, Japan had adopted a new constitution, modelled after Prussia's, and became a constitutional monarchy.

A modern army soon followed. Six years later, the embers of Hideyoshi's far-fetched dream were alight once more. The First Sino-Japanese War (1894-1895) was a raw display of Japanese tenacity and firepower in the face of superior Chinese numbers. Humbled, the diplomats of the Qing dynasty agreed to a humiliating peace deal in the Japanese city of Shimonoseki.

Not only did China lose the Korean Peninsula for good - granted 'independence' under Japanese supervision - but the island of Formosa as well. Worse, resource-rich Manchuria was now within Japan's grasp. The only hindrance was the Imperial Russian Navy's presence in the Kwantung Peninsula, a state of affairs brought about at the last minute as Japan imposed its terms on China.

A decade later it was Russia's turn to be on the receiving end of Japan's army and navy. In a series of spectacular battles from Port Arthur to Tsushima, Japan's sheer fighting prowess during the Russo-Japanese War of 1904-1905 established its credentials as a formidable adversary. It had become an exemplar for every nation suffering under the yoke of colonialism and rapacious European dominance.

Japan's latest triumph against a larger adversary caused another chilling side-effect. After the war, like the decrepit Qing dynasty with its increasingly tenuous hold over China, the Russian Empire's own seams would begin to unravel in a torturous decline that climaxed with the 1917 Bolshevik Revolution.

Rather than bask in its new-found status as an ocean-going power, another problem faced the Japanese elite - a rigid alliance of landed families-turned-industrialists and the political status quo. The country had become too successful and was resource poor.

The gifts of the 20th century were too generous to Japan. An archipelago of three

A STATE

1937
OF WAR

JAPAN 1937

ABOVE Japanese soldiers fighting in a town near to Nanking

中國歷史

main volcanic islands prone to earthquakes, with little arable land and no fossil fuel deposits, Japanese industriousness created a population boom that grew year on year. As an Asian power with a Prussian cast imposed by its constitution, a convivial and democratic outlook on national life never figured in the nation's political discourse.

Japan needed to be strong - if the world did not accommodate its needs, it would accommodate itself. The revolution that swept China in 1911 was a boon that allowed further Japanese gains into its main rival's economy. By this time Japan had mastered planning its economic foundations of coal, railroads and factories. Korea was its offshore base for cheap labour. This was not enough though; Japan needed to be stronger, even unassailable. An opportunity lay beyond Korea, across the Yalu River, in glorious Manchuria.

AN INDUSTRIAL UTOPIA

Manchuria was an exciting, rugged and unforgiving place. Until the 20th century Western travellers were only able to describe it in the most basic terms - its geography and the weather. The region's ill-defined borders were the Yalu River and the Yellow Sea to the south and the Ussuri and Amur rivers to the east and north, natural boundaries separating it from Russia where the steppes merged with the tundra and taiga. To the west was Mongolia's grasslands.

At the end of the First Sino-Japanese War, Manchuria was coveted by Russia as the last piece of its Siberian domain. With the blessing of France and Germany, Russia was able to position herself as China's defender, seizing Port Arthur and keeping Manchuria out of Japan's clutches.

In reality, Russia was just as eager to lay down railways and set up factories. Timber, minerals and vast tracts of arable land were for the taking. Harbin, China's northernmost city today, was founded by the Russians, who quickly turned it into a boomtown with its attendant ostentation.

Manchuria's forbidding mountains and steppes were home to the indomitable Jurchen tribes. During the 11th century these mounted nomads federated and subdued northern China long before Genghis Khan's hordes did the same. In the mid-17th century, their descendants repeated history. Organising themselves into an army, the Manchus toppled the Ming dynasty and ruled China at its height as the Qings.

At the end of the Russo-Japanese War in 1905, Manchuria was ripe for the taking. Japan could not take it, however, since this would provoke another conflict. The stratagem that suited its designs best was a cunning one. If modernisation had a single impetus, it was the

> "Japan needed to be strong – if the world did not accommodate its needs, it would accommodate itself"

cycle of accumulating and investing capital, and the imperial state had perfected modernisation.

According to Louis Livingston Seaman, a surgeon who served in the Spanish-American War and the Boxer Rebellion, Japan's arrival in mainland China bode well for the future. As explained in his book *From Tokio Through Manchuria*, published in 1905, the Japanese Army and Navy were models of efficiency.

Dr. Seaman insisted their presence was needed in order to stop Russia. "It would indeed be a peril and terror to civilisation were these hardy peasants of Manchuria and the countless hordes of China transformed into minions of the White Czar," he wrote.

Nine years before WWI, long before the Treaty of Versailles and its limitations on the Imperial Japanese Navy's tonnage, Dr. Seaman believed Japan acted as a regional balancer. "The present hope of security against this lies in a complete victory of the patriots of the Land of the Rising Sun, which shall effectually stem the tide of Russian aggression for this generation at least, thus giving China one more chance to put her house in order."

THE BATTLE OF SHANGHAI

When two massive armies clashed over the greatest city in Asia, the continent witnessed carnage on a scale that had never been seen before

Eager to secure their control over Manchuria, Japan's militarist clique planned to invade the mainland and force Chiang Kai-shek from power. The first domino to fall would be Shanghai.

The problem was the only Japanese forces stationed in Shanghai were a detachment of naval infantry, and sending more would arouse suspicion. There needed to be a reason for the arrival of Japanese troops. Taking their cue from the Mukden Incident and the outbreak of the Philippine-American War in 1899, it was decided that a single ambiguous crisis would launch the war.

After Chinese sentries allegedly gunned down a lone Japanese officer in Shanghai, one clash led to another and by 13 August thousands of Chinese and Japanese troops were already fighting within the city.

Lasting for three months, from 13 August to 19 November, the battle would be the most savage fought in the pre-WWII era and included a daring amphibious assault by the Japanese on the mouth of the Yangtze River.

The Imperial Japanese Army (IJA) and Navy would use all of their assets to quash the National Revolutionary Army defenders, who fought heroically despite high casualties. These qualities made battles like the struggle for Sihang Warehouse the stuff of legend.

In typical fashion, the well-equipped but poorly led Chinese lost up to 250,000 soldiers defending Shanghai and only succeeded in slowing down the IJA, who razed the provincial capital Nanking a month later.

LEFT Japanese soldiers in China in 1937

Support for China

A conflict between two hegemonic Asian giants, the war's intensity inspired an outpouring of propaganda

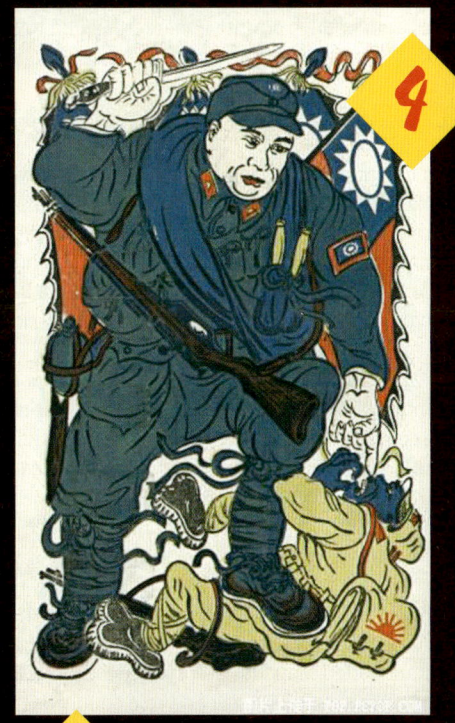

1 UNITED CHINA RELIEF
Massive U.S. aid to China did not begin until mid-1941, replacing the generosity of France, Germany and the USSR.

2 NAVY, ARMY, AIR FORCE
In this scene, Chiang Kai-shek looks on as his air force and navy arrive to thwart a Japanese armada.

3 EIGHTH ROUTE ARMY IN SHANXI
By 1937, the Republic of China already had a vast and modern army with which to defend itself thanks to foreign aid.

4 NRA ANTI-JAPANESE WAR POSTER
In this undated poster, a hulking NRA infantryman clutching a gleaming bayonet overwhelms his child-like Japanese rival cowering beneath him.

In the final chapter of *From Tokio Through Manchuria*, Dr. Seaman was earnest in his best wishes for China, then the proverbial 'Sick Man of Asia'. "So long as England, Japan, and our own land (the United States) stand for the integrity of this great unwieldy empire, the machinations of her foes will assuredly be circumvented," he wrote.

Perhaps something that was beyond Dr. Seaman's ability to foresee was just how sinister the Imperial Japanese Army's administration of Manchuria would become. In the ensuing decades they turned it into a colony with its very own state within a state, the Kwantung Army.

A less dramatic though insightful account of Manchuria's importance to Japan's progress comes from a book titled *The Economic History of Manchuria*. Published in 1920, it was prepared by men from the Chosen Bank (pronounced Choh-San), a financial institution based in Seoul, South Korea, run by the Japanese.

The book's author was very frank about Chosen's activities in Manchuria, where it had more branches than in the whole Korean Peninsula. This was necessary because "Manchuria had ever been a tempting field for the bank but then the trade of Chosen with the country was anything but such to justify its financial policy".

Founded in Seoul in 1909, a Japanese Imperial decree in 1917 made Chosen Bank the sole provider of Japanese bank notes in Manchuria. Of course, such a captive market needed to be kept – by force if necessary.

ABOVE As the Japanese invaded, civilians fled from cities such as Peking

FROM COLONIALS TO CONQUERORS

The Second Sino-Japanese War was actually just the bloodiest phase of a long struggle to capture the Chinese heartland. 30 years previously, the Empire of Japan had secured a crucial toehold in Manchuria after emerging victorious in its bloody struggle for the region against Russia.

In the following years its control of the region grew exponentially, so much so that this mutation of Japan's borders, which now spread across East Asia, created the dangerous strains that paved the way for its devastating defeat at the hands of the Allies in WWII. One of these strains was the ambiguous existence of the Kwantung Army.

Despite its ominous name, the Kwantung Army began as a small garrison tasked with protecting the Japanese-owned railroads that transported Manchurian produce to Korea. But as time went on its size and role changed. With the benefit of hindsight and historical records, it appears the Kwantung Army's distance from Tokyo made its officers more autonomous, more daring, and as a result, more reckless.

On 4 June 1928, Chinese warlord Zhang Zuolin was assassinated by a bomb in his railway car.

THE RISE OF HIDEKI TOJO

Taciturn, single-minded and a ruthless empire builder, Tojo was an oriental Spartan and the unwitting architect of Japan's humiliation

When Hideki Tojo became prime minister of Japan in 1941, Asia was at the mercy of an unremarkable man. Born in Iwate Prefecture to an army sergeant and the daughter of a Buddhist priest, Hideki was the eldest of three sons and groomed for a military career from an early age. As a result, his world view was framed by his martial upbringing.

Five feet, four inches tall, with poor eyesight and a career that was mostly spent in staff positions, Tojo was a hard worker with simple tastes. Serving as military attaché to Germany during and after WWI left a deep impression on him, and he was obsessed by the idea of national industry subordinate to national will. These experiences led to his involvement with the One Evening Society and the Kōdōha movement – each being secret militarist initiatives to prepare Japan for total war.

Other than leading the Kempeitai intelligence service in Manchukuo and orchestrating the invasion of Inner Mongolia in 1937, Tojo had little combat experience. As minister of war and then prime minister, he had absolute faith in Japan's destiny as a great power and believed any means necessary should justify this end, like the attack on Pearl Harbor. He was executed for war crimes on 23 December 1948.

RIGHT As war minister, Tojo earned the nickname 'the Razor' for his ability to make extremely quick decisions

BELOW Japanese soldiers fire through holes in a brick wall during the Battle of Shanghai

BELOW The city of Wuxi, near Shanghai, burns as Japanese soldiers move on

This attempt to subvert Manchuria was far from conclusive, but three years later the Kwantung Army overran the area. The following month a bomb blast on the South Manchuria Railway led to further military action and the establishment of 'Manchukuo'. It was a daring endeavour to found an industrial colony in China's unforgiving frontier. The deposed Qing emperor Puyi was even rustled out of his post-imperial life to serve as the nominal head of state.

What made these land grabs so frequent was China's weakness. The republican era that began with Sun Yat-sen's revolution in 1911 was a disappointment. By the 1920s the Kuomintang government only had nominal control of China and warlords ran fiefdoms that included whole provinces. So the Kwantung Army, with or without the approval of Tokyo's civilian leaders, took the initiative to expand its territory until it neared its deadliest rival: the Soviet Union.

All the years of subterfuge and belligerence in northeast China were minor acts in a grander drama. The Kwantung Army needed to be secure should the day come when the rival Red Army came crashing down the steppes, across the Amur River and right into the intended breadbasket of Japan.

THE TWO SIDES PREPARE

What is often missed when assessing Japan's national character before WWII is that the political and military leadership were routinely at odds. As the Kwantung Army and its officers went about the task of colonising Manchuria, the Imperial Japanese Army and Navy were making preparations for the next war. Even when anachronistic concepts like Hakko ichiu – best described as a Japanese version of Manifest Destiny and The White Man's Burden – gained popularity in the 1930s, it took an unstable officer class to intimidate the government before Japan could fulfil its imperial goals.

The same year the Kwantung Army overran Manchuria on a flimsy pretext, a pseudo-putsch took place in Tokyo. From 1932 to 1936, there was a campaign by the military, the police and the Kempeitai to snuff out communists, subversive elements and politicians who disagreed with the ideals of Hakko ichiu.

It was apparent a campaign was being waged by a deep state. It had no membership list or manifesto, but it had a name. The mysterious Kōdōha believed the first step towards realising an unassailable Japanese empire was seizing power by whatever means. In 1936, the Kōdōha's clout meant that the Imperial Japanese Army (IJA) and Navy (NJA) were readied for the greatest war in Asian history.

Preparations for this momentous struggle had been under way for years. When the U.S. War Department commissioned studies on Japan's military, the results revealed an efficient fighting machine. The IJA's Air Service had thousands of trained pilots and aircraft. The IJN was the best in the Eastern Hemisphere.

The Japanese infantryman, airman and sailor were formed in the same mould. No matter the branch, training was exacting, harsh and literally painful. The Japanese soldier was often portrayed as a yellow-skinned and bow-legged malefactor. In reality, he was a young man who was punished, beaten and humiliated by his superiors on a regular basis. But he had an excellent rifle in the 6.5mm Model 38, which was later replaced by the more powerful 8mm Model 94, colloquially known as the Arisaka. Japanese infantrymen also had a quaint muzzle-loaded 50mm grenade discharger for intermediate ranges as well as a semi-automatic 20mm anti-tank rifle. A lethal variety of machine guns and mortars were available to IJA companies, as well as light tanks and towed artillery. Simply put, Japan's military was ready for its next war.

By comparison, in 1937 the Kuomintang's National Revolutionary Army (NRA) was in questionable shape. Ever since Chiang Kai-shek assumed power in 1928 he had gone about setting China's house in order. At first he almost got rid of the communists under Mao Zedong, then he subdued the provincial warlords to assert the Kuomintang's authority.

Both efforts were a success, encouraging the European powers to make resources available for the NRA's modernisation. Western advisors had an important role in moulding the NRA into a professional military that ranked among the world's largest. Most prominent were an unspecified number of Germans, including WWI veteran Colonel General Hans von Seeckt.

Von Seeckt and a succession of officers gave Chiang Kai-shek a well-trained and highly motivated corps of 300,000 men by 1936. Added to this were between 900,000 to 1 million auxiliaries. Thanks to foreign aid, the NRA had access to a modern – albeit limited – arsenal. Small arms like the 7.92mm Mauser 98K and the 8.5mm ZB-26 machine gun gave the NRA infantry top-of-the-line firepower.

Limited amounts of modern artillery and light tanks – French Renault FT-17s and Soviet T-26s

> "The Japanese infantryman, airman and sailor were formed in the same mould. No matter the branch, training was exacting and painful"

ABOVE Japanese soldiers cross the moat to enter the Gate of China, Nanking's southerly city wall

RIGHT Bodies of victims stack up on the bank of the Qinhuai River near Nanking's west gate

BELOW A baby sits among the ruins of Shanghai

– also reached the NRA. On the eve of war with Japan the NRA was laying the groundwork for what would become the Republic of China Air Force. This time it was the USSR that provided the hardware to the Chinese in the form of 500 propeller-driven light fighter aircraft and more than 300 bombers. The navy, on the other hand, possessed modern gunboats and cruisers.

A STUMBLE INTO HELL

As it turned out, it took a bizarre string of events to set the NRA and the IJA against each other. Two incidents, one in Shanghai and the other in the former imperial capital Beijing, would spiral out of control and start an epic battle involving millions.

In July 1937, units of the Kwantung Army seized Beijing's historic Marco Polo Bridge, then in August a Japanese navy officer was killed by Chinese sentries in Shanghai. There continues to be speculation that NRA General Zhang Zhizhong orchestrated the incident to provoke a war at the behest of Stalin. Apparently, Zhang was a high-level Soviet agent.

The resulting three-month battle for Shanghai, from August 13 to November 19, was a futile one. Over the span of 100 days, the NRA was almost eliminated, but the IJA had received a rude awakening. The Chinese could put up a tremendous fight, and rising Japanese casualties posed a threat to any invading force's momentum.

The Kuomintang and its military had the worst of it, however. The IJA might have been slowed in the city fighting, but the NRA's losses were in the hundreds of thousands. Gone were its best officers, half of the air corps and most of its tanks and artillery. Meanwhile, the Kwantung Army in the north had seized Beijing and Inner Mongolia.

Chiang Kai-shek's options were all dire. With the national armed forces in disarray and the IJA on the march, on 1 December the Kuomintang abandoned its capital Nanjing, known to Europeans as Nanking, and relocated to Chongqing. The NRA general left behind to defend Nanking, Tang Shengzhi, had the manpower at his disposal but not the will or strategy to block the oncoming IJA. Nanking fell and its inhabitants were at the mercy of the IJA. What followed was a grim and baffling period that still echoes down the years to haunt Japan.

THE RAPE OF NANKING

From 13 December until the end of January, foreign missionaries and members of the diplomatic community witnessed arson and looting by Japanese soldiers in Nanking. A week before, the retreating Kuomintang had tried to destroy any structure of value lest they be captured by the IJA. Now, entire neighbourhoods were razed and civilians rounded up.

Soon the killing began. What has astounded historians since is that the atrocities perpetrated in Nanking had no precedent and seemed to have little purpose other than to inflict cruelty on its citizens. The earliest testimonies from Nanking during the first two months of Japanese occupation come from two unlikely American conspirators: Reverend John Magee and George Fitch, the head of the local YMCA.

Together they smuggled 16mm footage out of China. The footage captured Japanese atrocities in and around the International Safety Zone, where the foreigners vainly tried to save as many as they could.

It was brave but futile. Constantly harassed by the Japanese, Fitch and a small group of foreigners, including the heroic German ambassador John Rabe, bore witness to the IJA's revenge on Nanking. Fitch kept a journal of his experiences. Just four days after the IJA stormed the city, mass rapes were routinely perpetrated. "Over a hundred women that we knew of were taken away by soldiers," Fitch wrote. "Refugees were searched for money and anything they had on them was taken away, often to their last bit of bedding… It was a day of unspeakable horror…"

In 1937, a new concept began to circulate in Japanese newspapers and radio broadcasts.

BELOW Soviet forces at Khalkhin Gol

> "There was no strategy to the slaughter. Men young and old were rounded up"

CHINA'S RESISTANCE

Doomed by its own incompetence, the Kuomintang military compensated with sheer numbers equipped with a vast selection of European arms

The NRA
By 1928, Chiang Kai-shek had unified the crumbling Chinese state with the massive National Revolutionary Army at his disposal. Millions strong, an elite corps of 300,000 officers and soldiers trained by German advisors were ready for a showdown with Japan by 1937.

Structure
This depended wholly on foreign advisors. Some units were staffed and run like their European counterparts, while others were mired in anarchy. Other units didn't exist except on paper. Sporadic warlord-led armies were cohesive but small.

Equipment
Between poor administration and a modest industrial base, it was only possible to equip the army with locally made small arms. Planes, tanks, ships and artillery were imported from abroad. This over-reliance on foreign aid meant the army did not have the capacity to replace its losses.

LEFT Chinese soldiers armed with ZB-26 guns

ABOVE The National Revolutionary Army had its own small armoured corps that used the French Renault FT-17 light tank

Effectiveness
The most effective divisions of the Chinese army perished during the Second Battle for Shanghai in 1937. Others became bogged down suppressing the communists in the interior provinces. If the Chinese had one advantage, it was sheer manpower. The record of the Republic of China's armed forces is an ignominious one. Though successful in almost quashing the nascent communists, it was completely ineffective against the IJA. Even when Chinese generals were often very competent, their loyalties and motivations were highly questionable.

It was an attitude - a national mindset - that would justify a long war with an unyielding enemy. It was called Seisen, and in its name hell was brought to millions of innocents. But just what did the IJA accomplish in Nanking?

There was no strategy to the slaughter. Men young and old were rounded up on the assumption they were Chinese soldiers in disguise and either shot or bayoneted. Accounts of mass immolation also trickled out from traumatised survivors.

Fitch recalls the story of a Chinese man he tried to save. "He was one of a gang of some hundred who had been tied together, then gasoline was thrown over them and set fire."

Women were deemed as being fair game by the invaders. Japanese soldiers would break into homes and take turns raping them. Sometimes the women were killed. Eight days before Christmas Eve 1937, Fitch wrote: "A rough estimate at least would be a thousand women raped last night and during the day."

"One poor woman was raped 37 times," he added. "Another had her five-month-old infant deliberately smothered by the brute to stop its crying while he raped her." On 27 December, he wrote, "A car with an officer and two soldiers came to the university last night, raped three women in the premises and took away one with them." On 30 December there were "three cases of girls 12 or 13 years old either raped or abducted." Finally, on 11 January, Fitch's diary notes, "I have written this account in no spirit of vindictiveness. War is brutalising..."

There are no exact figures of civilian deaths in Nanking, or even deaths from the surrounding countryside - the Japanese burned every village in the capital's outskirts. The numbers that have endured are largely estimates. Allowing for a bare minimum of 50,000 killed would mean that the IJA murdered at least 1,200 men and women every day for six weeks. However, the number could easily be as large as 300,000, meaning the rate of murders by bayoneting, beatings, execution and decapitation takes on an unimaginable scale. What cannot be denied is the depravity of the Japanese occupiers. Aside from the 16mm film that Fitch smuggled in his overcoat to Shanghai and then to the US with the help of Magee, photographs survive of mutilated corpses, pyramids of severed heads and women stripped bare and taken as trophies.

The IJA looted Nanking, but the value of this wealth has been forgotten by history. In the face of this carnage, the mistaken bombing of the gunboat U.S.S. Panay that killed two Americans and an Italian journalist is understandably a footnote. For this incident the Japanese Government apologised and paid reparations.

THE END OF THE BEGINNING
After the atrocities at Nanking the war raged on, with China's generals bungling their operations despite foreign aid and expertise. In August 1939, the IJA embarked on its last northern adventure. The goal was the same as before: expand the boundaries of Manchukuo. The consequences were catastrophic.

In a place the Soviets called Khalkhin Gol, whole IJA divisions were encircled and wiped out by a methodical combined arms operation that was led by a certain former cavalryman named Georgy Zhukov. The Soviets had better artillery, more tanks and a lethal new doctrine that annihilated infantry formations.

After the battles of Khalkhin Gol, the IJA had no stomach to fight the Soviets. Manchukuo and the Kwantung Army's fate was sealed on 9 August 1945 when two great pincers of the Red Army crushed the last hope of Imperial Japan.

However, 1937 remains the year when the curtains were first drawn wide open and the stage of the last century's most catastrophic period was set. ★

中國歷史

Mao's

毛主席革命路

108

DISASTER PLAN

HOW A LETHAL MIXTURE OF ARROGANCE, FEAR AND BLIND FAITH CONDEMNED MILLIONS OF CHINESE TO DEATH

WRITTEN BY **CHRIS FENTON**

In 1940 China was in a state of utter turmoil. The country was overrun with foreign invaders, the government was powerless, and the workers fought among themselves for the scraps falling from the tables of petty warlords. How did the celestial kingdom come to this? The communists knew the answer – through the arrogance and pomposity of China's noble emperors. Communism had changed all that and chased away the foreign devils, pushed aside their rightist puppets and by 1949 had established a people's China. The self-styled driving force behind this revolution was Mao Zedong, the chairman of the Chinese Communist Party and a man of the people. Rising from proletariat beginnings in rural Hunan, Mao had grown up with revolution fervour in his veins. Having witnessed the destruction of Chinese power and heritage during the early 20th century, he had become a committed nationalist and later a communist, dedicating himself to the restoration of Chinese power through collective struggle. He had seen the Chinese people's spirit when properly motivated during the Communist Party's retreat into the mountains, which would later be dubbed the Long March, and the triumph of communist ideals after the destruction of the fascists led by Chiang Kai-shek, his greatest rival. Now, under his leadership, China would be great again.

Mao's plan was to instigate a radical industrialisation of the Chinese countryside, creating mass communes to produce grain, rice and steel to turn the country into a superpower. The population was to be organised on a mass scale. This was no time to think small – the Chinese strength was in its population and the entire country had to be put to work. These reforms would combine to form the Great Leap Forward. Mao ignored economists who argued for a gradual industrialisation process rather than a single quick bound and those who said that the post-feudal Chinese society couldn't handle so much change so quickly. Anyone who got in the way of his vision was deemed to be against Mao and therefore an obstacle to China recognising its true potential. So, in May 1958, the Communist Party agreed to Mao's proposals. China braced itself for its Great Leap Forward out of hell into a workers' paradise. What followed was one of the worst humanitarian disasters in history.

The mobilisation and ideological conditioning of the Chinese people was absolutely key. Under Mao's plans, all private property and private action was to be banned. Every Chinese rural worker was forced into communes thousands strong to create a mass land army to produce grain that would pay for new equipment from abroad and lead to the production of steel. Under the commune system workers would sleep in dormitories, eat in huge communal kitchens and work a "48-hour working day, with six hours for rest" as the *People's Daily*, Mao's propaganda newspaper, proudly proclaimed. There was not even room for traditional Chinese family roles in the new collectivist utopia – children were sent to mass crèches and women into the fields to work.

Party officials would "herd villagers in the fields to sleep and to work intolerable hours, forcing them to walk to distant additional projects". Some villagers wept as they watched their homes being destroyed to make way for the mass communes. One villager cried, "Destroying my home is even worse than digging up my ancestor's gravestone!" Mao was delighted and commented: "The notion of utopia mentioned by our predecessors will be realised and surpassed."

Initial results sent back to Beijing were more optimistic than Mao could possibly have hoped for. The harvest was so good that communist workers were encouraged to eat five meals a day in the communal food halls. As one commune worker put it, "It was real communism... we got to eat things made from wheat flour every day and they were always slaughtering pigs for us. For a while it seemed that they were telling the truth and we were going to enter heaven."

Mao saw no need to wait for grain production to start rendering export capital and commanded steel production to start immediately. He instigated a cottage industry for the steel programme - Chinese urban dwellers and rural workers were told to make steel in their backyards with primitive furnaces. Foreign visitors were impressed when they visited Beijing and saw the cityscape lit up with the contained fires of Mao's mini steel plants in the back gardens of his comrades. As one commune member recalled, "The more metal you collected, the more revolutionary you were."

Mao instructed grain harvesting to be switched to cash crops such as cotton and for steel production to be given the highest priority. The figures for the 1958 harvest showed there was more than enough food to go around so, as far as Mao was concerned, China should continue to bound forward. In August, Mao raised the target for steel production from 6 to 9 million tons. Provincial leaders spoke of unleashing surprise attacks into the fields with shock armies of mobilised labour to gather in cotton and begin collecting metal for steel production. War was also declared on flies, rats, mosquitoes and grain-eating sparrows. As the weather closed in and Chinese workers began to feel the grind of their 48-hour days, loudspeakers in every commune boomed out Party propaganda: "Our workers are strong, the people's communes are good!" By now grain was being left out in the field as workers frantically scrambled through their communes trying to find raw material for their backyard steel plants.

Party ideology was relentless and the eradication of sparrows became fanatical, but by killing the sparrows there were no longer any predators that could kill the insects that were now destroying crops. Other such contradictory policies emerged. Mao's obsession with steel production meant there were no longer enough workers to bring in crops and they sat uncollected in fields, rotting away as food reserves diminished.

The ideological pressure worked so well that no one really knew China was marching headlong into a disaster until it was too late. The 1958 harvest was modestly successful, but no one wanted to be the one to tell Mao that it wasn't a resounding success. A poor harvest followed but the workers were encouraged to 'fill their bellies until they burst' and as a result the food supplies were quickly consumed. Since the commune system had not envisaged transporting large amounts of food to other locations, food could not be moved to the areas that were now suffering from famine. In a Guangdong commune a six-month supply of rice was eaten in 20 days. The old and weak soon started to die of starvation.

The violent hysteria Maoism had created was now directed against the people, as starving Chinese workers began to weaken through malnutrition and the nightmare poverty of the commune system. Special criticism sessions were established by Party officials within rural villages and miscreants who were not meeting the required working standards were paraded in front of the village as Communist Party members forced other villagers to beat and humiliate the accused. The good harvests indicated by the official statistics meant that Mao continued to insist that steel was brought in to build his great utopia.

Thousands of rural peasants were forced through beatings and intimidation to abandon food production and concentrate on making steel from their furnaces despite the hunger they were now experiencing. One communist inspector

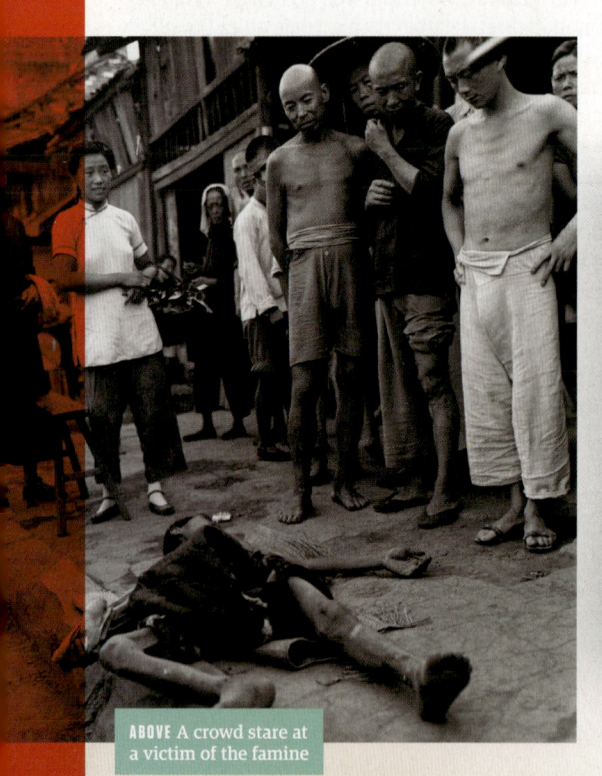

"Mao's ideology had shackled a grim existence of absolute poverty to the provinces and killed millions"

ABOVE A crowd stare at a victim of the famine

THE LITTLE RED BOOK

Mao's *Little Red Book*, more formally known as *Quotations from Chairman Mao Zedong*, details the deepest aspects of Mao's world view. It was first compiled during the Great Leap Forward by committed Maoist Lin Biao in 1960. While the original text is a tedious diatribe collecting over 400 selected quotes about the evils of capitalism and the need for continuous revolution against the bourgeoisie, its condensed version, the *Little Red Book*, was used extensively during the Cultural Revolution by Maoists after the failure of the Great Leap Forward. The book preached non-violence to solve internal disputes and democracy among the instruments of the Communist Party but also highlighted unity and a continuous form of revolution as key to a successful communist state. These contradictory lines resulted in violence among fanatical Maoist supporters and the supposed enemies of the state during the Cultural Revolution. Critics have argued that the book's publication was little more than an attempt to raise the profile of Mao after the failure of the Great Leap even though Mao insisted the book represented his inner thoughts about the subject of Marxism. Despite Mao's disapproval of profit-making enterprises in the book, he wasn't above claiming millions in royalties when it became a bestseller – only the Bible has more copies in circulation.

MAO'S DISASTER PLAN

ABOVE Mao announces the creation of the People's Republic of China in 1949

BELOW The Kuhsien steel mill in Changchi city added about 220 small local-type furnaces in seven days, increasing the daily steel output from 90 to 2,150 tons

noted on the punishments, "Commune members too sick to work are deprived of food. It hastens their deaths."

The persecution within the rural areas was terrible, but things were even worse in urban dwellings. Constant Party propaganda, mixed with the terrifying prospect of being selected for 'criticism', meant that urban dwellers had to toe the line and endure the endless working hours. Industrial accidents in factories were commonplace due to exhaustion and Soviet advisors teaching the industrial techniques left after abuse and molestation by Mao's officials, taking with them their expert knowledge. When asked about production figures, a typical response from one foreman was, "Day in, day out, they telephone for figures… who cares if they are true or false? Everyone is just going through the motions!" One man had his ears chopped off, was tied up with iron wire and branded with a white hot tool after he stole a potato from a communal plot near a factory. The worker's utopia had become a proletarian nightmare.

As the summer of 1958 turned into the harsh winter of early 1959, the supposedly glorious Great Leap had turned into a cold drop into the abyss. The decision to carry on regardless rested with the workers' paradise itself – China and its rotten communist system. There was no doubt in the mind of Mao that the Great Leap was working at the end of 1958, but this was because the system had fostered die-hard communist rhetoric and by 1959 that's all that Mao was hearing.

Part of the great Maoist vision was to enable communes to organise themselves – subject to strict Party controls – and give them centrally dictated grain and produce quotas that the provisional leaders had to meet. Of course, it would take a brave man – or a suicidal one – to return to the communist leadership anything other than glowing reports of fabulous harvests and content workers. Local leaders from Sichuan province were often compelled to revise their grain figures upwards if the original amount was felt to be not what the Party wanted to hear. Doctored photos were taken for the *People's Daily* of children lying on tightly packed wheat 1.8 metres (six feet) high. It was a delusion; the people were starving, but the Party swallowed the lie and Mao insisted on bigger targets, which created a culture of deceit. If one area had a high grain production, whether falsified or not, its neighbouring area would double their figures. Even the Mao-endorsed furnace was a fabrication. The high-quality steel Mao saw from the prototype was probably imported from one of the Soviet-model factories outside of Beijing.

This was Mao's fantasy world, and it was lethal. By the end of 1959, as the full force of the disaster unfolded, the time China would need to overtake Britain economically was slashed from 15 years to five and then down to two by the Party. One of the first test communes in Henan was named 'Let us overtake England'. Its inhabitants starved after their farmers were sent to produce steel and their fields flooded due to poor irrigation control. Locusts ate what was left of their crops. Terrified provisional leaders carefully managed tours by Party leaders.

At the beginning of 1959, Marshal Peng Dehuai, a ranking People's Liberation Army soldier who was deeply committed to the wellbeing of the peasant farmers, visited the communes and was appalled. He was convinced that the Leap had been an utter disaster. He talked to the emaciated peasants trying desperately to manufacture steel even though they were starving and asked, "Hasn't any one of you given a thought to what

111

you will eat next year if you don't bring in the crops? You're never going to be able to eat steel." The response was typical: "True enough, but who would stand up against this wind [command]?" Even Peng himself thought better of saying anything to the Chairman.

Then in the summer of 1959, after seeing the latest fabricated figures from the communes, Peng could restrain himself no longer. He wrote Mao a letter describing the Great Leap as a 'wind of exaggeration.' Mao's response was to throw a temper tantrum and in a speech to the Party he described Peng as a 'bourgeois rightist' who needed to strengthen his backbone. Peng was promptly forced out of Mao's inner circle to live among the peasants in a run-down area of Beijing. The standard line from the Party was spoken by a Mao favourite, Shanghai leader Ke Qingshi: "We should obey the Chairman to the extent of total abandon, in every respect – thinking, perspective, foresight and method – we are way behind [Mao]." There was only one man who could stop the Great Leap from bounding into greater destruction: Mao himself.

The beginning of 1960 brought with it grim statistics. Average available grain per head had dropped from 311 kilograms (686 pounds) in 1958 to 191 kilograms (421 pounds) in 1960. Mao's ideology had shackled a grim existence of absolute poverty to the provinces, and coupled with the corrupt, sycophantic communist system, it had killed millions. People were eating tree bark and gnawing the flesh off corpses lying in the streets in a country that was supposedly producing 596 million tons of grain a year.

Mao was convinced it was everyone else's fault. He blamed the provincial officials for not following his reforms closely enough, then for following them too rigidly. He blamed the Party in 1959 when he sensed that the officials were starting to move away from him, which after the Leap's failure was becoming glaringly obvious. His rants became more drawn out, claiming the revolution was "under a combined attack from within and outside the Party". A new anti-fascist campaign was launched by Mao, which purged anyone who wasn't feeding him the lies he wanted to hear. In the end, he blamed communism itself. In a heated speech to the Party after reports that peasants were dying of exhaustion, he said: "If you don't follow me, I'll do it myself… even to the lengths of abandoning my Party membership and even to the extent of bringing a suit against Marx himself." The Great Leap was no longer about grain, communism or even China. It was about Mao and his unquenchable ambition, as well as the forces of reality that were blocking him in his great quest.

As the months rolled by in 1960 and the population became weaker and weaker, Mao began to realise the country was in turmoil. The United States offered humanitarian aid and, in a final act of humiliation, so did Japan. They were all refused and Mao descended into a depressive stupor. The Party members became more vocal in their dissent, but Mao used his traditional form of intimidation. He threatened to purge dissenters, even going so far as saying, "I will go into the countryside to lead the peasants to overthrow the government." The intensity of these misguided tantrums was only matched by the gulf between Mao's delusions and reality. The famine had crippled large parts of the country's infrastructure; the only official organ that was working was the

"The Great Leap was no longer about grain, communism or even China. It was about Mao and his unquenchable ambition"

Communist Party and its lackeys. Even if Mao's supporters were willing to follow him through another civil war, the population was no longer physically capable of fighting one.

Finally, in 1960, Mao approved some roll back on the Great Leap. He allowed the economic planner Chen Yun to cut back on steel production and concentrate on farming grain. The farcical quota system was made more attainable and thousands of industrialisation projects were cancelled. It was all far too late. Over 30 million Chinese citizens lay dead, mostly due to starvation but a good portion due to the savage punishments imposed by Party officials. Some official Communist Party figures put the figure at 40 million dead. Mao's doctor had to order in more sleeping pills for the great leader.

By the end of 1960 China was in hell once again, however, this new hell was called Maoism and it was digging China's grave. Mao's ideology and propaganda had convinced the people to starve themselves and forced the communist system to hasten their fates.

On Mao's birthday that year Party officials dined on bird's nest soup, baby doves, shark's fin and the finest wine. The event was noted for the vast amounts of alcohol consumed, with at least one top-ranking official falling down drunk.

Around the same time a Chinese peasant recalled the death she had witnessed due to the widespread famine: "The people were numb, you just carried on as usual – no fear of death, no emotion for the living." ★

MAO'S VISION

May 1958 – The Great Leap Forward begins. Millions of Chinese workers are inspired and motivated by Maoist communism, striving to shake off their feudal existence and become happy, productive state workers.

Harvest 1958 – The harvest in 1958 is so bountiful and the commune system is working so well that Mao insists that workers eat five meals a day in the communal kitchens, fulfilling the ideal of the workers' paradise.

April 1959 – The timetable for overtaking Britain is shrunk from 15 to two years. The workers are producing grain, cotton and steel in such large quantities that export capital is building huge industrial cities.

June 1959 – Mao addresses the Luschan Party conference in triumph. He has stared down the capitalists in America and the class traitors in the Soviet Union that told him he couldn't make China into a world power.

1960 – China has become so powerful that the Western imperialists are forced to treat with Mao on his terms. American bases in Japan are forced to close and a cowed Soviet Union now takes its lead from a dominant Beijing.

CHINA'S REALITY

May 1958 – The Great Leap Forward begins. Millions of Chinese workers are displaced and forced to relinquish all private property, leave their ancestral homes and begin grinding 48-hour work shifts.

Harvest 1958 – The 1958 harvest succeeds, but the Party overestimates its success to please Mao. In reality there is not enough food in the country for the workers and reserves are depleted by the communal kitchens.

April 1959 – Fifteen provinces are now suffering from drought and 25 million people need urgent food relief. There is no help forthcoming from the government as the Party had not planned for such an eventuality. The workers are suppressed.

June 1959 – Mao is forced to fight for his position at the Lushan conference. Loud voices in the Party are now saying that the country is in chaos. As a final act of humiliation, China is offered food aid by America and the old enemy Japan.

1960 – With the country in chaos and over 30 million people dead, Mao's power within the Party weakens. He is forced to accept partial blame for the Great Leap and allows Party officials to roll back his plans.

ABOVE Mao visits farmers in 1958 to congratulate them on high yields

FAILURES

Communal eating
Maoist communism commanded the people to live side by side in communes and eat together in communal kitchens. When the Great Leap started workers were encouraged to eat as much as they wanted in the communal kitchens. What followed was severe food shortages as the harvests could not support such demand for food and the communist system wasn't strong enough to provide food aid to all parts of the country. This led to famine.

Steel furnaces
Mao's backyard steel industry was a disaster from the beginning and the prototype he saw probably did not produce the high-quality steel he was told it did. Feeding low-quality metal into the furnaces only served to create low-quality produce, meaning the workers were wasting their time. After millions of starving workers tried to produce steel rather than food, Mao was convinced to leave steel production to proper industrial facilities and skilled workers.

Irrigation
Thousands of starving peasants died creating ill-conceived and poorly planned irrigation projects throughout China. Mao knew the importance of irrigation to a country that had a vast amount of land and an unpredictable climate, but he had expelled the Soviet engineers sent to help China establish such large projects. The irrigation projects that were built created droughts in some areas and flooding in others as poorly trained Chinese agriculture engineers were ordered to set about irrigating Chinese fields without expert advice.

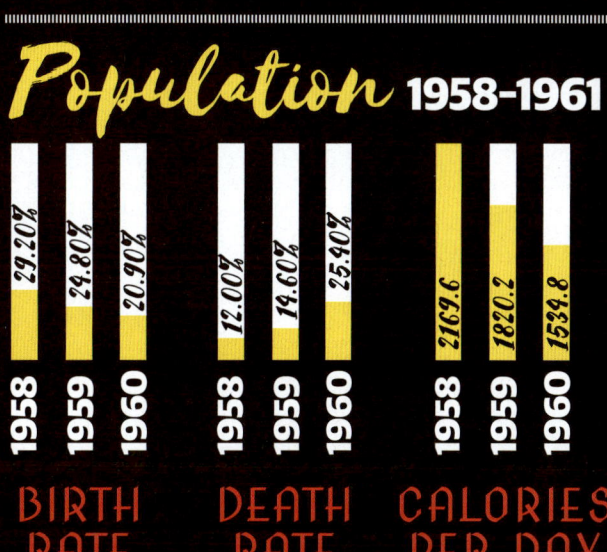

ABOVE A prisoner is subjected to public criticism

Production 1958-1961

GRAIN
million metric tons

Years	
1958	215
1959	170
1960	143.3

STEEL
1958	8.8
1959	13.87
1960	18.66

RICE
1958	80.8
1959	69.3
1960	59.7

Population 1958-1961

BIRTH RATE
- 1958: 29.20%
- 1959: 24.80%
- 1960: 20.90%

DEATH RATE
- 1958: 12.00%
- 1959: 14.60%
- 1960: 25.40%

CALORIES PER DAY
- 1958: 2167.6
- 1959: 1820.2
- 1960: 1534.8

OVERALL FIGURES

38,000,000 estimated deaths due to starvation

10,729,000 estimated deaths due to punishment/internment

Specific events

Henan
Party militias fanned out across the country and brutalised the population to force them to work. According to one researcher in Daoxian county, ten per cent of those who died during the Leap were "buried alive, clubbed to death or otherwise killed by Party members".

Yunnan
As a high-profile Mao supporter, the leader of Yunnan instructed his workers to work 'day and night' for two weeks to increase steel and rice production. Thousands died from exhaustion as a result.

Anhui
In one of the areas worst affected by the famine, workers resorted to cannibalism as their fellow workers died around them. Some even sold their wives and children in return for food.

Tiananmen Square Massacre

3–4 JUNE 1989

Timeline

1988 — China relaxes state controls of prices to help grow the economy. Corruption and profiteering sends inflation soaring to 26 per cent by October.

15 APRIL 1989 — Free market reformer and Communist Party General Secretary Hu Yaobang dies of a heart attack. Students gather in Tiananmen Square to express sympathy.

26 APRIL 1989 — The *People's Daily* newspaper publishes a piece that is critical of the students. Rather than forcing them to back down, this only antagonises them further.

13 MAY 1989 — Thousands of students begin hunger strikes in Tiananmen Square to embarrass the authorities prior to the upcoming state visit of the Soviet leader, Mikhail Gorbachev.

TIANANMEN SQUARE MASSACRE

WHAT WAS IT?

The Tiananmen Square Massacre was the brutal climax to three months of protests and demonstrations in China in 1989. The protests spread to 400 cities across the country and were led by university students who were concerned about the soaring inflation rate, restrictions on political participation and the challenges faced by graduates as China transitioned to a free-market economy.

The Chinese political elite were divided in their reaction. General Secretary Zhao Ziyang argued for peaceful dialogue with the protesters, but Premier Li Peng and Chairman Deng Xiaoping (the paramount leader of China) saw the unrest as a direct challenge to the government and pressed for a swift end by whatever means necessary.

On 20 May 1989, martial law was declared and 30 divisions of the army were mobilised around the country in an effort to restore order. In the late evening of 3 June, tanks and 10,000 armed troops advanced on Tiananmen Square. They opened fire without warning. Protesters were shot in the back as they fled; others were crushed under the wheels of military vehicles.

WHAT WERE THE CONSEQUENCES?

China's recent political liberalisation was abandoned. More than 1,600 students and workers were arrested and tried. Wang Dan, one of the student leaders, spent seven years in prison. Reformers within the Chinese Communist Party were expelled, demoted or placed under house arrest. The Chinese Government continued with economic reforms but rolled back earlier measures that had begun to separate the party from the government.

Today, any discussion of the Tiananmen Square protests is still banned in China. Films, books, newspapers and even whole publishing companies have been suppressed and shut down for breaking this rule. Chinese authorities have also attempted to censor the internet when it comes to the protests but with less success. Search terms such as 'June 4' are blocked, but increasingly social media has turned to more oblique code names.

WHO WAS INVOLVED?

Premier Li Peng
1928-2019
An opponent of economic reforms, Li Peng was also responsible for ordering martial law to end the Tiananmen protests.

Zhao Ziyang
1919-2005
The general secretary of the Communist Party argued for peaceful dialogue. He was placed under house arrest for 15 years.

Tank Man
Unknown
The morning after the massacre, one young man blocked the advance of a column of tanks. His identity is still a mystery.

Did you know? The Chinese Government's official death toll for the massacre is 241, but many independent estimates put it closer to 1,000.

---

20 MAY 1989 — The Chinese Government declares martial law. Thirty army divisions are mobilised and between 180,000 and 250,000 troops are sent to Beijing.

3 JUNE 1989 — At 10 p.m., troops open fire without warning. Song Xiaoming, a 32-year-old aerospace technician, is the first confirmed fatality of the night.

Hong Kong Returns

WHY DID CHINA LOSE THIS REGION, AND HOW HAS LIFE THERE EVOLVED SINCE THE HANDOVER?

WRITTEN BY **AILSA HARVEY**

Hong Kong is an archipelago of 263 islands that lies on the south coast of China. Boasting an impressive skyline, iconic harbour and diverse culture, it is part of China but operates as a Special Administrative Region (SAR), meaning it has a high degree of autonomy, with its own police force, judicial systems, currency and economic policies.

For 156 years, China lost autonomy of Hong Kong to Britain, who occupied the region following the First Opium War (1839–42). During this war, the British Empire fought the Qing dynasty of China, who wanted to stop Britain's illegal opium trade from smuggling the drug from its Indian colonies into China, where the government had introduced a ban. This was not the only cause of conflict at the time but is the conflict that provided the war with its catchy name. Following its defeat, China was forced to sign the Convention of Chuenpi, which required it to cede the territory of Hong Kong Island to Britain.

During the next 50 years, Britain claimed all the major regions of Hong Kong. This included the Kowloon Peninsula and the New Territories, which makes up the main landmass of modern Hong Kong. One of the signed treaties, the 1898 Convention for the Extension of Hong Kong Territory, cemented Britain's rule over Hong Kong for 99 years.

Hong Kong quickly changed under the principles of its new rulers. It experienced rapid economic growth, becoming a major trading centre, and was highly industrialised. The British Government built transport networks and ports and modernised the city's infrastructure over time. The English language also became a priority in schools and Western culture was forced upon the area.

In 1997, when 99 years had passed, Hong Kong was handed back to China. Because of the very different political approaches between the British and Chinese governments, Hong Kong's legal system didn't match China's, which had become a communist country in 1949. Around 100,000 people moved to Hong Kong to avoid communist rule in China. Hong Kong had also acquired elements of British culture. With such clashing lifestyles evolving alongside each other for over a century how could these regions hope to combine again seamlessly?

In 1984, before the return of Hong Kong to China, British Prime Minister Margaret Thatcher met with Zhao Ziyang, the third premier of the People's Republic of China. The politicians signed the Sino-British Joint Declaration, which was an agreement stating how the handover would take place. One of the points of this agreement was that Hong Kong would keep its social and economic systems in place for at least 50 years, so that there were no drastic changes for the people.

On 1 July 1997, there was a formal handover ceremony of Hong Kong from British rule to Chinese sovereignty. As of this date, the region became the Hong Kong Special Administrative Region (HKSAR). Hong Kong follows the One Country, Two Systems principle designed to stay in place until 2047. Until this year, despite belonging to China, Hong Kong isn't required to abide by all of China's laws. Hong Kong has its own border control and rights. For example, the free speech of the press is protected. The return to China was met with mixed reactions from the people of Hong Kong. For some, they were happy to be more closely connected to mainland China and felt that their national identity was being restored. Others were anxious about the drastic changes this could bring. A poll in 1997 found that around 65 per cent of people in Hong Kong thought British rule had more good implications than bad.

Due to being separated from China for over 150 years, more recent studies conducted by the University of Hong Kong show that 71 per cent of people there don't feel proud to be a Chinese citizen, with indications that younger people are more likely to feel this way. However, China is

ABOVE This 19th-century illustration depicts the signing of the Treaty of Tientsin

BELOW Victoria Harbour shows how built up areas of Hong Kong are

ABOVE The handover ceremony in 1997 took place at the Hong Kong Convention and Exhibition Centre in Wan Chai

"As China reduces Hong Kong's autonomy, its wealth is predicted to decline"

introducing laws that make it increasingly difficult for Hong Kong to hold onto its autonomy, despite the One Country, Two Systems principle not being set to expire until 2047.

For example, in 2022 China introduced a new security law for Hong Kong. The law prevents Hong Kong citizens from breaking away from the country, protesting with violence or intimidation, forming new agreements with foreign countries or committing subversion against the Chinese Government. This law was introduced just before the 23rd anniversary of the handover ceremony from Britain to China and means that Hong Kong citizens could even be charged with the maximum sentence of life in prison for breaking the law.

One of the biggest changes this law dictates is which power is responsible for interpreting the law. Chinese law will take priority over any independent ones in Hong Kong that are put in place. Although Hong Kong has laws in place to maintain human rights regarding privacy, the new security law means that people can be wiretapped and put under surveillance if they are suspected of breaking the law. Since it was introduced, hundreds of non-violent protestors and activists have been arrested in Hong Kong.

As China begins to reduce Hong Kong's autonomy, the country's wealth and economic status is predicted to decline. While Hong Kong was largely independent the region built external trade, communications and tourism relations. But with China soon to take full control, some investors have lost confidence in Hong Kong's stability and predictability.

Hong Kong became a global financial centre as a region following the rule of law. This means having an independent judiciary. Any future reversal of this aspect of law can impact businesses and investors as there is no guarantee of the same legal protections.

ABOVE Hong Kong's current flag was adopted on 4 April 1990

Further integration with China lies on Hong Kong's horizon. Its population of over 7 million people face changes to its governing and economic systems. However, Hong Kong lost part of its Chinese identity when it was handed over to Britain in 1841. Fifty-three per cent of adults there today identify as being both from Hong Kong and China and around ten per cent as solely Chinese. Despite the hazy implications of the return to China, Hong Kong will finally cut all ties with its coloniser.

Epic Engineering

INHABITANTS OF A VAST AND VARIED LAND, THE CHINESE HAVE LONG HAD TO RESORT TO INCREDIBLE FEATS OF CONSTRUCTION IN A BID TO TAME NATURE AND ADAPT TO AN EVER-CHANGING WORLD

WRITTEN BY JAMES HORTON

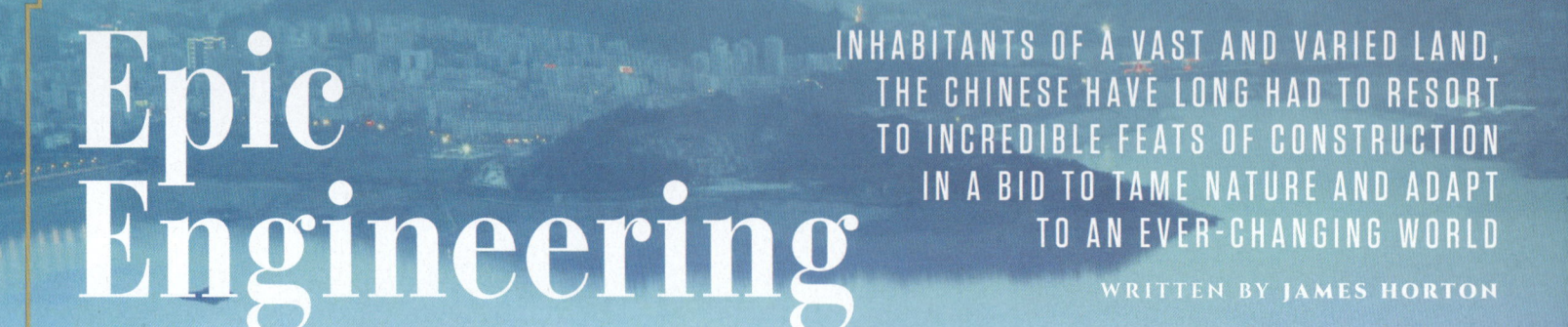

Three Gorges Dam
MEET THE HYDROELECTRIC JUGGERNAUT THAT DIVIDES CHINA'S YANGTZE RIVER

LOCATION SANDOUPING, CHINA
COMPLETED 2006

The Three Gorges Dam is a monster. Its 2.3-kilometre (1.4-mile) length, 115-metre (377-feet) base width and maximum height of 185 metres (607 feet) spans the Yangtze River, making it the largest hydroelectric power station in the world. By incorporating 27.2 million cubic metres (96 million cubic feet) of concrete and more than 460,000 metric tons of steel into its design, the dam supports an enormous reservoir that is capable of holding up to 42 billion tons of water.

Suffice to say, this dam can put out a lot of power. Estimated to generate 22,500 megawatts at maximum capacity, or around 11 times the energy output of the Hoover Dam in the U.S., the Three Gorges Dam has been pivotal to China shifting away from its reliance on fossil fuels and towards sources of renewable energy.

ABOVE As well as generating energy, the dam was designed to alleviate flooding of the Yangtze Basin

Hong Kong-Zhuhai-Macau Bridge
THE HUMAN-MADE THREAD OF IMMENSE SCALE BUILT TO CONNECT THREE OF CHINA'S MOST INTEGRAL CITIES

LOCATION LINGDINGYANG CHANNEL, CHINA
COMPLETED 2018

Since the foundations of the cities of Hong Kong, Zhuhai and Macau were first laid interactions between the three were hindered by the Pearl River Estuary that separated them. But thanks to human creativity they are now all linked by a land bridge that spans around 55 kilometres (34 miles) – 20-times longer than the Golden Gate Bridge.

ABOVE It took nine years to complete the bridge, which can withstand earthquakes, super typhoons and being struck by a cargo vessel

Did you know? The Three Gorges Dam has raised so much water it has slowed the rotation of the Earth by 0.06 microseconds.

BELOW The Beijing Daxing is the world's largest international airport

Beijing Daxing International Airport

THE WORLD'S LARGEST AIRPORT WILL SOON CATER TO 100 MILLION PASSENGERS A YEAR

LOCATION BEIJING, CHINA
COMPLETED 2019

Despite its size, the People's Republic of China had long struggled with a relatively low aviation capacity. However, all that changed in September 2019 with the opening of the impressive Beijing Daxing International Airport.

This gargantuan airport, designed in collaboration with Zaha Hadid Architects, boasts an intricate, flower-inspired terminal space built using 1.6 million cubic metres (5.6 million cubic feet) of concrete and 52,000 tons of steel and operates four civilian runways and one military runway. In total, this pioneering transport hub encompasses an area of 47 square kilometres (18.1 square miles), and it has rightly been described as a testament to China's production capabilities.

Initially, Beijing's latest airport is predicted to transport 45 million passengers per year, but this figure is expected to grow to a whopping 100 million passengers, making it one of the busiest airports in the world.

ABOVE The Three Gorges Dam cost $37 billion to build

BELOW By 2025 it is hoped that the airport will be able to accommodate 630,000 flights a year

> "The bridge will lower travel times from four hours to just 40 minutes"

A considerable portion of the bridge – almost 30 kilometres (18.6 miles) of it – straddles the estuary, and vehicles travel over the water in three lanes on both sides. Artificial islands connect the bridge section to a 6.9-kilometre (4.3-mile) underwater tunnel, which is submerged to allow ships to traverse the water. The bridge has reduced travel times between the cities from four hours to just 40 minutes, and what a sight people behold as they travel across it.

中國歷史

CHINA'S FIRST *Olympics*

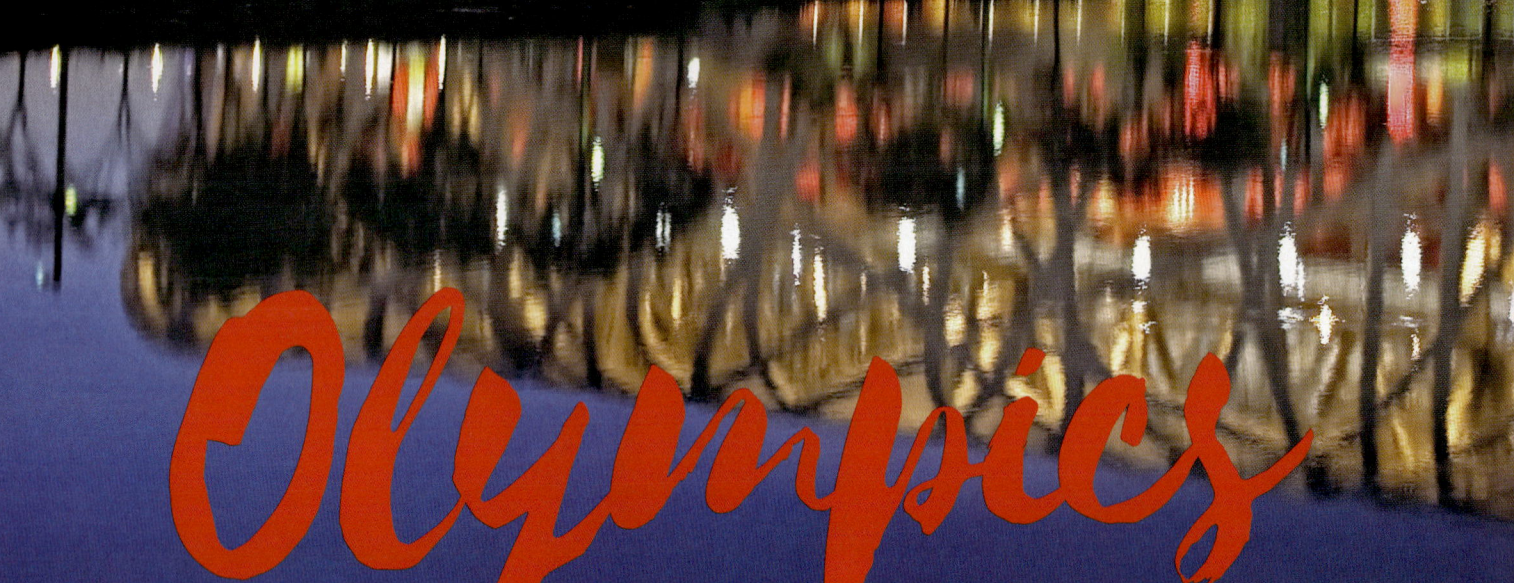

THE HIGHS AND LOWS OF THE BEIJING 2008 OLYMPIC GAMES

WRITTEN BY **SCOTT DUTFIELD**

On 8 August 2008, over 1 billion people tuned in to watch Beijing host the 24th Summer Olympic Games. Over the course of 16 days of painstaking competition, athletes from around the world convened in the Chinese metropolis to fight for the coveted 302 gold medals on offer across 28 sports inside 37 arenas.

Hosting the 2008 Olympics was a first for China having made a successful bid back in 2001. Over the following seven years Beijing got a modern makeover. To prepare for the inevitable spotlight placed on the city, China reportedly invested nearly $40 billion on its infrastructure, including transport renovations, new city-wide facilities and various upgrades.

As an institution, the Olympics has also preached the word of unity and world peace, something China clearly had in mind when it announced its slogan for the 2008 games – 'One World, One Dream' – in 2004. However, this fell on the sceptical ears of the world's media, who had largely criticised the nation's human rights policies.

One of the biggest challenges for any host nation is constructing the Olympic-sized stadium to house the athletes and its spectators. For Beijing, China commissioned the construction of a 91,000-seat stadium. The Beijing National Stadium, nicknamed 'The Bird's Nest', took around three years to build and cost £300 million ($380 million).

As the name suggests, the architectural design for the stadium is reminiscent of an avian creation, albeit 69.2 metres (227 feet) tall. The stadium comprises 42,000 tons of criss-crossed steel beams collectively spanning 26 kilometres (16.1 miles) and was designed by German architectural firm Herzog and De Meuron Architekten. At the time of its construction the stadium held the record as the world's largest steel structure.

Although its final unveiling was a moment of pride for Beijing, the road to its completion caused conflict with the city's residents. The Centre on Housing Rights and Evictions (COHRE), a Geneva-based international NGO, claimed that people were being evicted from their homes to accommodate redevelopment for the Olympics.

ABOVE The Beijing National Stadium, also known as The Bird's Nest

BEIJING OLYMPICS 2008

ABOVE Drummers perform during the opening ceremony

ABOVE It's estimated that hosting the Games cost China a whopping $40 billion

The group further purported that during the lead up to the games some 1.5 million people were "forced to relocate" out of their homes. However, the Beijing Olympic organising committee and China's Foreign Ministry disputed COHRE's claims and instead proclaimed that only 6,037 people had been displaced to make way for the construction of the stadiums.

Following on with the theme of unity, the Olympic torch relay, which leads the Olympic flame from Athens to the current Games, was called the 'Journey of Harmony' by organisers. The 129-day relay from Greece to Beijing saw the torch cross 137,000 kilometres (85,128 miles) via the hands of 21,800 torchbearers, which included travelling along part of the Great Wall of China. Once in Beijing, the torch headed towards China's newest national stadium to begin the Games.

Around 1.5 billion people sat in front of their television screens to witness the spectacle that was the Olympic opening ceremony. The ceremony started with the sound of 2,008 drummers beating in perfect harmony. What followed was four hours of patriotic presentation from 15,000 performers. The entire ceremony was produced by filmmaker Zhang Yimou, director of the movie *House of Flying Daggers*. The ceremony's budget was reported to have been more than $100 million (£78.8 million).

However, several incidents of fakery were reported in the media following the ceremony's broadcast, including pre-recorded firework displays across the skies from Tiananmen Square to The Bird's Nest. Audiences were also left uncertain about the live vocals of a nine-year-old singer named Lin Miaoke, who sang *Ode to the Motherland*. The ceremony's musical director, Chen Qigang, later told Beijing Radio that she was not singing but lip-syncing to the vocals of another young girl called Yang Peiyi. Qigang suggested the reason was that Peiyi didn't meet the visual requirements to sing live.

The opening ceremony came to a close when former gymnast Li Ning was lifted to the stadium roof on strings, seemingly running to the Olympic cauldron before igniting it. In doing so, Ning signalled the start of a fierce competition between 204 nations.

Many milestones were achieved in Beijing, including a lot of firsts: Afghanistan won its first-ever medal when Rohullah Nikpai took home bronze in the men's 58-kilogram taekwondo; Benjamin Boukpeti placed third in the men's single kayak slalom event – the first Olympic medal for Togo; and Tuvshinbayar Naidan won the first-ever gold medal for Mongolia for his victory in the men's 100-kilogram judo. There were also several new events, including the 3,000-metre steeplechase, men's and women's BMX and women's foil and sabre events.

"Michael Phelps went down in history as the athlete to win the most gold medals in a single Olympic Games"

The 2008 Olympics also saw some athletes smash worldwide records. Overall, 25 world records were broken during the Games. However, two competitors in particular dominated the headlines for their world-class achievements.

As the first man to ever win in three sprinting events at a single Olympics, Usain Bolt was very much the man of the hour on the racing track. The 2008 Olympics saw the hot-footed athlete breaking not one but three running records. Firstly, Bolt set the new record for the 100-metre sprint at 9.69 seconds, then he smashed the record for the 200-metre race in 19.30 seconds. Finally, he broke the relay record with his fellow Jamaican teammates, completing four 100-metre sprints in just 37.10 seconds.

ABOVE (From left to right) silver medallist Nastia Liukin (U.S.), gold medallist He Kexin (China) and bronze medalist Yang Yilin (China) at the medal ceremony for the women's uneven bars

ABOVE Michael Phelps broke seven world records in nine days in Beijing

ABOVE Usain Bolt sets the world record at 9.69 seconds to win the 100-metre dash final

BELOW Athletes pass a section of the Great Wall of China during the men's road cycling race

STRIPPED OF GOLD

The 2008 Olympics will down in history as a record-breaking Games. However, it will also be remembered as the Games that saw the most athletes stripped of their medals.

Looking back on the 2008 Games, many will remember some of the best athletic performances in Olympic history. However, during the years that followed revelations regarding athletes' using performance-enhancing drugs have been brought to light. In total, 50 medals (nine gold, 21 silver and 20 bronze) have been stripped from the 2008 winners due to doping.

Unfortunately, because of the decisions of one of his compatriots, Usain Bolt lost his gold medal for the 4x100-metre men's relay. Bolt's teammate, Nesta Carter, was one of 454 selected samples from the 2008 Games that were retested by the International Olympic Committee back in 2016 for banned stimulants. Carter's sample tested positive for methylhexaneamine, which has been on the World Anti-Doping Agency prohibited list since 2004.

ABOVE (From left to right) Nesta Carter, Michael Frater, Usain Bolt and Asafa Powell, winners of the gold medal for the men's 4x100-metre relay

Taking home even more gold medals was American swimmer Michael Phelps, who went down in history as the athlete to win the most gold medals in a single Olympic Games. The title had been previously held by fellow American swimmer Mark Spitz, who won seven gold medals back in 1972. However, Phelps snatched the title during the 2008 Olympics when the 23-year-old competed in 17 races over nine days, winning each of the eight finals he reached.

The overall winner for the most wins during the Games was the United States, taking home 36 gold, 38 silver and 36 bronze medals. Evidently inspired by hosting the Games, China's athletes won the most gold medals of any country – 51 in total.

With great praise can come equal scrutiny, and the 2008 Olympics had its fair share of controversies. During the Games themselves several scores and referee calls were challenged, although this is typical of any Olympic Games. However, when Cuban taekwondo fighter Ángel Matos was disqualified from a match that could have won him the bronze medal, he did not take it well. Feeling anything but magnanimous, Matos lashed out and delivered a high kick to the referee's head. Matos was almost immediately issued a lifetime ban from all World Taekwondo Federation championships as a result.

One of the biggest sporting scandals to hit the newsstands, however, involved the host's female gymnastics team, and what started as media rumours quickly turned into one of the biggest stories of the 2008 Games. For qualification into the gymnastic events, athletes from all countries need to meet the minimum age requirement of 16. However, rumours stirred that one or more of the Chinese gymnasts might have been a few years away from their sweet 16th. *The New York Times* reported that three of the six members of the Chinese gymnastic team were potentially underage. While the Chinese Government produced passports for all six athletes, confirming they were the right age and appeasing the Olympic Committee, many spectators around the world were sceptical.

Along with a sense of pride in hosting a successful showcase of the world's finest athletes, China was left with the opportunity to advance education and energy consumption. From the get-go the hosts presented the Olympics as an opportunity to address the growing problem of pollution within Beijing. At the time, the Chinese Technology Minister Wan Gang estimated that the Games would generate some 1.2 million tons of carbon dioxide, predominantly through air travel by competing athletes, so China introduced a tree-planting scheme and emission restrictions in an attempt to offset the extra carbon dioxide.

It worked: a study by NASA found that through various motor vehicle restrictions during the Games carbon dioxide emissions fell by between 26,500 and 106,000 tons. Using the momentum of environmental awareness the Olympic Games had generated, China went on to implement further policies to tackle its pollution problem. For example, 15,000 coal-burning boilers throughout the city of Beijing were replaced with cleaner energy sources. The city also increased the number of solar heaters by 17.6 per cent. The Games were a win for China and the environment.

The legacy of the 2008 Games was harnessed in 2022 when Beijing staged the Winter Olympics, thereby becoming the first city to host both editions of the Games.

中國歷史

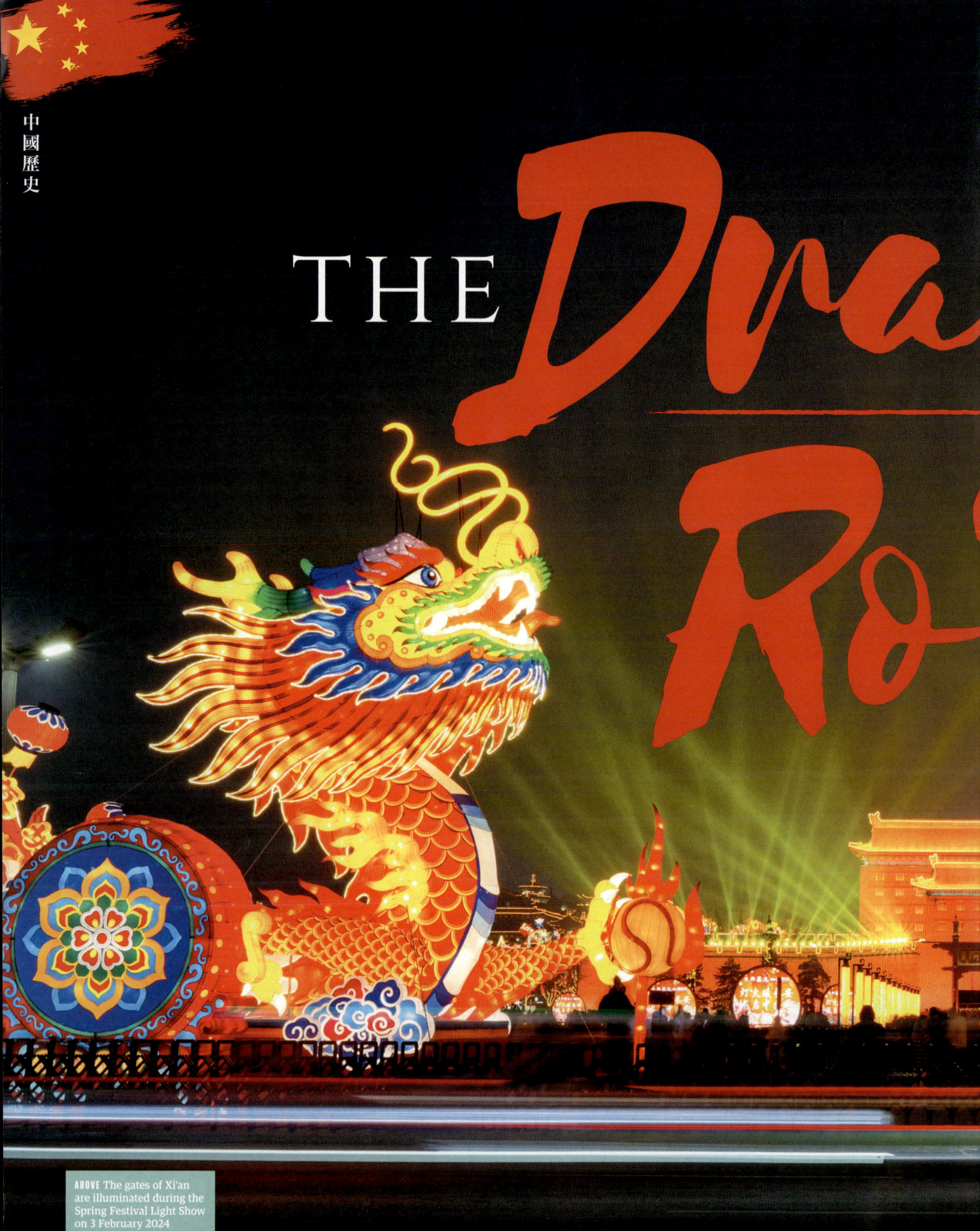

THE Dra
Ro

ABOVE The gates of Xi'an are illuminated during the Spring Festival Light Show on 3 February 2024

Dragon Roars

RISING WEALTH, MILITARY EXPANSION AND GRAVE HUMAN RIGHTS VIOLATIONS ARE DEFINING FEATURES OF THE 'CHINESE CENTURY'

WRITTEN BY **NEIL CROSSLEY**

THE DRAGON ROARS

ABOVE President Xi Jinping clawed his way to the top and has been in power since March 2013

ABOVE China's annual defence budget is estimated to be a colossal $700 billion

On 23 October 2023, at the 20th Chinese Communist Party (CCP) Congress in Beijing, the party's general secretary, Xi Jinping, was approved for a third term. It was an unprecedented appointment and the culmination of a transformative decade. Xi had been general secretary since 2012 and president of the People's Republic Of China since 2013. Not since the death of Mao Zedong in 1976 had there been such a dominant ruler.

Xi's tenure has witnessed rising wealth, rapid economic growth and massive military spending. It's an era that scholars and economists have dubbed the 'Chinese Century'. But this is also an age in which government repression and grave human rights violations have cast a significant shadow over any achievements in the eyes of many in the West.

CENTRALISING POWER
From the very outset of his leadership, Xi decided to reject the collective leadership practices of his post-Mao predecessors, opting instead to centralise his power. Xi set up working groups with himself as the head in order to expunge government bureaucracy and also make himself the undeniable centre figure of the new administration.

In 2013, Xi created a series of Central Leading Groups to bypass existing institutions, cut through stultifying bureaucracy and make policy-making a far more streamlined process. Within the first decade of his leadership, Xi tightened his own grip on the CCP and the Party's hold on the entire country.

ECONOMIC TRANSFORMATION
As positive narratives go, it's China's massive economic growth that really makes headlines. Now the second-largest economy in the world, some financial experts have forecast that it will overtake the size of the U.S. economy by as early as 2050. If the economy were represented by purchasing power parity (PPP), China would eclipse the U.S. as the largest economy with a purchasing power of more than $30.3 trillion, compared to $25.4 trillion.

It's a staggering accomplishment. China has gone from a poor country devastated by WWII, a civil war in the mid-20th century and decades of stagnation under disastrous communist rule to a feared and respected leviathan.

Xi has achieved this by reducing China's reliance on exports and increasing domestic consumption. He also boosted state control of the economy and suppressed certain segments of the private sector, such as online platforms and for-profit education.

It's no shock that academics and economists have labelled the 21st century the Chinese Century, as the People's Republic of China underwent a profound change.

WEALTH DISTRIBUTION
In 2021, Xi announced plans to spread "common prosperity" in what has been one of the world's most unequal economies. One of the key aims of Xi's leadership has been the elimination of extreme poverty, and in February 2021 he announced that this "miracle" had been achieved.

"According to the current criteria, all 98.99 million of the poor rural population have been taken out of poverty, and 832 poverty-stricken counties as well as 128,000 villages have been removed from the poverty list," he said.

But some believed that Xi's drive for economic equality came at a precarious time. In an interview with *The Guardian* in September 2021, economist and analyst Diana Choyleva, an expert on China's economy, highlighted how a shortage of raw materials and a resurgence of the coronavirus Delta variant could upend Xi's whole strategy.

"Xi Jinping has embarked on an ambitious but uncharted path as he aims to make good on the Party's promise of a socialist system that does not put the needs of the few over the needs of the many," said Choyleva. "But he is taking the

> "Xi made himself the undeniable centre figure of the new administration"

ABOVE A model of the Zhurong rover, which landed on the surface of Mars on 14 May 2021

ABOVE Protesters in London call for an end to the persecution of China's Uyghur Muslims

risk that his comprehensive income and wealth distribution agenda will undermine [what has] powered China's strong catch-up growth over the past 40 years."

MILITARY MIGHT

Military expansion is another key feature of Xi's leadership. Xi has overseen a major restructure and modernisation of the People's Liberation Army (PLA) - the military wing of the CCP - with a specific focus on Taiwan, an island lying approximately 161 kilometres (100 miles) off mainland China in the South China Sea.

Taiwan is situated in the so-called 'first island chain', territories that are vital to the U.S.'s foreign policy in the region.

There have been rumbling tensions between China and Taiwan for decades, but in the last few years the potential for conflict across the Taiwan Strait has escalated. On 9 April 2023, the Chinese launched a major military drill around Taiwan in what it called a "stern warning" to the self-ruled island. This was in response to a meeting between the Taiwan president, Tsai Ing-wen, and Kevin McCarthy, former speaker of the U.S. House of Representatives on 5 April.

Not surprisingly, the Taiwanese population has grown increasingly wary, with many joining civil defence groups and making preparations for a potential invasion. In September 2023, the three main contenders in Taiwan's general elections put 'the China threat' at the forefront of their campaigns.

"All three presidential candidates have acknowledged the potential risks of Taiwan becoming the next conflict zone," said Jing Bo-jiun, a senior research fellow in Taiwan studies at the University of Oxford, in an interview with *The Guardian*. "They aim to convince voters that they are the most capable leaders who can ensure peace and stability across the Taiwan Strait."

Upon winning the election on 13 January 2024, new president Lai Ching-te made his views on China's threats clear: "The election has shown the world the commitment of the Taiwanese people to democracy, which I hope China can understand."

GLOBAL GAINS

Modernisation lies at the heart of Xi's vision for China. In September 2013, during a visit to Kazakhstan, Xi announced the creation of the Belt and Road Initiative. This is a revitalised series of road and rail routes connecting Europe and Asia and built largely with Chinese expertise. The project is frequently described

ABOVE With approximately 22 million residents, Beijing is the most populous capital city on Earth

THE DRAGON ROARS

ABOVE President Xi Jinping attends the 15th BRICS Summit in Johannesburg, South Africa, August 2023

as a 21st-century maritime Silk Road, one made up of a 'belt' of overland corridors and a maritime 'road' of shipping lanes. It is the centrepiece of Xi's foreign policy, which rests on China taking a leading role in global affairs.

Yet while the scope of the plan is impressive, it has sparked global concern. The Belt and Road Initiative has been perceived in the West as economic imperialism, a project that could give China too much leverage over smaller and poorer countries.

"They've presented this very grand initiative which has frightened people," Jane Golley, an associate professor at Australian National University, told *The Guardian*. "Rather than using their economic power to make friends, they've drummed up more fear that it will be about influence."

Some have argued that this transport infrastructure could just as easily be used for more ominous means. "If it can carry goods, it can carry troops," said Jonathan Hillman, director of the Reconnecting Asia project at CSIS.

DEALING WITH DISSENT

Xi has seemingly reduced the gap between urban and rural incomes via his 'common prosperity' policy, but his rule has also seen a sweeping crackdown on civil society. He launched a series of anti-corruption purges, weeding out enemies and rivals, and has cracked down on dissent by tightening censorship and surveillance. Many non-government organisations have been shut down, journalists and human rights lawyers have been arrested and outspoken media tamed.

Xi's government has invested heavily in a colossal surveillance system to monitor its citizens' movements and activities. Once again, he placed himself firmly at the centre of this initiative, becoming the leader of the Central Leading Group for Internet Security and Informatization, the body in charge of cyber security and internet policy. Xi also chairs the National Security Commission of the CCP, another body that has helped him to consolidate power over national security affairs.

HUMAN RIGHTS VIOLATIONS

Without doubt, the most alarming outcomes of Xi's leadership are the grave human rights violations that have allegedly taken place during his tenure.

It's believed that since 2014, around 1.8 million Turkic-speaking Uyghurs and members of other Muslim minority groups have been incarcerated in internment camps located in the Xinjiang region in northwest China. These camps (which China claims are now closed) have been criticised by the governments of many countries and human rights organisations for carrying out alleged human rights abuses, including mistreatment, rape, torture, forced labour and involuntary sterilisations.

The Chinese Government calls these facilities "vocational education and training centres" and has claimed that 'attendees' have now "graduated and found good jobs". However, human rights organisations and the media describe them as internment, detention or concentration camps.

A statement released by Amnesty International on 23 October 2022 said: "President Xi's decade in power has been characterised by sweeping arbitrary detentions, a ruthless nationwide crackdown on freedom of expression and association, crimes against humanity against Muslims in the Xinjiang region, and a dramatic escalation of repression in Hong Kong… there can be no excuse for failing to hold the Chinese authorities to account over atrocities committed in President Xi's name."

RIGHT A robot croupier deals playing cards at the Macau Gaming Show, testament to China's modernisation

RIGHT Officials outside the Wuhan Institute of Virology

PUBLIC DISSENT
Mass protests and violent conflict have been a prevailing feature of Xi's tenure to date. On 1 October 2019, during the 70th anniversary of the founding of the People's Republic of China, there were clashes between protestors and police in a number of districts in Hong Kong. These resulted in the first use of live rounds by police.

Cultural and economic differences are also widely considered as a primary cause of the conflict between Hong Kong and mainland China.

THE PANDEMIC
In late December 2019, a new threat appeared in the form of a deadly virus. From the outset of the COVID-19 pandemic, Xi's administration pursued a zero-COVID strategy that enforced mandatory isolation. By summer 2020, the authorities had largely brought the disease under control. Even so, China was widely criticised for its censorship and lack of transparency.

Rumours were rife that the virus could have leaked from a laboratory in Wuhan, a so-called gain-of-function mutation, where the organism develops new abilities or functions. This theory gained momentum in the U.S., where some Republicans claimed to have seen "ample evidence" that the Wuhan lab was working to modify coronaviruses to infect humans. This theory was firmly rejected by Dr. Anthony Fauci, then the director of the National Institute of Allergy and Infectious Diseases in the U.S.

By November 2022, growing frustration with the zero-COVID policy prompted mass protests, with many calling for Xi to step down. Confined to their homes, unable to work or buy basic provisions, thousands took to the streets in what became known as the White Paper Protests.

> **"China's economy was in a dive and Xi's government needed consumers to spend"**

RIGHT In January 2024 a judge ordered the winding up of the Evergrande Group, which has debts of over $300 billion

COVID POLICY U-TURN
In early December 2022, almost overnight, the Chinese Government ended the zero-COVID measures. The result was inevitable. While Xi assured the nation that the latest strain was little more than a common cold, the death rate soared. According to a report by the Centers for Disease Control and Protection, 90 per cent of China's population was subsequently infected, resulting in 1.4 million deaths.

By June 2023 the virus was surging in the form of a new subvariant known as XXB and cases were reaching record highs of 65 million a week. In direct contrast to its previous policy, the government urged people to get out into the shops, malls and restaurants. China's economy was in a deep dive in 2022 and Xi's government badly needed consumers to start spending. The economy duly rebounded strongly in 2023, but in the absence of any kind of exit strategy, the human toll was nothing short of devastating.

NEW WORLD ORDER
Over one year into Xi's unprecedented third term, all the signs are that he has a sweeping vision to reshape the world of the future. Under his drive for common prosperity he has sought to reduce inequality, expand the middle classes and penalise large private companies who he perceives as hoarding the nation's wealth.

Now he is aiming to topple America as the most powerful nation on Earth (China is a key member of BRICS, a group of nations that hopes to challenge the West's economic and military hegemony) and reshape the international system. A 13,000-word document released in Beijing in September 2023 outlined his vision for a "global community of shared future".

The documents explain that this is a future free of "universal values defined by a handful of Western countries". What concerns the West about this is how assertive and authoritarian China's vision is. For many countries, it is hard to see past the reported systematic persecution of Uyghur Muslims and others. Xi countered such concerns when he launched China's 'Global Civilisation Initiative' in early 2023 in front of representatives from 150 countries. "Different civilisations," he argued, "have their own perceptions of shared human values."

He is not without allies. In the last few years, even those countries that have had close relations with the U.S. – such as Pakistan – have been drawn towards China's vision. Ultimately, the future could be one in which China and its close allies distance themselves from the West and its values.

"What the Chinese are saying... is 'live and let live'," Yun Sun, director of the China programme at the Stimson Center think tank in Washington, told CNN. "You might not like the Chinese political regime – but if you want security, you will have to give them the space to survive and thrive as well."

THE DRAGON ROARS

HISTORY OF CHINA

Future PLC Quay House, The Ambury, Bath, BA1 1UA

Bookazine Editorial
Editor **Charles Ginger**
Art Editor **Thomas Parrett**
Head of Art & Design **Greg Whitaker**
Editorial Director **Jon White**
Managing Director **Grainne McKenna**

All About History Editorial
Editor **Jonathan Gordon**
Art Editor **Kym Winters**
Editor in Chief **Tim Williamson**
Senior Art Editor **Duncan Crook**

Contributors
Harriet Knight, Perry Wardell-Wicks

Cover images
Alamy, Shutterstock, Getty Images, Harriet Knight

Photography
All copyrights and trademarks are recognised and respected

Advertising
Media packs are available on request
Commercial Director **Clare Dove**

International
Head of Print Licensing **Rachel Shaw**
licensing@futurenet.com
www.futurecontenthub.com

Circulation
Head of Newstrade **Tim Mathers**

Production
Head of Production **Mark Constance**
Production Project Manager **Matthew Eglinton**
Advertising Production Manager **Joanne Crosby**
Digital Editions Controller **Jason Hudson**
Production Managers **Keely Miller, Nola Cokely, Vivienne Calvert, Fran Twentyman**

Printed in the UK

Distributed by Marketforce, 5 Churchill Place, Canary Wharf, London, E14 5HU
www.marketforce.co.uk – For enquiries, please email:
mfcommunications@futurenet.com

All About History History of China First Edition (AHB6296)
© 2024 Future Publishing Limited

We are committed to only using magazine paper which is derived from responsibly managed, certified forestry and chlorine-free manufacture. The paper in this bookazine was sourced and produced from sustainable managed forests, conforming to strict environmental and socioeconomic standards.

All contents © 2024 Future Publishing Limited or published under licence. All rights reserved. No part of this magazine may be used, stored, transmitted or reproduced in any way without the prior written permission of the publisher. Future Publishing Limited (company number 2008885) is registered in England and Wales. Registered office: Quay House, The Ambury, Bath BA1 1UA. All information contained in this publication is for information only and is, as far as we are aware, correct at the time of going to press. Future cannot accept any responsibility for errors or inaccuracies in such information. You are advised to contact manufacturers and retailers directly with regard to the price of products/services referred to in this publication. Apps and websites mentioned in this publication are not under our control. We are not responsible for their contents or any other changes or updates to them. This magazine is fully independent and not affiliated in any way with the companies mentioned herein.

FUTURE Connectors. Creators. Experience Makers.

Future plc is a public company quoted on the London Stock Exchange (symbol: FUTR)
www.futureplc.com

Chief Executive Officer **Jon Steinberg**
Non-Executive Chairman **Richard Huntingford**
Chief Financial and Strategy Officer **Penny Ladkin-Brand**

Tel +44 (0)1225 442 244

Part of the
ALL ABOUT HISTORY
bookazine series

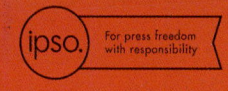

Widely Recycled

ipso For press freedom with responsibility